FLASH POINTS

FLASH POINTS

LESSONS LEARNED AND NOT LEARNED IN MALAWI, KOSOVO, IRAQ, AND AFGHANISTAN

Jade Wu

excelsior editions

AN IMPRINT OF STATE UNIVERSITY OF NEW YORK PRESS

Published by State University of New York Press, Albany

Printed in the United States of America

Excelsior Editions is an imprint of State University of New York Press

For information, contact State University of New York Press, Albany, NY
www.sunypress.edu

Production, Diane Ganeles
Marketing, Kate R. Seburyamo

Library of Congress Cataloging-in-Publication Data

Names: Wu, Jade, 1970– author.
Title: Flash points : lessons learned and not learned in Malawi, Kosovo, Iraq, and
  Afghanistan / by Jade Wu.
Other titles: Excelsior editions.
Description: Albany, NY : State University of New York Press, 2017. | Series:
  Excelsior editions
Identifiers: LCCN 2016031499 (print) | LCCN 2016039843 (ebook) | ISBN
  9781438465456 (hardcover : alk. paper) | ISBN 9781438465470 (e-book)
Subjects: LCSH: Economic assistance, American—Malawi. | Economic assistance,
  American—Kosovo (Republic) | Economic assistance, American—Iraq. |
  Economic assistance, American—Afghanistan.
Classification: LCC HC60.W85 2017 (print) | LCC HC60 (ebook) | DDC
  338.91/73—dc23
LC record available at https://lccn.loc.gov/2016031499

10 9 8 7 6 5 4 3 2 1

For Bruce.
For the brave men and women who tried to make
their professions better by speaking truth to power.
And for the American people, whose hard-earned tax dollars
funded innumerable programs overseas.

It is easy in a time of great events . . . to overlook one of the hard facts of history: a nation may lose its power and integrity slowly, in minute particles.

—William J. Lederer and Eugene Burdick,
The Ugly American (1958)

Contents

III
Surprise in Iraq

IV
Numbers in Afghanistan

V
Bureaucracy in Washington

Illustrations

Note on Names, Terms, and Statements

Names . . .

For the protection of all concerned, except for public figures and the author herself, all names of individuals and some identifying characteristics have been changed.

For security reasons, the names of TONI and Newport compounds are pseudonyms.

Terms . . .

U.S. foreign assistance encompasses a large number of overlapping but related fields, including development, humanitarian assistance, and peace-building, reconstruction, and stabilization. The terms denoting these fields are used throughout the work. The author is fully aware that there may be distinct differences among these fields that nevertheless are often simultaneously pursued or blend from one to the other. This work is not about defining these terms but about examining our conduct in the field of helping others abroad.

Statements . . .

This work is based on the author's observations and experiences. The statements of the author should not be construed to be the official statements of the entities mentioned. The author has no intention to embarrass, slander, defame, or malign anyone. The important point here is that these events took place and what we can learn from them to improve the way we conduct ourselves in the field of U.S. foreign assistance.

Introduction

Flash! Flash! And *flash*! The memories kept coming back. Walking down the street from my apartment in Arlington, Virginia, I saw moments from my time overseas return. A branch would fall, a squirrel would jump, a motor would roar—and boom, scenes from the past flashed back.

Like many young Americans who went overseas to poorer countries with little life experience and a big bag of hope, I wanted to "save the world." I wanted to fix things, solve problems and make life better for the less fortunate. Yet once in the field, not only had I found intricacies on the ground more difficult to navigate than I had imagined, I was surprised and aghast at the quality of many Americans working abroad. Whereas in the "do-gooders'" world one would have expected to find devotion, compassion, knowledge, and creativity, I witnessed a great deal of ignorance, nonchalance, poor judgment, and a proclivity toward waste—much of which went unchecked and was repeated in one developing country I went to after another. From Peace Corps volunteers to American subcontractors, these mentalities and actions affected how the locals perceived Americans and eventually worked against many U.S. policies and programs.

But that wasn't all.

Where money was big and greed was bigger, as they were with overseas contracts in Iraq and Afghanistan, I saw the alarming saturation of huge contracting companies that brought in a different kind of workforce and politics. Thriving on appearances, statistics, and the bottom line, these companies brought in many Americans whose focus on their big salaries detracted from their relationships with the locals and the purpose of their programs, corrupting the reasons why the U.S. was in these countries in the first place.

xvii

This story is my personal, unvarnished account as an implementer, the "little guy" on the ground who was part of executing U.S. policy and programs. There have been many books by renowned policymakers, top government advisors, and high-ranking military officers but too few by those whose faces were closest to the soil, the local people, the programs, and the problems.

It is the story of how I entered the field of U.S. foreign assistance and what I saw as America spent large amounts of money, time, and lives to "make the world a better and safer place." From the hot savannah of Malawi through the cold damp gray of Kosovo and into the volatile war zones of Iraq and Afghanistan, I tell my version with candor, humor, sadness, and irony.

I tell this tale as a conscientious civilian who became so appalled by what I found that I felt compelled to speak truth to power. I speak because the American people have the right to know. They have the right to know what types of activities, mentalities, and personalities their hard-earned tax dollars paid for—and continue to pay for.

As the U.S. encounters difficulties in many developing countries, particularly in the Islamic world, this story is about the lessons learned—or, more accurately, many that *should* have been learned—when dealing with people in another country of a different culture and religion. It was written to stimulate thought, questions, and, hopefully, action for the better.

As of this writing I have worked in foreign assistance in six countries besides the United States. Yet I am only discussing incidents in four because my memories from these flashed the sharpest and the clearest, and their experiences carried a stronger message.

So sit down, focus, and read. Put yourself in my shoes. What would you do?

Would you laugh, cry, speak up, or run?

—Jade Wu
Patriot Day
September 11, 2016

I

Fresh in Malawi

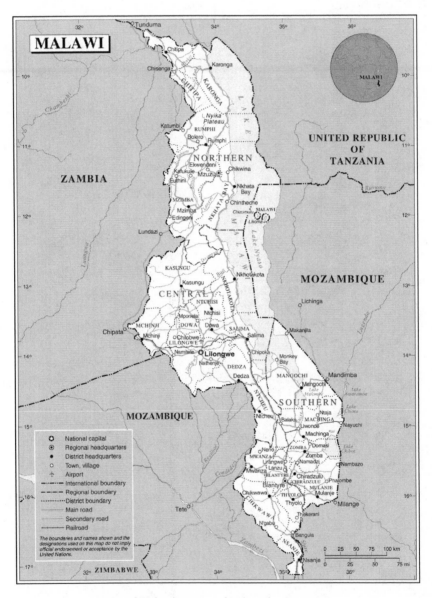

Map of Malawi courtesy of Wikimedia Commons.
https://commons.wikimedia.org/wiki/File:un-malawi.png.
Image is in the public domain. No part of it was altered.

Flashback One

In the village of Lunzu just outside Blantyre, Malawi, a country deep in the southeast part of Africa, I stood in front of the class. There were about eighty school kids in the audience, all Malawians. With their dark skin, short curly hair, and school uniforms, they all looked the same to me. They all stared curiously at me, the new Asian teacher who claimed be an American. One by one the brave kids raised their hands. They have questions for me. Where am I really from? Do I have a husband? Am I friends with Michael Jordan? How about Janet Jackson? Finally, a shy skinny boy in the back raised his hand halfway. I asked him to stand up and speak up. He stood. The whole class fell silent. He looked around anxiously and asked, "Madame, we have heard rumors that Chinese people eat people. Do you eat people too?"

1

_____

Decisive Call

Ring! Ring! The telephone kept going. Ring! Ring! No one was at home to answer. Ring! Ring! The answering machine picked up. Beep! The caller was finally able to speak: "Hello, this is a message for Jade Wu. Jade, this is Nancy Thomas from Peace Corps headquarters in Washington, D.C. Your application has been approved and you'll be leaving for Malawi in approximately four months. Please call me back so we can discuss the details. You can reach me at 1-800—."

I was a California girl. Except for being born in Hong Kong and living my first five years there, the only international travel I ever did growing up in Los Angeles was crossing into Tijuana, Mexico. Instinctively, I knew there was more to see. There was more beyond the big blue ocean when my brother and I played on the beaches of Santa Monica and more beyond the hills of Los Angeles County where our family hiked on weekends.

Growing up in a house with only one sibling, there wasn't much fighting over the television. Usually, my brother and I would be pretty good about watching cartoons, Westerns, or movies, but whenever my father came home from work we would watch the news. The constant scenes of people in distant lands suffering from starvation, disease, natural disasters, and war bothered me. I remember once watching news coverage about HIV in Africa, seeing all the deformed and sickly individuals dying of this deadly virus and wondering why no one around me was doing anything about it. As a kid the scenes to me were horribly graphic and haunting, but it appeared that they were only real when the TV was on.

Once it was off, friends and family went about their business as usual. Real life for most southern Californians revolved around work, traffic, the beach, restaurants, and Hollywood. People overseas in less fortunate circumstances were just news, not right outside one's front door.

One day when I was twelve my father bought me a big globe. We took it home and put it on my desk. I stared at it. Just the size of the world and the number of countries put me in a state of awe. Thereafter, whenever there was news about a faraway place, I went to the globe and found it. Foreign issues such as the Iran-Contra Affair, the Falklands War, and the AIDS epidemic helped increase my knowledge of geography. Like many young people with little life experience and save-the-world ideals, I wanted to travel overseas, roll up my sleeves, and fix these problems.

My first opportunity at this came when I joined the U.S. Peace Corps in July 1995. After completing a stimulating but rather theory-oriented master's degree in political science at the University of California, Santa Barbara, I felt it was time to leave studying behind and get out into the real world.

The only interview I had with Peace Corps took place in the federal building at 11000 Wilshire Boulevard in Los Angeles. It was early January and I was the only one sitting in a rather sterile waiting area on one of the upper floors, listening to the droning noise of the air-conditioning, when a middle-aged woman with puffy white hair appeared.

"Jade Wu?" she asked, looking at me.

I nodded.

"Hi, I'm Barbara Lorne," she said smiling, extending her hand.

We headed into her office.

Barbara was a woman in her fifties who had served as a volunteer herself somewhere in Latin America years before. Although her clothes were dated, her manners formal, and her big out-of-fashion eyeglasses took up most of her face, there was something underneath. There was a spark, a flash that came out every time she described her overseas experience. One could tell she really treasured her Peace Corps days.

She looked straight at me and asked various questions, expected ones of course: What skills do you have? Can you survive in a remote village? How do you feel about not having running water or electricity?

I did my best to answer all her questions, but then came an obvious one I hadn't thought of.

"Where would you like to go?" Barbara asked, studying me carefully. *Where?*

I was surprised. I didn't have a ready answer. I just thought they'd assign me to one of those African places I had seen on TV with starving children.

"Anywhere that doesn't snow," I finally answered.

It sounded lame but it was true. I didn't want to freeze. In southern California it didn't snow. I could not imagine functioning in a developing country with lack of resources in temperatures below 55 degrees Fahrenheit.

Then Barbara threw another curve ball at me.

"Do you have a boyfriend?" she asked, falling back into her less flashy self. "If so, how serious is the relationship?"

I hesitated. I thought about tall, blond Aaron whom I had been dating for years. But it seemed to be going nowhere.

"Yes, but it isn't serious—" I answered, my voice trailing off a bit.

Barbara gazed at me intently through her big glasses.

"We are going to need a statement from him," she said matter-of-factly, handing me the form.

Weeks after completing the forms and passing the medical checkup, I received that decisive phone call from Nancy Thomas. I was in. I was going to Malawi. The truth was I didn't even know where that country was other than it was in Africa. So before returning Nancy's call, I went to my globe and started searching. I found it: a skinny, vertical, landlocked country that was just a little above South Africa and far, far away from Los Angeles.

I was excited.

It was early in July when Aaron and I went to our last dinner prior to my departure. We had been dating since our days at UC Santa Barbara. We had met as undergraduates in the Reserve Officers' Training Corps and had had lots of fun. But something was missing; something was not quite right. Aaron was a nice, affable, straitlaced guy, but he lacked curiosity and passion for many things. He didn't question why things were the way they were, and having a job as an administrator at St. John's Hospital in Santa Monica, where most of his work was routine, he didn't have to. Born and raised in southern California, he had traveled no further than

Tijuana too. He told me once that he had everything he needed in Los Angeles and felt no desire to look beyond.

When we ate at a local Italian restaurant in Torrance that evening, Aaron was quiet. Obviously, something heavy weighed on his mind. But it was not until afterward, when we took a drive up to Palos Verdes Peninsula not far from what used to be Marineland, that Aaron bothered to speak. The night sky was clear and the moon was bright. Aaron parked the car and looked at me.

"I am going to miss you," he whispered.

I smiled.

"I'm going to miss you too," I said.

He let out a deep sigh, his hands still on the wheel.

"I wish you would go to Malawi, do your two years, and get *it* out of your system," he stated in a frustrated tone.

I was aghast. Yet this was typical of our relationship. I would think that things were all right and then he would say something, revealing things weren't. Up until this point, we had talked about things and I did not know he felt this way about my Peace Corps service. I did not know that Peace Corps was an *it* that needed to be gotten out of me.

"It's just that I don't understand you," he continued. "You have everything here. Why do you need to go far away and leave it all behind? Leave me behind?"

"Because I don't have everything here," I answered with conviction. "There is so much in the world to see and I want to see it."

He looked down at the dashboard.

"Well then, go and get it done," he said quietly. "When you get back we'll get married and have children. I hope the kids will look like me."

The last statement gave me pause.

"What?" I asked, staring at him. Aaron was golden haired and of European descent. I was Chinese.

He turned to me.

"I want my children to be blond," he said firmly. "I want them to look like me."

My blood pressure began to rise. Did he know what he sounded like? Why was he telling me this now?

"I don't think you can control what children look like," I answered, trying to sound calm. "Are you saying you don't want kids if they don't look like you?"

Aaron fumbled with his keys and mumbled something inarticulate.

"I just want them to look like *me*," he reiterated. "I know it's possible even with you."

I looked out beyond the peninsula into the deep dark Pacific. Suddenly everything became quiet and clear.

I was going to Malawi.

2

Biggest Fear

At the Peace Corps Malawi orientation in Washington, D.C., I met the other volunteers who were going with me. There were approximately a hundred of us in the class from all over the United States: California, Oregon, Washington State, Montana, Colorado, Michigan, New York, and so forth. The majority were in their twenties and just freshly out of college. We were going to be teachers, health workers, nutritionists, parks and wildlife attendants, community organizers, and engineers. Many had plans and talked about how they wanted to help Malawians. One young lady, who was going to be a health worker, told me excitedly what she planned to do.

"I want to implement the 12-Step Program," she said breathlessly with a smile.

I didn't even know what that was.

Walking through the large hall, I saw and heard excited exchanges. Bright-eyed, bushy-tailed, and eager for adventure, many spoke animatedly about what they had packed and what they had heard about Malawi. A few even showed off their newly bought REI clothing, sleeping bags, and water bottles. The excitement in the room reached a fever pitch. It was apparent there was more anticipation than knowledge or experience.

We sat through several days of presentations, most of which were helpful but mainly large doses of common sense. In one session the Peace Corps staffer asked us to write down the biggest fear we each had about going to Malawi.

"Write it down and drop it in the bag. Then we'll discuss it," she directed.

A brown paper bag was placed in the center of the room.

I knew exactly what to write. While others looked pensive, I quickly scribbled, "the outhouses," and dropped it into the bag. Though it might appear a small matter, I was not one who liked camping, especially without plumbing. I was not fond of American port-o-johns and could only imagine the equivalent in Malawi being worse. They were not something anyone could avoid. Everyone had to deal with them.

Later, the staffer reached into the bag and pulled out our pieces of "fear." She read them out loud, one by one.

"Failure to adapt, missing family back home, unable to learn the local language, missing home-cooked food," she read on. "These are all legitimate concerns," she said, nodding.

Then she pulled out one fear, read it to herself, winced, and set it aside. I did not know whether it was mine, but it was quickly apparent that the concerns others had were very different. I focused on something immediately practical. If she had read mine out loud, I was sure everyone would burst into laughter.

The day we set out to the airport, I noticed that a few volunteers were no longer with us. Their terminations were quiet, of course, but I thought it strange that, absent an emergency, they would have done all the paperwork and jumped through all the hoops only to decide at orientation that Peace Corps wasn't for them.

Hadn't there been time and money invested to recruit them?

After many hours of fly time and several changes of planes, we finally landed at Lilongwe International Airport in Malawi, deep in the southeast part of Africa. I was one of the first passengers to get off. When the aircraft door opened, a searing July heat ripped in. I had never been to a place this hot before.

"Whoa!" I yelped, flinching back from the heat. As a natural reflex, I put my arm over my face to protect it from the intense change of temperature.

The area around this smallish one-building airport seemed very flat with red-colored dirt everywhere. A bit beyond the airport were small shrubs and lots of undeveloped land. But no high-rises, skyscrapers, or anything resembling the outline of a major city appeared. Later, as we bumped along in two old shuttle buses into the capital city of Lilongwe, on a road full of potholes, we encountered many single-story buildings with broken windows and in need of new paint. This was very different than what I had expected of a capital city. Moreover, poverty was apparent. The sidewalks were all cracked and chipped. The Malawians, and there were many, were small, dark, thin people. They seemed to jump out and cross streets whenever and wherever they wanted. The men wore old t-shirts and jeans, while the women wore blouses and chitenjes, a cloth wrapped around the waist like a skirt. For one who grew up in a part of America where the majority was white, it took some getting used to, now that the majority was black.

Suddenly, I felt very noticeable. As an Asian American, I did not blend in physically. I never thought I would ever feel "too white" in life, but now I did. I could only imagine what my Caucasian friends were feeling.

Every Malawian I met the first week was friendly and tried to help me settle in. It took some getting used to looking into their dark brown faces, the whites of their eyes, the white of their teeth, and listening to the soft lilt in their accent. Peace Corps had put us in the Kalikuti Hotel in Lilongwe, introduced us to its local staff, and gathered a number of young people from the local community to welcome us.

"You will learn to adapt!" Jacintha said confidently to me. "You will survive!"

Jacintha was the first Malawian I ever spoke to. Peace Corps had given her my name, and during a welcome reception in our hotel lobby, she approached me. Jacintha was bubbly and young, probably no more than seventeen. With a big bulb of curly black hair and lots of energy, she smiled at me, someone who wore a deer-in-the-headlights look. She tried to reassure me that everything was going to be all right.

"You will like it here," she continued confidently.

I nodded my head hesitantly.

"Come," she said gesturing toward some chairs. "Let me teach you a few phrases in Chichewa."

We sat down, and I laughed with her all afternoon.

A few days later Peace Corps revealed our assignments. I was to teach English to junior high and high school students in Lunzu, a village in the southern part of the country. I looked at the map. Lunzu, hours south of Lilongwe, was along the M1 highway, Malawi's major north-south road and about fifteen kilometers north of Blantyre, Malawi's financial hub. I was excited. I couldn't wait until I got there to start sharing my knowledge with my students. I was here to *help*, and I wanted to get moving. Like most of my fellow volunteers, I was anxious to get to my village and start work. I had so much to share, to teach, and to *fix*.

But not before a few volunteers resigned. At the end of one training session, a volunteer named Chrissy stood up.

"I just found out that my mother has cancer," she stated matter-of-factly. "Peace Corps will always be here but my mother will not. It was an honor knowing all of you. Good-bye and good luck."

Then she was gone.

More flew out in subsequent weeks. We would hear rumors that the reasons had to do with family or health, but I could not help wondering if these individuals realized that Peace Corps was not a good fit.

Then I learned we all had to do several weeks of a "village stay" in a village other than the one to which we were permanently assigned. The point was to experience living with a host family, pre-screened by Peace Corps, and learn about the local way of life.

"This feels weird," a fellow volunteer whispered quietly to me. "Can you imagine, we're each getting 'adopted' by a Malawian family in our twenties!"

I blinked as her words sank in.

I was "adopted" by a family who lived in Matawale village near Zomba, about 330 kilometers southeast of Lilongwe. Zomba was a big city. It had an open-air market, a university, a plateau, and a luxury hotel, in addition to all the small mom-and-pop businesses along its main road. Like Lilongwe, its dirt was red-colored and its shrubs were small. My new family was the Pilolos. The husband and wife were both school teachers, and they had two children: one an infant and the other about five years old. The day Mrs. Pilolo came to pick me up from the Peace Corps' training camp in Zomba, it really felt like an adoption, except that I was no longer a child. I was standing in a dirt parking lot waiting for someone to collect me. Many of us stood there together, like slaves in a market waiting to be claimed. For the first half hour, it felt so strange to watch each of my friends greeting his or her new "parents" while no one came for me. I just stood there, dejected, for the longest time.

Finally, she came. Mrs. Pilolo was a slim woman in her early twenties wearing a colorful dress with loud patterns made from coarse local cloth. She walked up gracefully to our coordinator and handed him a slip of paper. As he called out "Jade Wu," I jumped forward and greeted my new "mother."

She gave me a warm smile that showed her white teeth and said, "Let me take you home."

Walking on a dusty road toward the Pilolos' house in the afternoon heat, I noticed the gentle beauty in my new mother. Her hair was black, thick, and curly, her eyes were brown, and her skin was the color of dark chocolate. But the most striking feature about her was her grace. Neither loud nor bossy, she was a woman of few words. When she spoke she was clear and precise.

Reaching the house, I saw it was not a hut but a small one-story shack made of concrete. Though it looked forlorn, lopsided, and unpainted, it was surprisingly homier than the other houses we had passed. The windows had curtains and the front door had a mat. But whoever had built the house appeared not to have measured things correctly. The whole structure reminded me of the tilted cartoon houses in Toontown Disneyland, except with much less animation and color.

"Your room is in the back," my mother said, leading the way.

We walked through a small rectangular living room with a cement floor and a low ceiling. I noticed that although the brown couch, the square coffee table, and the few chairs around were not new, everything was clean and tidy. My room, just as clean but smaller, was square in shape and had a bed frame with an old mattress on it. Sharing a wall with my room was Mr. and Mrs. Pilolo's bedroom. Its old wooden door was closed so I could not look in. Nowhere in the house did I notice electric outlets, light switches, or lights. Nor did I see a television or radio. I was going to have to do without.

That afternoon my mother patiently walked around the entire property, which was on a dirt lot, showing me where things were: the separate bath house, the outside kitchen, and the outhouse. I came to realize we did not have running water either. Worse, my "biggest fear" was about a hundred yards from our house. I looked worriedly at my new mother.

"I may have to come here at night," I said, somewhat embarrassed.

"You must not come out here alone, daughter," she answered. "You must wake me so I can accompany you."

The thought of a twenty-something young woman having to be accompanied to an outhouse seemed ridiculous. What if I had stomach issues and had to run out here several times in one night?

But, as my new mother explained, it would be extremely dark and there might be wild animals. One should never walk alone in the dark.

Settling in for the next several days and meeting the entire Pilolo family was interesting and heart-warming at the same time. Mr. Pilolo was a small, slight man with an authoritative voice but a kind heart. He was always making sure that I had everything I needed. My five-year-old brother, Clifton, was a whiny, thumb-sucking little guy who often threw tantrums when he saw our mother attending to our baby sister. My baby sister, Ana, was only five months old; she didn't say much but cried and giggled at me once in a while. Most of the extended family lived around Matawale, often coming by, smiling and staring at me as if I were a new specimen to be studied.

"You are from America?" Mr. Pilolo's brother asked one day, looking at me intently. He was taller than my new father but less clever.

"Yes," I answered, brushing a bug off my arm.

"But you don't look like the others," he said, stating the obvious.

"That's because America is the coming-together of many races," I explained. "I am Asian American."

He studied me from head to toe. It was as if he was learning for the first time that Americans were made up of a multitude of colors.

There were new things for *me* to learn too: adapting to the outhouse, bathing with a bucket, cooking over a small campfire, and eating with my hands. I grasped haphazardly and bungled along, learning what I could about the local culture. It was not difficult for me to realize how ignorant I was and how much I needed my new family to survive.

But *I* was going to help fix Malawi.

One afternoon I was sitting in the shade with a few volunteers. They were "adopted" by other families in the neighborhood. We each shared stories about what happened. Mike, a round, pleasant young man from Michigan, began to voice his dissatisfaction.

"Gosh, I miss McDonald's, ordering in pizza, and just sitting in front of the TV," he mumbled. He looked a little bored and a little lost.

"You need to chill," Shaye said, somewhat answering him. She was an older volunteer in her fifties. "We need to learn how to just hang out. Don't you guys notice how Malawians spend their downtime? They just sit and talk under trees!"

We all looked at each other.

Every one of us missed things from home. I missed not having dirt on my clothes, another girl said she missed her boyfriend, and one guy missed his car. But this was to be expected, especially after all the information Peace Corps had given us.

Then there were other challenges.

While staying with the Pilolos, drinking the water from the neighborhood well was a problem for me. Filled with sediment, it was very brown. Moreover, I had to boil it for ten minutes to kill the germs. When I poured it into my Eddie Bauer bottle, the liquid looked like tea. When I put this "tea" to my lips, it burned. With the weather being unbearably warm, it was equally unbearable to drink hot water.

Nor did boiling kill all the germs. Within several days my stomach started to rumble and twist. Soon I was rushing to the outhouse. My "biggest fear" had come to life.

The rushing continued into the night, sometimes even during early morning hours. I would get up in haste, knock on my mother's door, and we would hurry over to the "great pit." Stomach hurting, I would dash into the mud-walled outhouse with a flashlight and a roll of toilet paper. The overwhelming smell of feces couldn't be avoided. Mrs. Pilolo waited outside as I blasted away inside, completely embarrassed by the noises I could not control.

Fumbling with my light in one hand and the tissue paper in the other, nocturnal creatures with unknown names crawled into view. I tried not to look, but they were all over the place: on the walls, in the crevices, on the ceiling, and near the pit. The only way I could comfort myself was to switch off the flashlight and pretend they weren't there.

Then, in complete darkness, I struggled to keep balance. As the ground was wet with urine, I could not set the toilet paper down. Cursing, I held on to the flashlight while unrolling sheets of tissue. Meanwhile, since that which came flying out of me was less than solid, it did not fall neatly into the pit. I had to "kick" much of it into the dark abyss. Ultimately, with legs soiled, stomach twisting, and countless creatures staring, my thoughts flashed back to my clean, state-of-the-art bathroom at home in Los Angeles.

I was indeed far away.

When my stomach problems continued and Mrs. Pilolo was deprived of her rest, I decided to take matters into my own hands. One night needing only to urinate, I decided to take care of things myself. After all, I had traveled halfway across the world without my parents. As a confident young woman, I lit a candle and started to search my suitcase for a container, something that could hold liquid. I found a plastic Safeway shopping bag.

As youth came with ignorance, I thought the bag would work. Thanks to the flickering light of the candle, I saw my shadow on the wall as I started to use the bag. At first things seemed fine, but then I heard droplets hitting the floor. When I looked at my shadow on the wall again, I could see drops of urine leaking from underneath the bag! Exasperated, I finished my business and threw the soggy, and sorry, plastic bag down in frustration. How could I be so stupid? I had a graduate degree and came from a first-world country! In the morning, I would be the moron who would have to tell her mother what had happened.

Morning came. I got dressed and went to speak to Mrs. Pilolo. She was preparing breakfast for her infant.

With a beet-red face I cleared my throat, "Good morning, Mother. Do you have a rag? I had a bathroom accident in my room last night and wish to clean it up."

Mrs. Pilolo was looking down at the porridge.

"I will clean it," she said in a muffled voice, trying to stifle a burst of laughter.

I was very embarrassed. Perhaps I had given my fellow volunteers a bad name. What if the Malawians in Matawale now thought that all young Americans had bladder control problems?

Despite this embarrassing conversation, I managed to find a rag and clean up my mess. Later, I sat under a tree with fellow volunteer Laura Smith, a lively girl from Oregon with social work experience. She laughed when I told her what had happened. Then she related her outhouse woes.

She had had the runs the last several days. In the evenings she had been regularly dashing to her outhouse with a flashlight and toilet paper too. On one of her trips she did not make it. Her pants were soiled, right down to her white socks.

We both rolled over laughing.

When the village stay was finally over, the volunteers all gathered together and shared their experiences. Not surprisingly, many of the stories were about no plumbing, no electricity, and adventures in the outhouse. Friends told me how they had urinated in cans, containers, anything they could find that held water to avoid running out to the mud shack in the middle of the night. By contrast, a few volunteers had come up with one excuse or another to stay at the Peace Corps camp in nearby Zomba where there were flushing toilets. It seemed they did not even want to try to adapt to village life. The realities of local hardships were quickly sinking in.

My "biggest fear" had not been unwarranted after all.

3

Settling In or Just Settling?

"Are you ready?" Chester asked me. "Our transportation is waiting."

I nodded as he helped me with my bags.

It was a bright, sunny day back in Lilongwe as all the volunteers gathered to say farewell to each other after the last hour of in-country training. Finally, after more than two months of discussions, classes, and a village stay, many of us were more than ready to disperse to our assigned villages. A Malawian counterpart from each of our places of work was supposed to be present and escort us to our respective sites.

Lunzu Secondary School had fulfilled its duty and sent its deputy headmaster, Mr. Chester Namba, to fetch me. I was introduced to him the night before and found his manners welcoming. Though only in his twenties, he appeared well informed, sensitive, and organized.

"It's going to be a six-hour ride," Chester informed me as our pickup truck started pulling out. He had the same brown skin, the same white in his eyes, and the same enchanting lilt in his accent that I had seen and heard in other Malawians.

Riding in the back of the pickup, we bumped along the M1 highway, which was paved but full of potholes. Though this road was long, it only had two lanes: one going in each direction. There were dirt and dust everywhere, and the hot sun only made things drier. Intermittently, I saw locals walking along the highway, usually without a hat or a water bottle, and wondered at how they survived the heat.

Poverty was apparent everywhere we passed. Small villages that paralleled the road were clumps of small mud shacks, with thatched roofs, huddled together for protection. No Malawian looked as if he wore new clothes. Everyone was dark-skinned, dust-covered, and weather-worn. At the end of the trip, I was weather-worn too. My smooth black hair was so knotted by the wind that it was impossible to get a comb through it.

Lunzu was a town of a few thousand people. The first thing I noticed was that there were no sidewalks. All the one-story concrete buildings with rusted-tin roofs were huddled together next to the open-air market, all of which stood on top of a big dirt lot. These were small businesses selling cloth, sheet metal, housewares, and renting out rooms for the night. The open-air market itself was a maze of about a hundred concession stands. Merchants sold fresh vegetables, fruits, meat, and household goods on top of wooden tables underneath roofs made from dried grass. Kwasa kwasa, the local folk music, filtered in from a bar, adding to the festive mood. Crowds of Malawians, wearing clothes made from coarse local material, roamed through the stands, chatting and bargaining. Women, gracefully balancing baskets of fruit and potatoes on their heads, walked by. A few young people stood under a tree, drinking their sodas.

I did not see one Caucasian in their midst.

When we drove into Lunzu Secondary School's driveway the headmaster, Mr. Alifand, came out to greet us. He was a small man, no more than five foot four, with big hair. Given his slight build, his Afro, which looked like a hairstyle from the seventies, was all the more accentuated. He appeared quick-witted, clever, and alert. Without wasting time, he introduced me to the staff who were present at the school's office. Within minutes I shook hands with a few teachers, the secretary, and the maintenance chief. They were all Malawians and looked no different than the ones I had been working and living with for the last two months. There was the same accent in their English and the same friendliness I had seen before.

The school's lot was in the shape of a big oval, sitting on a slope overlooking a valley that was very green. Clustered together in the middle of the oval were several rectangular brick buildings that made up the school's offices, classrooms, and auditorium. To one side there was a huge dirt field that one of the teachers told me was their sports ground. On the other side were the students' dormitories: one for girls and the other for boys. Apparently this was a government-subsidized, coed boarding school. All students graduating from primary schools in Malawi who wished to attend Lunzu Secondary had to compete for a seat here.

I saw that the inside perimeter of the oval was dotted with teachers' houses, situated equidistant from one another. A dirt road, which started at the school's driveway, brought one from the M1 highway through the school's entrance and all the way around the property.

I had a good feeling. I thought the place was beautiful and ideally located. It was not far from Blantyre, Malawi's financial center, and Mlambe hospital was right across from us on the M1.

Then Mr. Alifand and Mr. Namba decided to walked me to my house.

"We have assigned you House Number 10," the headmaster said, pointing ahead.

All of the teachers' houses, which were identical in size and appearance, were numbered. They were all one-story, rectangular in shape with brick walls and slanted tin roofs. Mine had a few windows that looked as if they did not shut properly. A few panes appeared to be out of their frames.

As we stepped up to my front door, Mr. Alifand pulled out a big key from his pocket and unlocked it.

"The last teacher who lived here also died here," he informed me gravely.

This stopped me in my tracks.

I looked quizzically at both men, but they said no more. We moved my bags in and walked through the entire house. It had a large living room, an enclosed kitchen, a toilet room, a bathing room, and three small rectangular bedrooms. Sparsely furnished with an old, scratched wooden dining table, six chairs, and three thin foam mattresses, nothing in the house was new. There were rough edges, worn-out wooden countertops, creaky doors, a cement floor and cobwebs. I could see there was a lot of work that needed to be done to make this a comfortable living space.

Then I looked out the kitchen window.

The view of the valley beneath was breathtaking. It was green everywhere. There were papaya trees, and someone had a plantation with rows and rows of crops growing. About fifty yards away, I saw a small, one-story brick building. It looked like a smaller residence resembling my house. It appeared that every teacher's house had one too.

"Oh, that's the boy's quarter," Chester said, sensing my curiosity.

"What's that? Who's the boy?" I asked, ignorantly.

"If you have a servant," Mr. Alifand explained, "he would live there."

If I had a *servant*, I repeated to myself.

Being an American and very egalitarian, I never thought I would ever have a servant, particularly as a Peace Corps volunteer. Yet I remembered Peace Corps saying we could hire household help if we wanted. Perhaps the help would live there.

Classes began about a week and a half after my arrival. The day before the first day of school, I saw swarms of students arriving at our front gate. They started entering our school well before noon. All dusty and weather-worn, these teenagers had traveled to Lunzu from different parts of the country. I saw them lug in old suitcases and backpacks and heard their excited chatter as they greeted each other after months of absence. Mr. Alifand informed me that we were expecting a little over six hundred students altogether.

"Teacher! Teacher!" Students shouted as they saw me from a distance.

On the first day in my first class about eighty students were waiting for me—and I had three classes to teach. As I entered the classroom, I saw a sea of teenagers wearing the same blue uniform: a blue shirt and blue trousers for the boys and a skirt for the girls, all of whom sported the same style of hair—short, black, and extremely curly. Inwardly, I gasped as I could not tell one brown face from the other. They all looked the same to me. When the students saw me, they all stood up as a sign of respect.

"Good morning, Madame!" the students said in unison.

I smiled, put my books down, and looked down at my attendance sheet. Name after name, many of them about thirteen letters long, was impossible to pronounce. Some names, for example, began with M-P-H. How does one pronounce that? I wondered. How can these Malawians have such long names? Mine altogether was only six letters!

After stumbling over the pronunciations, I introduced myself and allowed the students to do the same. They stared curiously at me, some amused and some suspicious. I could tell that I was the first American in their midst, let alone an Asian American. They must have wondered how this Asian who claims to be an American came to be their English teacher. It was apparent the school had never told them I was coming.

During our first lesson, the students asked me a myriad of questions: Are you *sure* you are American? You don't look like the others. Can you drive? Why did you come to Malawi? Are you friends with Michael Jordan? What's Hollywood like?

Then came the ultimate get-to-know-me question, something Peace Corps did not prepare me for. A timid boy in the back of the room asked whether I ate people, because Malawians had heard that Chinese people ate people.

At that moment the room became so quiet that one could hear a pin drop.

I looked out onto the sea of apprehensive faces. Being in a classroom where the walls were scratched, the windows cracked, and many desks mangled, what could one expect these students to know?

"If you don't all sit down and pay attention, I'll gather you up and throw you into a big boiling pot!" I said, gesturing with my hands.

The class roared with laughter as the ice was broken.

Later, when I returned home, I spoke with my neighbor, Mrs. Maluzi, who lived in House Number 9. She was a plump, middle-aged widow who taught home economics. Revealing she lived with one teenage son and a teenage niece, who were also students at our school, she asked me how my first class went.

"Oh, fine," I answered, not wanting to tell her how I mispronounced a bunch of names.

Then I asked her about the previous teacher who occupied my house.

"Who was he?" I asked. "What did he die of?"

"He taught French," Mrs. Maluzi answered, bending down to pull some weeds in front of her house. "He died a few months ago—back in April, I think."

"What did he die of?" I pursued. I really wanted to know.

Mrs. Maluzi gave me a grave look.

"He was very ill," she said quietly, looking away. "He died in that house," she said, gesturing at my house.

Either Mrs. Maluzi didn't know what this teacher died of, or she didn't want to say. The only other fact that she revealed was that he died in my bedroom in the very bed I now occupied. Though this bothered me, I had now met my first class and saw how the students needed me. No ghosts or scary tales were going to chase me away.

About a month later, I went into Blantyre to meet with several volunteers who were stationed there. Only a fifteen-minute bus ride away, it would be the city that I would travel into on a weekly basis to do banking, shopping, and a host of other errands. Blantyre was the second largest city in Malawi, approaching a population of a million people. In addition to its supermarkets, restaurants, banks, hospitals, and small businesses, there were paved streets and tall office buildings. Blantyre was the closest I ever got to feeling like I was in a modern city in Malawi. Yet, though it was the financial center, traces of poverty were still apparent. Sidewalks were chipped, roads were bumpy, and building facades had serious deterioration. Beggars, usually with some physical deformity or another, were regular sights at street corners.

Sitting down to lunch in a sandwich café, several of us chatted about our new assignments. Our group was made up of teachers, health workers, and project coordinators.

"I love my schedule," Jeannie said between bites. "I'm only expected to teach a few days a week."

I was surprised. At Lunzu Secondary, *I* was expected to teach five days a week as well as hold office hours and participate in afterschool activities.

"You're lucky," Amy, a health worker, said to Jeannie. "At my hospital no one has told me what I'm supposed to be doing yet. As far as I'm concerned, I can come and go as I please."

As our group chatted on, it was apparent that many had very flexible work schedules. They came and went whenever they wanted, sometimes not even showing up for days with little or no backlash. Since Peace Corps was paying our stipend, the actual places of employment only needed to provide a job and housing. Though this arrangement sounded great in theory, some local institutions were either too slow or never got around to detailing the job description and the schedule its Peace Corps volunteers were supposed to fulfill. As a result, there was little accountability and some volunteers took full advantage of this.

But it wasn't just the lack of clarity in work hours or job description that was disconcerting; it was the attitude that I now saw surfacing. In contrast to the eager, energetic desire to do good in Malawi, which was apparent in Washington, D.C., a sense of indifference, a nonchalance, was now appearing. A number of the volunteers saw that Malawi's poverty wasn't going away. They decided that no matter how much time and effort they put in, the country's problems involving government, health, education, employment, sanitation, and corruption would not be solved.

"It will be like this for years to come," Janet said, yawning. It sounded like she was just settling for what she had found rather than settling in.

"The people here are different," Ben said with equal indifference. "They just don't seem to get it."

Then the group moved on to talk about other things: restaurants in Blantyre, nightclubs, who was dating whom and which volunteer was going to host a weekend bash.

Figure 3.1. Lunzu, 1995

Figure 3.2. Me, shopping in Lunzu market, 1996

Figure 3.3. My students, Lunzu Secondary School, 1996

Figure 3.4. My house at Lunzu Secondary School

Figure 3.5. Blantyre, 1995

4

Navigating Intricacies

Lots of Malawians, young and old, were dying in the country. In addition to the former occupant of my house, another teacher at the school passed away due to a "mysterious" illness. It happened about six months after I arrived. One minute he was on medical leave. The next minute we were told he was dead.

None of the Malawians I met liked to speak about the exact causes of death, but AIDS was rampant throughout the country. Often I would make a Malawian acquaintance in Blantyre through banking and shopping, not see him or her for a few months, and then find out later that he or she had died. Many times these individuals were young. I suspected many of them had died of AIDS, including the two teachers at my school. When the latter one was on leave, I had heard he had immune deficiency issues as well as shingles, usually signs of carrying HIV.

Even the M1 highway that ran right through the heart of town had several gravestones lining it. Death was all around.

One day I met a young Japanese woman who worked at Mlambe hospital. Chikako Naguchi, a Japanese International Cooperation Agency (JICA) volunteer, was a lab technician. We met at the Lunzu *msika*, the open-air market. She was thin as a rail but carried herself with grace. When she saw me, she stepped forward and nodded. She spoke broken English and I did not speak Japanese. But somehow we managed to communicate in a mixture of English and Chichewa. It must have struck onlookers as strange: two Asians speaking two languages to each other.

She told me that she was going to be in Malawi for two years too and invited me to her house subsequently for tea.

Sitting in Chikako's tidy but small square-shaped living room near the hospital, I asked her what a lab technician did.

"Test vials of blood—every day," she said.

My ears perked up.

"How many on average test positive for HIV?" I asked.

"Random day, oh, about sixty percent," she stated without hesitation.

I gulped, wondering why this virus had spread so quickly. All around there were advertisements for condoms and stores selling them. The locals must have heard about this contraception and yet HIV had strongly taken root. Why? One fellow volunteer had told me it was about the level of acceptance—the acceptance of using protection. Apparently, many Malawians were still having a hard time with this. It seemed a no-brainer to me that important lessons should have been learned. But no, my fellow volunteer had explained, it was not that simple. There were many factors involved: education, income, cultural acceptance, religious acceptance, and accessibility, particularly in the rural areas.

The problem was a lot bigger and more complicated than we had imagined.

◆ ◆ ◆

About nine months into my stay in Lunzu, I experienced my first break-in. It happened one morning around ten thirty. I had left my house to go to class. When I returned an hour later, one of the large window panes in my front door was completely shattered. Luckily, I was walking with two teachers who were also returning to their houses after class.

"Jade! That's broken!" Mr. Mbeza shouted, pointing at the spot where there used to be a glass pane. He was the first to see it.

Startled, I felt a wave of fear spread through me. Who did this? Who had been watching me? Was a burglar inside now?

I didn't want to go in the house alone and it wasn't as if I could just call 911. I looked at Mr. Mbeza and the other teacher, Mr. Matufa.

"Will you both enter the house with me?" I asked.

They nodded. Both men knew I should not go in by myself.

When we entered the house, we did not find anyone. Except for a few chairs and mattresses that had been overturned, the only thing that the burglar took was my backpack, one I had conveniently emptied out the night before. It appeared that whoever it was had very little time.

"He or she was small enough to enter through this," Mr. Matufa pointed at the opening in my front door where there used to be glass.

I stared at that opening in disbelief, unnerved that someone had been watching my schedule that closely.

That evening Chester used the school's pickup truck to drive me to the local police station.

"We haven't had a break-in like this at the school in many years. Perhaps we should ask our head prefect to guard you," he chuckled softly. Chester was trying to make light of a disturbing situation.

When we got to the police station, I saw it was a one-story building situated on top of a dirt lot. No parked cars were around, nor were there any street lights. A small faint light came through one of the windows. As we entered the small dusty office, I saw a wooden table, some papers stacked on it, and an old black landline telephone. No computer, radio, or television was in sight. Looking straight ahead behind the table down a short hallway, there was a cell with two men in it. Except for the occasional moaning of the prisoners, it was a fairly quiet office. After a few minutes, a small Malawian man wearing a police uniform came out from the back to greet me. I told this officer what had happened.

"Fill out this form," he said nodding, handing me a sheet of paper.

I looked down at it. The copy was so faint I could hardly make out the words.

I looked at the officer.

"Is someone going to come to my house tonight to do an investigation?"

The officer gave me a wry smile.

"Well," he said, "we would like to but we are short on vehicles. Many of us travel on foot and by public transportation. We have to do many investigations. Maybe in several weeks we could be there."

Several weeks? I was aghast. I turned to Chester. He didn't seem surprised. How could the police protect the community with so little resources?

At that moment, one of the prisoners let out a loud screech and the officer excused himself. I could see there was no use in prolonging my visit.

In the next several days, I felt a need to do something about my security. I had heard about the few break-ins my fellow volunteers suffered, and even the Malawian teachers at the school now told me to beware. Apparently, none of them had experienced a burglary in their current houses, so it must be that as a foreigner I stood out. Lunzu's open-air market was a hub for thieves. I had been warned that these thieves worked in groups. Sometimes they would slither their way through crowds, agilely picking pockets. Other times they would hide under the Lunzu bridge near Mlambe hospital and come out at night when pedestrians were at a disadvantage. Reputedly, burglaries, robberies, and pickpocketing were rampant.

Peace Corps had informed us that if we wanted to hire a guard, we would be reimbursed. I asked around the school's community for recommendations but did not receive any viable interest. Mrs. Maluzi suggested I seek assistance from Blantyre's human resources department.

"There should be candidates," she said.

Thus I took the bus one afternoon to Blantyre and disembarked near the human resources building. As I approached its old, gray building, I saw crowds of Malawian men sitting on the grass outside waiting. I correctly assumed that all of them were candidates looking for work. When I headed for the front door, hundreds of eyes turned to me and stared. I could feel their interest peak. Entering the building, a clerk wearing a starched white shirt and a skinny black tie asked if he could help me. I told him that I was looking for a guard. He escorted me into his office and asked me to have a seat. I plopped myself down on an old dusty vinyl armchair placed under two open windows, one on each side.

The clerk stepped outside and shouted something in Chichewa to the men on the grass. Within seconds, numerous resumes were being shoved through the open windows on each side of me. It was a small room. I could literally hear the *swoosh* of papers pouring in. I looked up and saw large pieces of white cascading down upon me, on my head, my shoulders, and my arms. The clerk returned and was aghast to see me drowning in resumes.

"I—I'm sorry!" he exclaimed.

That afternoon I spent a long time sorting and stacking these papers into piles.

Because there were so many resumes, I was not able to read every one. I picked three out where the grammar was clear and correct. I told the clerk I wanted to interview these people. He walked outside again and shouted their names.

The first two men seemed all right, but we did not connect. The third man, a Mr. Dockwe Chlimbe, was interesting. Though he appeared a bit older—probably in his late forties—was missing a front tooth, and wore clothes that were wrinkled, he was respectful of me. He managed to answer my questions with his broken English, and I warned him of the dangers of being a security guard for a foreigner. I reminded him that thieves worked in groups and there could come a time when he would have a confrontation with them. He said he was aware of this, and I saw no reason to waste more time. I told Dockwe that I needed him to start that evening.

At six that evening Dockwe reported on time.

"Good evening, Madame!" he exclaimed as he stood at attention and saluted me.

We walked around the outside of my house and I gave him a general overview of what I expected. But something must have been lost in the communication, because after I went back inside, he spent the next several hours marching nonstop around my house like a soldier with a stick! Not even Prince Charles got this kind of service. As I peered out, I shook my head. Nothing about Malawi was going to be perfect: not its economy, security, high unemployment—but at least I was able to hire one of those men sitting on the grass.

As if the week wasn't surreal enough, several evenings later, I was inside my house correcting essays when I heard a soft knock on the door. This was unusual as I did not have guests after a certain hour. Dockwe was standing outside.

"Madame, you have a student," he said, gesturing behind him.

As a rule, pupils did not go to teachers' houses. Thinking this must be an emergency, I opened the door and peeked out into the darkness beyond Dockwe. A tall, skinny young man wearing a t-shirt and cut-off shorts walked toward me. I did not recognize him as he was not a student from any of my classes. I was teaching the equivalent of ninth and tenth graders. He looked a little older. Likely, this student was a senior at the school.

He looked sad.

"Madame, can I talk to you?" the young man asked in a soft voice. "We must speak."

He stood on the doorstep but did not enter. I stepped outside with a flashlight and closed the door behind me. I told Dockwe that the student and I were heading back to the teachers' conference room. I wanted to make sure things looked appropriate.

The student's name was Roderick and he was indeed a senior. I asked him to accompany me back to the school as we should not be talking in my house.

As we walked, he sounded forlorn.

"You must help me, Madame," he wailed. "There is *nothing* for me here in Malawi. You must help me get out! I want to go to the U.S!"

I heard him, not just the words but the meaning. He was right. Malawi was very poor and offered few opportunities to its younger generation. The unemployed men sitting on the grass in Blantyre underscored that. What future would Roderick have here? Why should he not desire to start a life elsewhere? European settlers had done so in North America during the 1600s followed by many subsequent generations of immigrants.

But as a Peace Corps teacher, what would be an appropriate answer? I did not wish to mislead this young man about his prospects in Malawi, nor did I wish to give him false hopes about leaving the country.

We walked quietly for several minutes. Reaching the school building, I told him that he should work hard to finish his studies at Lunzu Secondary. That must be the first step. I also told him that I did not have a magic "in" on how to get to the U.S. He nodded sadly, seemed to appreciate my time, and did not push the topic further. Then we said goodnight and I returned home.

The next morning, I was in the teachers' lounge early. This was the room where each teacher at Lunzu Secondary had a desk. It was like one big office with two rows of desks lined up side by side facing each other. There were school announcements tacked to the bulletin board, a telephone for staff use, and cubbyholes with each instructor's name on them.

Still ignorant of the local culture, rules of the teaching profession, and the delicate nature of being the only American at the school, I started talking about my meeting with Roderick the night before.

"What?" a fellow teacher asked in dismay. "He came to your house? No student should disturb a teacher at her house!"

All the teachers nodded in agreement. Apparently, there were sensitive school rules I wasn't aware of.

I explained that he never entered my house and that my guard was present the whole time Roderick stood by the door.

"Doesn't matter," another teacher cut in. "He should not have been there."

My only purpose was to share the deep insight this student had. Unfortunately, the teachers focused only on the impropriety of the action. Before I knew it, one of the teachers went and revealed the entire story to the headmaster and Roderick was expelled for good. Effective immediately.

"For good?!" I exclaimed, appalled upon learning of it.

This was going too far. I had to do something.

I went straight to Alifand's office after class. I explained to him what happened the night before, emphasizing that Roderick did not enter my house. Alifand, a small man sitting behind a huge desk, took his time and rolled his eyes from side to side.

It was apparent that he had already made his decision.

"Ms. Wu," Alifand said slowly in a grave tone, "you are new and do not know this student. He is very troublesome. The expulsion is for the best."

"But what about Roderick's degree?" I demanded. "Where will he go to finish it?"

Alifand did not give a clear answer. I had a sinking feeling that Roderick was going to either do without or have to compete for a seat at another school.

As I left the headmaster's office that afternoon, I hung my head. Wasn't I supposed to be here to help students learn? How was it that I got one expelled instead?

I was walking morosely toward the parking lot when I saw Roderick coming my way. His bags were packed and he was no longer wearing a school uniform. He looked even sadder than the night before as I stopped to talk to him.

But he spoke first.

"It's not your fault," he said quickly. "Another teacher here was unhappy with me and took revenge."

I was lost for words. I told him that I had spoken to Alifand and asked that the expulsion be removed. Roderick nodded helplessly and walked toward the exit with his bags. Slowly and quietly he disappeared into the horizon.

That was the last time I ever saw him.

As the semester continued, I understood better who my students were and where they came from. Each morning I would come into class, work through a grammar lesson, and listen to what my students had to say—in English. I learned many of them came from small villages where the family was the basic unit, and where most people knew each other. Many had parents who were school teachers, day laborers, and farmers. Contact with the outside world was rare, and luxuries such as a television, a daily newspaper, a family-owned car, running water, and electricity were almost nonexistent. Moreover, a number of them had never been to the country's three big cities: Lilongwe, Mzuzu, and Blantyre. What they knew and what they believed to be true were gathered from their community. For many, attending a boarding school was the first time they were away from home for long periods.

And because it was a boarding school there were problems beyond those encountered at a day school. We had water and electricity outages, food shortages, medical problems, and sexual activity within the student population. Sometimes the sex was consensual, and sometimes not. I was especially disturbed by the latter.

In the teachers' lounge one day, I could not believe what I was hearing. Apparently one of my students, Gladys Mphinga, had had an affair with a male student. When Gladys found out she was pregnant, she was so alarmed that she drank laundry detergent to abort the fetus. As a result, she became so ill that she had to be admitted to Mlambe hospital.

"Sometimes you even see a fetus lying in the ditch!" one male teacher exclaimed, cackling.

I winced.

My male colleagues continued to banter about the various sexual encounters of the students. Some of the females chimed in too.

"Are you kidding?" I asked, sticking to the point. "Is this the way we get rid of pregnancies here?"

A few teachers nodded. But somehow the level of concern in the room was lacking. It appeared that there were those present who thought that pregnancies were entirely the fault of the female.

"What do you expect if a man comes upon an attractive woman?" one male teacher demanded. "Nature must take its course!"

I bristled. I didn't know which was worse: the news about Gladys' sexual activity or the beliefs of my colleagues.

5

Disturbing Trends

One morning I traveled to Lilongwe for a medical appointment. A five-to-six-hour one-way bus ride from Lunzu would bring me into the capital city whenever I had business to do at the Peace Corps office. Entering the waiting room, I was not surprised to see a handful of volunteers sitting around hoping to see our country director. There were usually always a few; sometimes they were the same ones who had been there before, and sometimes they weren't. The general vibe one got from them was that they wanted the director to do or fix something.

Understandably, some volunteers had very legitimate concerns about health, housing, employment, and security. But others mainly just wanted to complain. Many times the solutions were not at the fingertips of our director, a soft-spoken gentleman in his fifties who had been a Peace Corps volunteer himself, but in the hands of the volunteer.

"I just don't understand why Peace Corps doesn't send someone down to my site to look at things!" one volunteer complained as I walked by. "If it did, it would understand what I was going through!"

The few sitting near him nodded their heads.

"I had a meeting with Sam the other day," one woman said dismally, referring to our deputy director. "*All* she did was listen."

Several in the room rolled their eyes.

It wasn't difficult to conclude that those few who stayed at their sites and worked through their problems were the ones who, ultimately, made it to the two-year mark. Others were mainly headed for an early termination.

Sitting down and catching up with a few friends was, nevertheless, relaxing—and informative. But these conversations sometimes took alarming turns. In addition to the usual updates about who terminated and went home, there was now the gossip about sexual activities. Chelsea, who was a health worker in Blantyre, told me about the promiscuous behavior of some of the Peace Corps women with local men.

"Are you sure?" I asked, alarmed.

She nodded.

"We go to nightclubs sometimes," she said. "People were hooking up left and right."

My jaw dropped.

"Hey, I live right by Lake Malawi," Susan said, chiming in. "You should see some of the guys in our group. They took bar girls home."

Being by the lake was a favorite weekend activity for many foreigners. But I couldn't focus on the beauty of Lake Malawi. I was highly disturbed by what I had heard. Was all this true? What about HIV?

I remembered the sessions Peace Corps had conducted during training about HIV/AIDS, safe sex, and abstinence. Had any of the information sunk in?

Days later while riding the bus back to Lunzu I still couldn't get the behavior of some colleagues out of my mind. Why were they so cavalier? Were they really that lonely? Moreover, if a volunteer irresponsibly put herself at risk, should our government's money be involved? Should American taxpayers pick up the tab for sexual indiscretions?

And yet given the length of our service, was it realistic to expect that all volunteers practice abstinence?

Disembarking at the Lunzu market and lost in thought, I accidently took a different turn. This path, behind the open-air market, was another way to get to my school. Passing a group of small mud huts with thatched roofs, a toddler saw me and began to scream.

I was startled.

The piercing screams continued as he pointed at me. Another child, around the same age, came out of a hut, saw me, and began to scream as well. Then a third child did the same. The whole scene was highly disturbing.

Taking a deep breath, I quickly walked on. I remembered what a fellow American had told me. Our light skin color frightened Malawian children, especially those who had never been exposed to foreigners.

It was hard to believe that in a country where foreigners had had a presence for more than a hundred years, which was formerly a British protectorate, and where I was trying to *help*, there were those who thought I was a scary creature, a ghost.

And this belief was not limited to toddlers.

A few days later I was on a bus again, this time headed to Blantyre. An old Malawian man, wearing no shoes and sporting a gray beard, sat down next to me. While the bus was moving and I was looking out at the vast undeveloped land between Lunzu and Blantyre, this man gently touched my arm every few minutes. I thought this was odd, and each time I turned to look at him, he looked away. Then, out of the corner of my eye, I could see he was getting ready to touch me again. I figured it was his way of seeing if I was real.

So before I got off the bus, I turned and gave his arm a good squeeze, just to let him know I was human.

◆ ◆ ◆

"What happened here?" I demanded, throwing up my hands. "Why are these windows opened?"

"I don't know, don't know," Dockwe mumbled, shaking his head helplessly.

It was happening again. Things had been moved around.

Every night I would check all my windows and doors before going to bed. But some of the windows were so old they would not shut properly so I used wire to tie them down. When morning came, every so often, I would find the chairs in my living room completely rearranged and one or two living room windows completely ajar. Someone, or several someones, had entered my house during the night. They never stole anything but made it clear that they could.

It was unnerving.

Whenever I confronted Dockwe, who did not have the keys to my house, he always professed lack of knowledge. I figured he was either "in" on the game or was asleep when it happened. When I shared this incident with my American colleagues in Blantyre, they revealed similar incidents that had happened to them. One volunteer, who kept several dogs for security purposes, said that she came home one afternoon only to find one of them dead, apparently of rat poison given to it by an unknown person.

"He was dead by the time I got home," she said sadly. "The others looked sick. I'm pretty sure whoever did this wanted to break into my house."

We all shook our heads in disbelief. While it wasn't surprising that some wanted to steal from us, we were, nevertheless, in this country to do good. As gossip spreads and we volunteers did not blend in, one would have expected that the surrounding communities would have wanted to protect us. Instead, we did not know whether the thieves were people from near or far. The whole situation was irksome and gave us a darker view about the realities on the ground. As a result, a few more volunteers terminated and those who stayed were left to self-help in a country where the police had few resources and were known to be corrupt.

6

Meeting the President

Spring 1996 had arrived and I received a notice in the mail. It was from our Peace Corps office in Lilongwe informing me of a great upcoming event. President Bakili Muluzi of Malawi had issued an invitation to the American community to have tea with him in Lilongwe, celebrating the United States Peace Corps' thirty-fifth anniversary in the country.

I couldn't believe it. As a lowly volunteer, I was going to get to meet the president!

When the appointed week arrived, I traveled to Lilongwe and checked into the Capital Hotel where Peace Corps reserved rooms for the volunteers attending. Reuniting with my group, it wasn't hard to see that the numbers were continually shrinking. Moreover, a few volunteers had shifted sites; they were no longer at the village to which they were originally assigned. From my observation those who moved around, dissatisfied with things, were often the ones who terminated.

The next day all of us put on our best clothes—best under the circumstances—and traveled in several minibuses to the State Lodge, the functional equivalent to the White House, where the president was waiting to receive us.

Nearing the State Lodge, I realized we were in a part of Lilongwe I had never seen before. This part of town was a huge contrast to the usual potholed, congested streets of downtown where most businesses occupied worn-down buildings. It was open and spacious with well-manicured lawns. When we arrived at an enormous gate, it seemed like we were about to enter a large estate in the English countryside.

One by one our minibuses stopped at the guard's booth. I had completely expected that we would be asked to disembark and be subjected to a search. Surprisingly, none of this happened. Our driver simply drove up to the guard who already had a list of names. The guard glanced into the minibus briefly and waved us on. There was no double-checking who was who.

The State Lodge itself was huge, but it looked more like a massive white office building with many windows than a place where a president would live. The bus pulled up to the main door and we disembarked.

Entering the building and walking with my group through several rooms, I saw elegant, Old World furniture. There were tables and chairs made of dark wood and sofas covered with velvety material. Indigenous figurines, proudly representing Malawian culture, were on shelves, coffee tables, and near doorways. Batiks, of all sizes, were tastefully hung on walls. Even the lighting fixtures on the ceilings were stylish.

It was apparent that a great deal of money had been spent to decorate these rooms.

Yet no matter how expensively each room was furnished, there was a noticeable emptiness about it. The rooms did not look used. Not a hair was out of place. Instead it seemed that the rooms existed more for show than for function.

Reaching the end of our walk, we entered a large meeting hall where rows of chairs were lined up facing a lectern. Sitting down, we heard the voices of other Americans approaching. Once they arrived, I recognized a few people from the U.S. Embassy, the U.S. Agency for International Development, and various other American entities.

There must have been over a hundred people in the room. Once we were all seated, several Malawian men dressed in serious-looking, dark-colored suits entered the hall. They were tall and stately. Then a huge Malawian man in a white suit, about six feet tall and over 350 pounds, walked with dignity to the lectern. I could tell, by the way he carried himself and by the deference others showed him, that this must be President Bakili Muluzi of Malawi.

"I would like to welcome you all today, especially Peace Corps," the president said with a light lilt, smiling.

If there were security guards in the area, I did not notice them. I was completely mesmerized listening to President Muluzi. He talked a bit about the history of Peace Corps in the country while many in the audience smiled, nodded their heads, and applauded.

Then all of a sudden the president asked, "You see this beautiful property here? The very one we are in? It is for sale. I am selling it. So if anyone is interested, please contact me."

I was surprised. What was he doing? Making a sales pitch? What kind of money were we volunteers making? It was not even a salary. Our survival stipend was barely equivalent to $12.00 a month!

The president did not appear to be joking.

After his speech, he invited everyone out to the garden for tea. Standing outside on an extensive patio, I could not avoid the sight of unending manicured lawns with their topiary and fountains. The bright sunlight and blue sky only accentuated their beauty.

But who could afford a place like this?

A few minutes later the president was standing near me talking to people from our embassy. But no photographs were being taken and no one dared to ask him. Then I thought, if I want a photo I need to ask now or it will never happen. Wasting no time, I walked up to President Muluzi. He was speaking to his vice president.

"Excuse me, Mr. President," I said, cutting off the vice president. "I am a Peace Corps volunteer and would like a picture with you. Is that okay?"

The tall, massive form turned toward me and looked down.

I felt extremely small.

"Is that okay?" he repeated smiling. "Of course it is!" he bellowed, grabbing my camera and handing it to his vice president.

"Take the photos!" he commanded.

Suddenly, I was standing there next to the president of Malawi while his vice president clicked away. A fellow volunteer who stood nearby got in some of the pictures. Then, as we finished, I saw more volunteers heading our direction. They wanted pictures too.

Afterward I walked back into the main hall and joined my friends who had gathered at the bottom of a grand staircase. Then I heard someone calling my name.

"Jade! Jade! I'm up here!" the voice shouted.

I looked up. At the top the staircase, leaning over the banister, were several volunteers. One of them was Ted Hirsch, a blond, lanky, energetic young man. Holding a liberal arts degree from a university in California, he worked at a hospital in northern Malawi. Ted motioned for me to come up and join him.

"Lots to see up here!" he yelled.

I was not sure that the president had opened the upper floor to guests. But a simple glance around assured me that not even the guide who originally welcomed us was concerned.

Now on the second floor of the State Lodge, Ted and I followed other volunteers on our self-guided tour from room to room. It was strange that all the bedrooms on this floor had connecting doors. Even more peculiar was that each bedroom was decorated in *a* color and almost everything in that room was *that* color. A pink room had a pink bed, pink walls, pink tiles and pink carpet—exactly in the same shade. But, just like the rooms we had walked through upon entering the Lodge, none of these looked inhabited. They were all too clean, too tidy, too untouched, and too lonely.

"What a place," Ted said as I nodded.

After a while, Ted had disappeared and I was alone.

"Jade! Are you there? Come look at this!" a familiar female voice shouted.

I walked toward the voice that led me farther and farther away from the others.

It was Trisha Myers. She was one of the few in our class who had been to this part of the world before. Prior to graduating, she had been to Uganda as part of a nonprofit project. During orientation she had shared her experience, which gave those of us who had never been here a clearer mental picture.

When I found her, she was standing in an ornamented room all by herself, staring at a painting over a fireplace. Entering, I saw the back of her head with its short, curly blond hair. When she heard me she turned around, causing the hem of her long black dress with its dainty petal pattern to swing open like a flower.

"Isn't this neat?" she said referring to the painting.

"Oh yeah," I answered. "Everything in this place is neat—and expensive."

We looked at the objects in the room for a few more minutes and then proceeded to the next one.

When it felt like it was time to go, we could not retrace our steps. Though we tried, we could not find the main hallway that would lead us back to the grand staircase. It appeared that the whole second level was arranged in some sort of a maze.

"It must be this way," I said pointing in one direction.

"No, I think it's that way," Trisha said pointing in the opposite direction.

The noise of people chatting downstairs no longer came through. I got the sense we were a lot deeper into the Lodge than we were supposed to be. We did not have cell phones, and I did not see a landline telephone anywhere. There were not even windows from which to look so that we could get our bearings.

I was starting to get worried.

As we continued in the maze we arrived at a hallway that had something that looked like an emergency exit door.

I looked at Trisha.

"Should we try it?" I asked.

"Go for it," she said shrugging.

I did not see any other alternative. If opening this door caused an alarm to sound off, at least someone would find us.

We opened it. No alarm went off. It was a back staircase that went down two flights. No lights came on to help guide our downward spiral. I reached the bottom first. I yanked open a door that took me outside to another part of the grounds. Again, no alarm went off. Trisha followed. It appeared that we were all the way on the other side of the Lodge. No one was in sight.

We walked around, came upon a few stately fountains, but did not see anyone. I wondered where the president and his security people were. Then we came upon a parked Peace Corps car. As we waited by it, I thought about the three decades that Peace Corps had been in this country. It appeared that the standard of living for most Malawians was still below the poverty line and its education, health, government, and business sectors were all suffering from numerous systemic problems. Yet somehow the country had managed to finance a State Lodge that had every appearance of wealth. How many more decades did we have to be here—how many Peace Corps volunteers would have to come and go—before the quality of life for Malawians would significantly improve?

I struggled for an answer.

In several minutes, we saw Peace Corps staff coming our way.

We knew *we* were going to be okay.

But I did not know if the *Malawians* were going to be.

Figure 6.1. President Bakili Muluzi of Malawi and me, thirty-fifth anniversary of U.S. Peace Corps in Malawi, State Lodge, Lilongwe, 1996

7

No Longer a Guest

On a hot afternoon the teachers of Lunzu Secondary were having a staff meeting. For more than a year, I have sat through these. Usually taking place once a month, Mr. Alifand would start by reading off a bunch of issues and then as a group we would discuss them. But today something unusual was on the agenda: a cemetery cleanup. The headmaster announced it was time to do one again. I was puzzled. What was this cleanup and why were our teachers involved?

"The time is coming again for the cleanup of Lunzu's cemetery," Mr. Alifand announced. "The place is overgrown with weeds. As part of the community we must go there and help. It will take place this Saturday. This is an important project. I encourage everyone to participate."

As the headmaster spoke, he only looked at the other teachers. He said he expected them to volunteer their time and that this would enhance the school's reputation in the community.

Then he turned to me and asked, "Would you like to go?"

"Yes, certainly," I said, nodding, not knowing what I was really getting into.

It was the first time that anyone in Lunzu really asked anything of me. I had no plans for that day, and I figured that since I lived here I could also die here. Perhaps there could be a time when I needed a space in that cemetery.

"Ah," Alifand continued, "you must abide by our traditions when doing this. I will have one of our female teachers come and talk to you first." He nodded at the female staff.

I was clueless. I did not know there was "tradition" when one was cleaning a graveyard. I had never even seen the place. What was I expected to do?

On Friday evening, two female teachers came to my door. As it was after work hours, they were both wearing a blouse and a chitenje. They told me that they would come fetch me the next morning at 5:30 a.m.

Five thirty! I groaned.

Somberly, the women reminded me that the temperature and humidity rose during the day so the custom was to have an early start.

"We plan to finish by noon," one of them explained.

There was more. They informed me that I must wear a chitenje as well as a head scarf to cover my hair. I told them that though I had a chitenje, I did not have a head scarf. One woman said she would bring one for me.

"And oh," one of them continued, "you must also bring a hoe."

A hoe! I was a teacher not a farmer! And even if I wanted to bring one, where was I going to find one at this late hour? It was not as if a Home Depot or Lowe's was nearby.

I looked worried. The women glanced at each other and told me that they would bring a hoe for me as well. I went to bed that night, setting the alarm. Early the next morning I woke while it was still dark. As I got ready I realized that I would be pulling out a lot of weeds that day. Yet I had no garden gloves or any kind of hand-protection gear. I looked down at my hands; they were smooth. I was anything but a field hand. My fingers loved playing the piano, having been taught by a Juilliard graduate. Now these digits were going to spend several hours fighting with weeds.

Five thirty came. There was a light knock on my door. A group of women, made up of the two female teachers and their friends, stood at my doorstep. All of them had on a blouse, a chitenje, and a head scarf. Though their attire was colorful, the grave look on their faces revealed it was a solemn occasion. One handed me the head scarf, which I quickly put on, and another handed me a hoe. As we walked gingerly out of the teachers' housing area, the sun was just barely rising. I did not see any men and wondered where they were. I was told they would go there separately.

As we walked on the dirt path parallel to the M1 going north, one of the ladies started giving me tips.

"When we arrive, we should listen before starting," she said.

Apparently a man was in charge and we were to wait for his instructions.

"And oh," she continued. "Be careful of the poison ivy."

I gulped.

A few steps more and we heard singing. Local songs were being sung by those already clearing weeds. As its location was a bit off the main road, the cemetery was not visible from the M1. Once we arrived I saw that the property was as unpretentious as expected. There were no fancy gates, fountains, tombstones, or statues. There was not even grass. All I saw were mounds of dirt, a few wooden crosses and weeds everywhere.

Then I saw people working. The man in charge came over and spoke in Chichewa. We were directed to work in one corner. As we got started, I could see the hoe was not much use. Following the lead of others, I began to pull weeds with my bare hands. Before long the sun was high and the heat unmerciful. I was sweating nonstop. Out of respect for the solemn occasion I had not brought along a water bottle. Now I was really parched.

One of the women pointed to the poison ivy nearby.

"Don't go there," she said. Thankfully, I had not. Someone else had and was already complaining of an itch.

As I was a bit superstitious I did not wish to walk on top of people's graves. But in this cemetery one could not help it. The place was full, and it looked like more would be buried here.

We worked for hours as songs were sung to make the time go faster. Every once in a while, I received stares from Malawians I did not know. They looked at me, smiled, and looked away. I could see this was an activity that brought the community together.

Finally, someone in my group gave me a tug.

"Are you ready to leave? It's noon," one woman said.

I nodded, wiping the sweat off my brow. It was terribly hot and I really needed water. My group of women gathered together and we left. Walking back to the school I noticed pink blisters and ripped skin on my hands. I chuckled to myself—this pianist's hands had never been so agrarian.

At the next teachers' meeting, Alifand went through his list of announcements as usual. When he got to the cemetery cleanup, he stated he was very happy that a number of teachers got involved.

Then he looked at me, smiled, and said, "I understand Ms. Wu also went."

Everyone in the room nodded with approval. I was no longer just a "guest" living in Lunzu. I had participated in a project that was locally initiated and important to the community.

8

Politically Correct

"Did you hear?" Micheline asked. "Several more people are going home. Mary flew out yesterday. Jane and Tyler are leaving next week."

I wasn't surprised. We were into our second year in Malawi and our Peace Corps class was experiencing a high rate of turnover. The reasons usually had to do with job dissatisfaction, adaptation, health, security, or a mixture of these. The energy and enthusiasm most people exuded in the beginning had quickly dissipated.

Sitting in my living room, I looked at Micheline Howard. She was a tall African American from Louisiana and very proud of her heritage. When she spoke her words were direct but well thought out, and she did not display the immaturity many volunteers did. In the past few months she and I had become friends. Living only three hours north in the village of Balaka where she served as a community organizer, she had decided to pay me a visit.

Exchanging information about our jobs and villages, I told Micheline about the odd questions I had received from my students because I was Asian.

"The kids asked me whether I ate people because they thought the Chinese did. Were you asked any odd questions being black?" I inquired.

Micheline shook her head. She told me that she did not feel the locals saw her differently than they did the Caucasian volunteers.

That's strange, I thought to myself, surely the Malawians must have noticed that she was the same color as they?

After a week in Lunzu, we decided to travel to Lilongwe together. We both had official business to do at the Peace Corps office.

When we walked down to the busy Lunzu bus depot, the heat of the day was intense. Flies buzzed around relentlessly on heaps of trash while bus drivers, with shirts drenched in sweat, walked around shouting out their destinations: Blantyre! Mzuzu! Lilongwe! Mangochi!

Many Malawians stood by, with family members and luggage, waiting for the right bus to come along. When we finally got to our bus, it was overcrowded. In addition to people, locals brought sacks of maize, vegetables, and cages with live chickens. Squeezing on board, Micheline and I barely made it. Once inside the overwhelming body odor and the stuffiness were unbearable. Gritting our teeth, we joined the many standing.

After an hour of bumping along the M1, our heavily-laden bus broke down in the middle of nowhere. As this was not uncommon, I was only mildly annoyed. Many of the passengers decided to stay on board and wait while the bus was being fixed. But Micheline and I took our chances. We disembarked and walked north along the main road, sticking our thumbs out to hitchhike.

"Maybe someone will stop for us," I said, hope trumping reality.

I was glad my parents were not here to see this.

Perspiration seeped through my shirt. Cars and buses passed without stopping. Dust was everywhere, in the air, in our hair, on our clothes, and on our skin. As there were no stores or gas stations nearby, we just kept walking. The sun was high. Then as my water bottle got lighter and lighter, I started to worry.

After what seemed like an hour, an old bus packed full of Malawians stopped for us. It was so decrepit that some windows were missing as was one of the headlights. This bus was so full that its doors could not close. As I approached, the locals scooted in to make room for me.

"Can you move in more?" I yelled. "I have a friend!"

The skinny locals bunched in and I stepped onto the bus. Micheline was behind me, maybe a few steps away.

The bus driver, a large Malawian man, looked straight at me.

"You can come in but not that nigger!" he exclaimed suddenly pointing at Micheline.

Shocked, I did not have a smart retort. My head turned a full 180 degrees from looking at him to her. Both the speaker and his object of disdain were equally black. I did not know whether Micheline had heard him. I was so embarrassed I could not look at her a second time. It was hard to believe that a black man would say this about a black woman.

I stepped closer to the driver.

"She is my friend," I said firmly, wiping the sweat from my brow. "We are traveling together."

He shook his head. Micheline had not entered the bus. By the look on her face, I could see she sensed something was wrong.

I looked at the driver again.

"We are traveling together," I said again.

"Okay fine," he finally sighed, rolling his dark brown eyes and wiping his sweat on his sleeve. Micheline boarded the bus and we were on our way.

After this incident, though I saw her several more times, Micheline and I never talked about what the bus driver had said. I was uncomfortable just thinking about it and too ashamed to bring it up.

But I could not stop wondering about it.

I thought about the history of Malawi, the poor conditions many of its people lived in, and the education level of the general population. None of this explained why a Malawian man would say this to a black foreigner. Did he feel superior? Did he know that *he* could be referred to this way? Or was the term "nigger" one that Malawians only used to refer to American blacks?

Weeks later back in Lunzu when Micheline visited again, I was in the teachers' lounge. This room, as usual, was booming with laughter and jokes.

"Ah, I see you have a friend visiting," a busy-body colleague noted.

I nodded.

Several inquired who she was, where she was from, and where she worked. I tried to answer all their questions.

Then one of the teachers blurted out, "She's a nigger!" And the whole room roared with laughter.

Bristling, I turned and told everyone that this was a highly pejorative term, not to be used in polite society. But no one in the room seemed to understand. My Malawian colleagues just looked at me and laughed. They were more relaxed. To them, it seemed that almost any subject could be discussed and any words could be used, even those that were unacceptable to Americans.

This took some getting used to.

It was apparent that what I had expected educated Malawians to understand was not being understood, at least not in the way I had wished it.

Quietly, I took a broad mental survey of the teachers in the room. Most of them were in their thirties and some in their early forties. None had the opportunity to travel abroad, but all had a university education. It became clear to me that, among different cultures, possessing a university degree did not mean that people necessarily understood each other, each other's values, or even agreed upon what was proper or normal.

Subsequently, another incident confirmed my suspicion. Returning from Lunzu's open-air market one afternoon, I decided to stop by the teachers' lounge to pick up some essays. As I entered, several colleagues immediately jumped up from their desks to peek into my shopping bag. They were curious as to what this American bought.

"So what did you buy today, good sister?" a colleague asked from across the room.

"The usual," I answered noncommittally.

"You mean meats, bread, and sweets," he suggested.

"No," I answered. "I'm a vegetarian."

Everyone stopped what they were doing and looked at me. I believed that I had mentioned I was a vegetarian before.

"What?" another colleague exclaimed, standing up. "You can *afford* not to be!"

This teacher's statement gave me pause. It was very telling. It reminded me of the poverty in this country and that even at the professional level Malawians were struggling, often going without meat for days.

At that moment one of the teachers stood before me.

"You are a *big* vegetarian then," he stated conclusively, studying me from head to toe.

This was said to a woman of five foot two and ninety-eight pounds.

◆ ◆ ◆

When I first arrived at Lunzu Secondary, the school had given me two books: one on English grammar and the other containing Malawian literature in English. Now well into my second year, I was assigning students more reading from the latter. I had flipped through this book several times, without noticing anything unusual, but one evening, while planning lessons, I came across something very interesting.

The tale was about a few young, poverty-stricken Malawians who fell asleep. When they woke up in the middle of the night, they noticed that everything in their house had changed. Everything was brand new: a state-of-the-art microwave, refrigerator, stove, and furniture. Moreover, when they looked in the mirror, they all had white skin! They expressed delight and wonder to each other. Yet this transformation was all based on them being good. Thus the theme of the story was that if one was good, one would become rich and white. A Malawian had written this.

I put down the book.

Was this story here because this was what many Malawians desired? Or was it here to induce discussion? Was it even politically correct to have such a story in Malawi's public school system? These teenagers were so impressionable. What did the Malawian Ministry of Education want to achieve with this?

Then I had an even stranger thought.

I was not white or black. Since my skin color was somewhere in between, did that mean I was just a little bit good and a little bit bad? Or perhaps I failed to make the successful transformation over to whiteness?

I was in a dilemma. The message in the story was against my beliefs and certainly against the spirit of Peace Corps. Was I going to teach it?

I talked to a few volunteers in Blantyre who were teachers, but they said they did not use this literature book. When I approached my Malawian colleagues at the school who taught English, they just shrugged saying I didn't have to use the story.

I scratched my head. There were plenty of stories in this book, so I moved on to the next one. But I could not help wondering how such a tale got into the curriculum and what other teachers who were using this book were doing about it.

Despite my ignorance, misunderstanding, and, sometimes, misgivings about the local culture, I wanted my students to be proud of their heritage. Even as a volunteer, still green in the field of development, I could never imagine that the way to improve a country was to suppress its culture. A strong cultural heritage, opened to new ways of doing things, was key to developing.

If I had stood in front of the class and read this story to my students, it would only reinforce their poverty and lack of opportunity, none of which needed reinforcing. But I was here to encourage growth and pride. I wanted my students to believe in themselves and what they can do, not to desire to be a different race.

I decided that this story had no place in my classes.

Figure 8.1. A few teachers, Lunzu Secondary School, 1996

9

Working the System

"Aren't you supposed to be at your school teaching?" I asked Mark over bites of a sandwich.

Mark Duncan, a Peace Corps volunteer who was a secondary school math teacher in a small village in northern Malawi, looked at me and shrugged. We were having lunch upstairs from the PTC Supermarket at the Regency, a small café that catered to the expat community in Blantyre.

"I don't worry about it," Mark said with his mouth full. "Whenever I am away I give the students notes to copy."

And he really wasn't worried. He just sat right there at the table with me in a room full of Britons and Americans eating his tuna melt and sipping his Coke.

I looked at him. He was young and affable. Originally from Iowa, he had joined the Peace Corps with a math degree. All through the village stay, Mark had been among the best at learning Chichewa. He was one of the few who could actually carry on a conversation in the local language beyond the initial greeting and a few primitive statements.

But he wasn't terribly responsible or dependable. He was one of those guys who, if he told you he was going to do something, there was only a fifty-fifty chance he was going to do it.

Over the past year, I had seen him wandering in Blantyre every now and then when the school year was in session. His school was located over nine hours away. Yet whenever I approached him asking how his classes were going, I always got the same answer: he had given notes to his students. I had heard this phrase before—many times. Some of the teachers at Lunzu Secondary would do this too when they didn't feel like teaching. It happened more often than was good for the students, and the teachers got away with it. For some reason Mr. Alifand did not crack down on things like this.

But, I thought, standards should be higher for a Peace Corps teacher, shouldn't they? As an American, Mark stood out. He should be setting the example for his Malawian colleagues, not falling into their indolent ways.

I could almost see those kids in Mark's classes, hours north of Lilongwe, waiting for him to teach. It was a sad thought.

Weeks later I was again running errands in Blantyre and ran into Cate White. Cate was a Peace Corps biology teacher whose school was located about an hour from Blantyre. We stopped in the street and talked.

"Nice to see you again," I said, wiping the sweat off my brow. It was a sweltering hot day.

She smiled. From a well-off family in New Jersey, Cate told me originally that she had joined Peace Corps to do good in the world. Young and pretty, she was one of the few women in our class who seemed to have a knack for the sciences.

But today she would tell me something different.

"How are your classes?" I asked.

"So, so," she replied, rolling her eyes. "My headmistress doesn't seem to like me so I am only teaching two days a week."

Two days a week?

I was aghast. I was teaching all five days, and so were other education volunteers who were reasonably committed to their schools. How could this be?

Cate didn't want to talk more about it. Apparently, this scanty schedule had been going on for some time. I asked her what she did for the remainder of her week.

"I come to Blantyre," she answered, her voice trailing off a bit. "I'm signed up for yoga and French classes."

Weeks later I was talking to a few friends in Blantyre who admitted they had seen Cate in the city on weekdays during work hours, wandering aimlessly.

I thought about Cate, Mark, and others like them who were doing minimal work. Peace Corps had sent us information months ago stating that there were opportunities for a "secondary" project for those who were able and had the time. The letter included a list of nonprofit organizations in various locations. Why didn't these volunteers sign up for these jobs? Were they earning their stipend and *helping* Malawi? If not, should they still be in Peace Corps? What happened to the great enthusiasm projected back in Washington, D.C.?

Understandably, most in my class were very young with little or no work experience outside of college. For many, it was the first time they had been abroad and away from family for long periods. Some indulgences were to be expected and should be allowed to a certain extent. Yet I could not help but wonder about those who took advantage of the system—the Peace Corps budget and, ultimately, American taxpayers' money—without giving much in return.

Could it be that this was a trend in the development field: great enthusiasm in the beginning that eventually petered out with many giving up hope and leaving while others stayed, some taking advantage of the system?

Then again, problems in the field were never that simple. Some volunteers had justified complaints. Teachers expressed concern about the lack of classrooms, chairs and desks, school books, chalk boards, chalk, writing paper, and so forth. Likewise, health workers lamented over the shortages in medicine, needles, bandages, beds, clean linen, and low sanitation standards. Mix all these problems with the lack of competent local staff, a relaxed work ethic, the differences in culture and language, a poorer socioeconomic background, and what does one get? Huge multifaceted issues with no easy solutions.

There were Peace Corps volunteers who worked very hard, but they were not in the majority. These were usually the ones who thought about things on their own and found creative solutions to problems. Some of them had secondary jobs, and others had applied for and received grants to do additional projects at their sites. One young man in our group, Will Samson, was a nutritionist who saw a need in the Peace Corps population. With his free time he wrote a cookbook based on items that could be found in local markets. It was published and distributed to all the volunteers, who found it very useful. Another woman, Sharon Crane, who was an organizer for the Parks at Lake Malawi, had a lot of initiative. When she lost her initial position, instead of complaining to the Peace Corps director, she wasted no time in finding a new one. Finally, Melanie Johnson, who was stationed in Blantyre, worked the hardest I had ever seen any volunteer work. Loving her job as an engineer, she put in so many hours that even her roommates commented on her dedication.

In all my time in Blantyre, I never saw Will, Sharon, Melanie, or those like them, wandering about aimlessly.

Perhaps working successfully in the development field was more than just merely doing one's job, it was about dedication and the creative solutions one came up with and acted upon along the way.

10

Lesson Learned

On a sunny day I was coming out of my house and heading toward the school when I saw a group of men—my fellow Malawian teachers—sitting on the ground in front of House No. 4, staring with stone-like expressions into the dirt.

I quickly grabbed a passer-by and asked what had happened.

"Mrs. Machimbe died last night," he said quietly.

Mrs. Machimbe was the wife of my colleague who lived in House No. 4. I had heard in the past month that she was sick and in the hospital. But I did not know it was fatal.

Instead of just coldly walking past I stopped at House No. 4, put my books down, and sat down on the dirt with the men. I did not see any women. As I copied the men by staring stonily into the ground, I could hear the women, the wives of these men, approaching. They all had scarves wrapped over their heads instead of the usual way of letting their hair free, and all had chitenjes wrapped around their waists.

The women entered the house and began wailing loudly to each other in Chichewa. The screeching, screaming, and crying were almost unbearable. I looked around. By contrast the men were motionless, expressionless, and quiet. I wondered just how many of these people were actually close to the Machimbes, particularly Mrs. Machimbe. She had not been particularly social.

The wailing continued and I winced. I sat quietly holding up my head with my hands. Maybe some of the screaming was genuine, but I had a feeling that a lot of it was done out of custom. After a while, some of the men got up and continued on to the school to work. I hurriedly did the same.

But no one talked about what the lady died of.

Weeks later, death came around again.

The Machimbes had been blessed with a baby boy earlier in the year. But the baby was a sickly child and was constantly in and out of Mlambe hospital. When the mother died, the baby was in the hospital, hooked up to a respirator that of course required electricity. While he was in the hospital, a storm buffeted Lunzu for several days. No one in the vicinity had power for a while. When the power finally returned, the teachers told me that Mr. Machimbe's baby boy had died, just weeks after his mother.

When I next saw the now childless widower, Mr. Machimbe's face was etched with pain.

"It should not have happened this way," he said quietly and walked away.

I felt even worse than before.

I went back to my house, threw my books down and yelled out—at no one. What the hell was the West doing in this country? Weren't we supposed to *fix* these kinds of problems? What good did I do? I was less than a kilometer away from this baby who had a problem with a simple solution and I wasn't able to do anything.

What good were my English classes anyway?

I was really down. I felt useless and ineffective. The save-the-world values I had prior to Malawi were fading, fuzzier in view, and no longer realistic to me. I saw the limits of what I could do and I saw the limits of what my Peace Corps friends could do. It was frustrating to acknowledge that we had been in a country for close to two whole years but made only a small amount of difference.

Still, in the middle of this inexplicable disappointment, I had learned something: development issues were complicated, nebulous, changeable, and often unclear. Some of the problems came from the locals and others came from the foreigners. Still there were those that no one knew exactly how they originated but that they were here and needed to be dealt with.

Perhaps success should not be measured against what we had set out to do but by what we could do, creatively and patiently, along the way.

Wiping up tears, I stood up. Though the process was humbling, I still wanted to try. In the few months I had left, I wanted to do what *I* could to help the locals with what I had.

11

Changed and Unchanged

It was September 1997, close to the end of our service. Princess Diana had just died in a car accident in Paris. Everyone who had heard the news was in a daze. Even the teachers at my school were questioning what had happened.

Entering the teachers' lounge, I had just picked up my last letter from our office in Lilongwe. It informed me that there was going to be a meeting in the capital between officials in the Ministry of Education and the Peace Corps teachers in my class. It encouraged us to attend. As I read on I realized that the point of the meeting was to allow us to give feedback to the ministry.

This was a great idea I thought.

A few days later I was in Blantyre and ran into a fellow Peace Corps teacher.

"Are you going?" I asked, referring to the meeting with the ministry.

"Nah," he said, waving a hand nonchalantly. "It wouldn't make a difference anyway."

I gave him a forced smile. Close to half my class was already gone for one reason or another. Very few teachers were left. When I arrived in Lilongwe two days before the meeting, I ran into a few more and asked whether they would be attending.

"It doesn't fit my schedule," Annie said, busily planning her exit trip from Malawi.

"Nor mine," Brandon replied, walking away.

"Who's bothering to go to that anyway?" Tim asked, looking at me as though I was a moron.

In the end only two volunteers would go to this meeting: Darren Jones and I.

On the day of the meeting Janet Chikondi, one of the associate Peace Corps directors, said she would accompany us. Janet was an educated Malawian who managed our program's education sector. She was bright, young, and articulate. As I arrived at the Peace Corps office that morning, Janet seemed apprehensive about what Darren and I would say to the ministers. She went over our lists, making sure what we had planned to speak on was appropriate for the occasion.

I thought this was a bit curious as the point was to give the ministry our honest feedback.

Always careful, Janet gave the example that at the previous year's meeting with the ministry, the teachers in the prior group made some inappropriate remarks. She emphasized that we were meeting with important government officials and that we should behave with decorum.

As the three of us drove up to an old grayish set of buildings, which made up the government complex in the capital city, I had a sudden flashback to two years earlier when my class first landed in the country. That week the hundred or so of us, all fresh-faced, eager, with clean clothes, unsoiled shoes, and no dirt beneath our fingernails, had been ushered into one of these buildings to be welcomed by Malawian government officials.

But it would be different today. It was only Janet, Darren, and me. We were escorted into a huge impersonal hall to wait for the ministers. When two finally appeared I recognized the woman immediately. She was a heavy lady with braids in her hair, and she wore a long dress all the way down to her ankles made from colorful local cloth. When she walked she had an air of dignity though her movements were slow. I had seen her the first time in our initial welcome meeting and then again at Lunzu Secondary School when she made a rare visit.

As the three of us took our seats in a huge auditorium facing the ministers in the center, the male minister began by saying how happy he was to see us. He was a tall gentleman with a large stomach and a round face. He thanked us for our service and made some remarks about improving the school system. While he spoke, I looked around the room. It felt so empty. One might have thought that there would be more teachers wanting to give feedback to the Malawian government.

Then Janet began to speak. She related how much Peace Corps enjoyed working with the ministry and hoped that the relationship will continue for years to come. After she finished, Darren shared his views. Darren was a skinny young man who taught science at a school located in the middle of the country. Having the air of a know-it-all and sporting a ponytail that hung down the back of his neck, he spoke with a tone of confidence. He told the ministers which school he was at, which subject he taught, some of the challenges he faced, and he made a few recommendations. The ministers nodded. Darren was polite, politically correct, and brief. Given his usual outspokenness, I thought his remarks were a little subdued. There were numerous problems many of us observed in the school system.

Everyone now looked at me. It was my turn. I told the ministers who I was, what subject I taught, which school I was at, and some of the good and bad experiences I had teaching. They nodded, looking a little bored.

Then I decided to go for it.

Prior to this meeting, I did not reveal to Janet what I wanted to say about the Malawian literature book, partly because I had not decided whether I would bring up the topic. But now, I saw this was my only chance to speak to these senior officials, and if there was anything I wished for them to know, this was the moment.

I looked them straight in the eye and told them about that story in their literature book for Forms One and Two, the one whose theme emphasized that if Malawians were good they would become white and have the privileges and material wealth of a white person. I reminded the ministers that the students were young and impressionable. They should be encouraged to be proud of their culture and work with what they have, not try to be somebody else and certainly not another race. Moreover, the story was inaccurate. Not all white people were good and wealthy. This story had no place in the school system and should be removed.

The ministers stared at me.

After a few minutes, one of them spoke.

"Did you say you are Jade Wu?" the male minister asked, breaking the silence.

I nodded.

"My nephew told me about you," the minister said.

"Who is your nephew?" I asked, taken aback.

"Wilson Mgambe," the minister answered. "He is in your Form Two class at Lunzu Secondary School. He talks about you."

I didn't know what to say. I didn't know whether this was bad or good. I knew Wilson. He was indeed one of my pupils, but he never told me that his uncle was a top ministry official. I certainly did not expect this revelation today.

Then the ministers spoke. They said they did not know such a story was in the literature volume. They agreed that it needed to be reviewed and thanked me for highlighting it. Arguably, it could have been there for discussion purposes, but these kids were impressionable.

As we left the ministry's building that day I could not believe that my Peace Corps service was coming to an end. Two years had passed so quickly.

But what have I accomplished here? How many lives, if any, have I helped, changed, or given hope to?

This was difficult to measure. In fact, I did not even know if it could or should be immediately. It would be nice if numbers on a chart did the job, but many times statistics were skewed. Just because I taught English to over three hundred Malawian students in a school year did not mean that all these students' English-language skills had improved. And just because their English had not improved did not mean they did not otherwise benefit from my presence. One had to take into consideration all the times I gathered my students together and shared with them what I had seen and experienced outside of Malawi, opening their eyes and minds to new things.

Then my thoughts turned to the country itself. It has had a Peace Corps presence for more than thirty years, not counting all the other foreign assistance entities it has been hosting. Yet what about the country has improved? Many troubling issues were not going away. Deep-rooted problems involving poverty, education, health, corruption, and government were alive and well. How was it that these problems failed to diminish even after foreigners and their influences have been in Malawi for more than a hundred years?

History tells us that not all foreign presence was helpful, even that which was well intentioned. I thought about my Peace Corps class. In theory, we came to Malawi to help, to teach, and share skills. Yet as time passed and difficulties arose, many volunteers terminated and went away. Not only did some offer little to the Malawians, they had a free trip to another part of the world, all on the American taxpayers' tab. Ultimately, those who had completed their two years of service had either *worked* or managed to find a way *to work* the system.

My last day in the country had arrived. Even as I boarded a taxi to take me to Lilongwe International Airport, I believed that things in Malawi could improve. There were locals who worked very hard, but it would take time, patience, creativity, and innovation, qualities not many foreign assistance entities encouraged in their employees as I would later learn.

Sitting in the plane next to Muriele Addams, another volunteer who had completed her service but who had long waited for this day, my beliefs were confirmed.

"Hooray! We're leaving!" she exclaimed as the plane started to move. It could not be soon enough for her.

Out the window the tiny airport was as I remembered it on the first day we arrived: a skinny airstrip with one small whitish building and a few shrubs. Nothing much about it had changed. *I* was the one who was different. It was amazing that I flew into this poverty-stricken country thinking that there were so many things I could teach it when, in the end, I was the one who ended up being taught.

While I was mulling over these thoughts, the plane took off. Within minutes Malawi, the country, had disappeared, but the lessons it taught me remained a lifetime.

II
_____

Crisis in Kosovo

Map of the Republic of Kosova (Kosovo) courtesy of Wikimedia Commons.
https://commons.wikimedia.org/wiki/File:Kosova%60s_Map.gif.
Author: Korrik Sofalia.
Source: http://technorati.com/politics/article/six-months-more-for-kosovo-acting/.
Licensed under Creative Commons Attribution-Share Alike 3.0 Unported.
No part of this image was altered.

Flashback Two

In the midst of the Albanian-Serbian crisis, I was told by my Kosovar staff that they had just found a new teenager staying at the World Vision shelter in Prishtina. When I went to meet her, Kaltrina told me that she had run away from home. Her father had raped and impregnated her elder sister with the help of their two brothers.

Shortly before running away while Kaltrina was lying awake in her room one night, she heard her sister give birth. A candle was lit and a baby was heard crying. Then suddenly the light was extinguished and there was no more baby noise. She heard the back door slam as her father walked out to the river behind their house. Kaltrina believed that he murdered the child and threw the body in the river. The next day her sister ran away and, Kaltrina believed, committed suicide. Days later, Kaltrina had an argument with her father. He picked up a hot iron and swung it at her. She could take no more. She ran away and found me.

12

Manhattan of Humanitarians

"Do—do you want to work here?" Tony asked, calling from Kosovo. The static on the phone was nonstop.

"Yes! Yes! Of course!" I shouted into the receiver excitedly.

"There—there are many international entities here looking to hire— if you buy yourself a plane ticket and fly out here, I'm pretty sure you'll find a job," Tony suggested.

Anthony E. Julius was a U.S. Foreign Service officer I had met in Los Angeles a year after returning from Malawi. He had been teaching foreign affairs at UCLA as the Diplomat-in-Residence when I did an informational interview with him. A tall, stately looking gentleman in his fifties, he had the air of an aristocrat. Yet once I started the interview I found that not only was he extremely well read, he was down-to-earth and funny. We kept in touch and months later, in the middle of 1999, the U.S. Department of State sent him to Kosovo.

The crisis in the Balkans was all over the news. Kosovo, unlike peaceful Malawi, had just emerged from a period of warfare, ethnic cleansing, and destruction. It had not even been recognized as a country yet and rule of law was virtually nonexistent. Its administration of government was under the United Nations, which was scrambling to sort out disputes and inject some law and order. The situation on the ground was very tense and there were frequent clashes between the Albanians and the Serbians. Hundreds of thousands of Kosovar Albanians who had been displaced earlier were starting to return from nearby countries. International entities of all sizes involved with humanitarian work flocked to the area and, as Tony informed me, were desperate to expand their staff.

It would be a risk, I knew. But I still wanted to work overseas helping others. I hadn't given up after Malawi, and Kosovo would be my first taste of what it would be like to earn money working in a full-blown humanitarian crisis, one which involved peace-building, reconstruction, and stabilization efforts.

So I took the chance.

I printed numerous resumes, put them in my suitcase, closed my apartment in Virginia where I had moved to by then, and bought a one-way plane ticket to Kosovo. It was December 1999. During the flight I remembered looking out at the clouds and wondering what I would do if this Kosovo gamble did not work out. I would be out, at a minimum, the cost of a plane ticket. On top of that I would have the bother of flying back, moving my things out of storage and back into an apartment, not to mention looking for another job.

With these thoughts in mind, after arriving in Prishtina, the capital of Kosovo, and finding a place to stay with the help of Tony and his office, I wasted no time wading through the slush in the main streets. Sidewalks were dirty, chipped, and uneven. Piles of trash abutted dilapidated buildings. Heaps of gray snow stood in the way of cars and people. Black smoke polluted the air as garbage was burned. Traffic lights failed to work causing congestion.

Prishtina was one of those cities where vehicles were parked on the sidewalks while pedestrians walked in the streets.

But the city did have one thing going for it: it was littered with the offices of any international development organization one could think of and even ones that one has never heard of. It was the metropolis of do-gooders, the Manhattan of humanitarians. I saw office signs for Save the Children, World Vision, International Red Cross, Catholic Relief Services, the Office of the United Nations High Commissioner for Refugees (UNHCR), the Organization for Security and Cooperation in Europe (OSCE), and so forth. I walked into one building after another, dropping off my resume, and watched as employees zipped in and out wearing jackets with company logos. The air was filled with excitement, hope, and energy.

We internationals were going to fix Kosovo.

Then, I saw an ad for a community services coordinator at an American nonprofit organization. The position called for a leader who had the ability to organize and communicate effectively. This person would be in charge of the distribution of information and emergency relief supplies to displaced Kosovars.

I entered the office and handed the receptionist my resume. She asked me to wait. In a few minutes, I was told that the director wished to interview me immediately. I was led into the office of Chia Chisomo. Chia was from Kenya. With her frizzy black hair, dark skin, East African accent and manners, she reminded me very much of a Malawian. I felt very comfortable talking to her. It was bizarre that I flew all the way to the Balkans only to find myself being interviewed by a woman from East Africa. After Chia interviewed me, she offered me the job. She needed me to start right away. I didn't even have time to change clothes or eat lunch.

My first assignment ended in embarrassment. Parked outside our nonprofit was a white Land Rover with the organization's logo on it. Chia asked me to drive this vehicle to a nearby village to deliver goods to Kosovars in need. When I stepped outside, the icy wind blew right through my bones. As I seated myself in the driver's seat, I saw the vehicle had a manual transmission. Not knowing how to operate one, I let out a big sigh. Just minutes after I had aced the interview, I had to return to the office to inform Chia of one of my many deficiencies.

She looked at me and laughed.

"Well, we'll just have to hire a driver for you," she concluded.

She called in a local assistant and told him to bring in some resumes for drivers. The next morning when I reported to work, I saw a line of young men, all Kosovar Albanians, waiting to be interviewed. I looked at these men. They were all bundled up in old winter clothes: worn-out coats, sweaters, and torn jeans. Many of them had uneven haircuts, the type one received at home with blunt scissors, and crooked teeth, all of which were quieter signs of the low quality of life and the lack of availability of services.

The assistant was busily meeting and interviewing each man. Then around 10:00 a.m. a good-looking young Albanian was introduced to me. His name was Eduard Jupa.

Eduard was about five foot nine, had short brown hair, brown eyes, and even features. With the help of the right makeup artist and the right clothes, I believed he could resemble Tom Cruise. Eduard sat down and we began to converse. His English wasn't great, but we were able to communicate.

"Do you speed?" I asked. "I can't have anyone who speeds."

He laughed and said that he was a careful driver.

"Do you drink and drive? I can't have any of that either," I continued.

He shook his head and answered that he did not drink.

As we went through the interview, his eyes sparkled with laughter. I guess he could tell that I wasn't as strict as I wanted to sound. Finally, I looked up and gave our assistant a signal of approval. Eduard was hired.

13

A New Class

The international community I met in Prishtina was diverse, made up of Europeans, Americans, Africans, Japanese, and many other nationalities. One could not get through a day without running into bunches of them. Young and old, they were all over the place. With their nifty North Face–type jackets, Columbia-type boots, fancy handheld devices, and SUVs sporting company names, they became the new, trendy class of humanitarians, one whose members could be spotted a mile away. Likewise, their employers were each fighting for a piece of the action, trying to land as many contracts as possible, and vying to raise their international profiles.

Every week there would be meetings after meetings, sometimes far too many. Those in the health, housing, gender, security, and good-governance sectors came together, ideally to share information and open up discussions, with the hoped-for purpose not to duplicate or contradict each other's efforts. Yet the more I attended these meetings, the more I saw how disorganized and chaotic the foreign community really was. It was the classic case of the right hand not knowing what the left hand was doing. Many seemed more interested in bragging about their entity's achievements than sharing critical information. Often an organization's representative would stand up and read off how many families his organization assisted that week, and where, without providing further information about the difficulties it had experienced while doing so.

Though English was the working language, so many in these meetings spoke it with such different accents it was often difficult to understand one another. Whenever this happened, one could see people in the audience straining their ears to listen or raising their hands to ask the speaker to repeat himself, which only added time and rarely clarified the confusion. On top of everything, very few were good public speakers. Their reasoning and organization of ideas often did not make sense.

In one meeting, I was sitting in the front row when a woman from Spain got up to speak. She was the international liaison with the Kosovo energy sector, and with the recent shortages in electricity we were expecting her to provide an update. Instead, she berated the international community for using too much electricity.

"Save energy! Save energy!" she commanded, pointing her finger at us. "Don't use more than you need!"

The audience was both surprised and taken aback. Most of us were experiencing the daily lack of a hot shower, working stove, and heat in our sleeping rooms due to constant blackouts. It was difficult to imagine saving anything one had so little of to begin with.

Looking around me, one of the main problems with the international community was the short duration most of its workers were here for. Most people were in Kosovo on temporary assignments, usually three to six months. Some were "on loan" from their regular duty stations in South America, Africa, and Asia. Even I was on a three-month contract. With this high rate of turnover, continuity was a problem, and what one individual promised to do weeks ago had little chance of being carried out, frustrating both Kosovars and foreigners alike.

Unlike what I had found in my Peace Corps class, the foreign community in Kosovo was a mixed bag. Some were very experienced in the humanitarian world, having over ten years with, say, the UN, and others were new to the field with little or no humanitarian experience. Given the great hurry with which many international entities tried to build their staff and the high rate of turnover they were experiencing, hiring requirements and procedures were often relaxed—which ultimately was reflected by the quality of the employees.

Shortly after I was hired, I saw an example of this in my own organization.

A weekend was arriving, and given all the stress and long hours at work, a few colleagues talked about "going away."

"It's going to be a blast," Liz said as she winked at Trae, who had crawled underneath a desk in our office to connect wires for a computer. He was our IT man.

Liz was a large woman in her twenties from Wisconsin. With freckles and frizzy red hair that flowed beyond her shoulders, she reminded me of an overgrown Raggedy Ann. Outspoken and outgoing, Liz gave me the sense she was in Kosovo more for the excitement than for the humanitarian side of things. She worked in our accounting department.

"Looking forward to it," Trae responded with a knowing smile from underneath the desk.

He was in his twenties, too, with a fit body and brown hair. But for his British accent, he looked like the typical white guy one would see on a college football team.

It was apparent that alcohol was going to be involved. New, I was not invited, so I passed the weekend quietly. When Monday morning arrived, the unenviable news trickled in. Liz, Trae, and two other coworkers took one of our entity's new SUVs and drove, without permission, across two borders to Sofia, Bulgaria. According to one written account, when they first arrived in Sofia, the group had parked the vehicle in front of a cinema and entered a restaurant. After a meal, they entered the cinema and stayed inside for several hours. When they came out, their vehicle was gone. Then came the rounds of helplessly going from one Bulgarian police station to the next, trying to find out who had taken the SUV. With no helpful information in hand, the group managed to gather up the courage to phone our employer. In addition to confessing to the unauthorized trip and the lost vehicle, they had to ask for transportation back. Upon their return to Prishtina, three of the four were immediately relieved of their positions.

I saw Liz as she was clearing out her desk, her eyes red.

"I still want to work here," she mumbled at no one in particular.

This unfortunate experience was only a preview to the lack of judgment of some who were rebuilding a country and people's lives.

14

No Perfect Solution

As often was the case in an area of the world where there was a frenzy of humanitarian action, organization was a challenge and my entity was no exception. Often we would not find out what our schedules were until we walked into the office that morning. Partly the field of humanitarian relief was to blame as one had to respond to whatever emergencies arose, and partly our management as it provided very little direction.

On a snowy day Eduard and I had our first assignment together. We didn't find out until we arrived at the office that we were to deliver a wood-burning stove to an Albanian woman living in the outskirts of Prishtina. Other than the directions to her house, all I was told was that she was expecting me and there would be people there to help us upon arrival.

After an hour on the road, we finally drove into her village. As we entered, I noticed several men lined up at the "entrance" as if to greet us. When we rolled by, they waved. Strangely, the four men looked alike, possibly quadruplets, except that each had a head a little smaller than the other. Meanwhile, their bodies were abnormally larger than their heads. I gasped as I had never seen such a deformity before.

I looked at Eduard.

He saw my face and tried to explain.

"This is small village," he said in broken English. "There are few people. They make family. This is small village."

I got the message: inbreeding.

When we spotted her house, we parked at the bottom of a hill since there was no drivable road up to the top where the house was. As we hiked up in the snow, the middle-aged matron came out and greeted us with the biggest smile. It was like sunlight on a dreary day. Even though she had white hair, wore an apron, and looked otherwise like a pie-baking grandmother, I thought she was beautiful. She expressed how happy and grateful she was to see us.

But then I looked around. There were no men other than the quadruplets I had seen at the entrance. I turned to the matron.

"Is your husband around?" I asked. "We need him to help us with the stove."

She shook her head.

"Killed! Killed!" She said, gesturing a stabbing with her hands. She then turned to Eduard and said something in Albanian, which he translated for me, that her husband had died at the hands of Serbians.

"Are there any male neighbors or relatives nearby?" I asked, horrified by her story. "The stove is very heavy."

She shook her head again.

By this time, a crowd of neighborhood children, approximately ages six through twelve, had gathered around to see *me*. It appeared that they had never seen an Asian close-up before. The woman pointed to them and said that these little ones were going to be the help.

I gulped.

The *heavy* wood-burning stove was inside our Land Rover—at the bottom of the hill.

I looked at the woman, the children with their sweet smiles, and I gulped again. How were we going to bring such an item uphill? What if the stove fell and crushed little toes and fingers?

But the woman exuded strength and confidence. She assured me that we could do it and I did not see another choice. We all walked down to the Land Rover. The pathway, though not long, was steep.

Suddenly, I had an idea.

I told everyone that we were going to carry the item up the hill in segments. I demonstrated using my hands. We would all count to three, pick up the stove, move it several steps, and put it down again.

"Ok, everybody got that?" I asked after explaining.

The woman, children, and Eduard smiled at me. We slowly took the stove out of the vehicle and set it down.

"One! Two!—Three!" the matron, children, Eduard, and I shouted together.

We picked up the stove, moved it several steps, and put it down again, laughing.

"One! Two! Three!" we counted again, moved the stove a bit, and set it down again.

Little by little, working as a coordinated group, we got the stove up the hill. I was sure anyone watching from a distance thought we were a strange sight. But the woman was happy, the kids were thrilled, and I was amazed. When we finally reached the top, the snow began to melt and sunlight streamed across the land.

Entering her front doorstep, I felt relieved and took a deep breath. We did it.

I never knew that determination and courage mixed with moving a heavy appliance would leave me so satisfied.

♦ ♦ ♦

"This is still Yugoslavia," Gina said loudly and confidently, walking through our office. She was in the middle of a conversation with another American and referring to Kosovo.

"It is Yugoslavia until a new government is recognized," Gina asserted, insensitive to the tense nerves she was already stepping on.

Several of our Albanian staff sitting nearby looked up. They were our administrators and translators. I could tell by their expressions that they weren't pleased with Gina's statements.

Gina Smithe was a graduate student in her thirties from northern California. Working as the community services coordinator out of our office in Ferizaj in southern Kosovo, she drove up periodically to Prishtina for supplies and staff meetings. Blond, pretty, and self-confident, she walked with a sure step, often offering strong opinions about the Albanian-Serbian crisis.

"I have problems with her," Vera whispered to me. Vera was a young Albanian who worked as a translator in our office. Though only twenty-five, she already showed the strains of a hard life. Her eyes had purple bags underneath them and her lifeless blond hair had started to thin.

Like many Albanians, her family suffered suppression under the previous government with several members experiencing violence at the hands of the Serbs.

"I don't like what she's saying," Vera continued, gesturing toward Gina. "Tereza has problems with her too."

Tereza, I knew, was our Albanian translator who worked in the same office as Gina in Ferizaj.

I nodded sympathetically at Vera, acknowledging that I heard and understood her. Then I looked at Gina and wondered why this woman was working in Kosovo. Did she know that her statements were inaccurate? It was already January 2000. Yugoslavia as a country had ceased to exist since 1992. Moreover, when it did, it was not a happy memory for most Albanians. Most of its government officials were Serbians who had treated the Albanians as second-class citizens.

Gina's job was to *help* the people of Kosovo, not to provide controversial political statements.

I looked around the office. Several of the Albanian staffers were whispering to each other, likely discussing what Gina had said. I asked myself whether the internationals in our office knew how essential our local employees were. They were our key to the local culture, language, ways of doing things—and its people. Without their help, our program would never succeed.

Days later, Vera came running up to my desk.

"There's a girl in the shelter who needs you!" she exclaimed, breathless.

I turned toward Vera. She began to tell me about Kaltrina Baliqi, the teenager she had found in the World Vision shelter just hours ago.

Little did I know that of the many sad and scary cases I would encounter in Kosovo, Kaltrina Baliqi's was the most heart-wrenching, with an eeriness attached. This case, like many others, required more than just humanitarian skills. It emphasized the need for social work experience, family counseling, and local culture expertise, skills that many internationals here did not possess, including me.

When I met her at the World Vision shelter with Vera, I knew hers would be a troublesome case, one with many layers of complications. Kaltrina was the teenage daughter of a Kosovar man who had mistreated his wife. The wife had left for Germany years ago, leaving behind daughters Kaltrina and Francesca and two sons. The man, Mr. Baliqi, was accused of raping his daughter Francesca, which resulted in her giving birth one night. Kaltrina had heard their father take the baby out to the back of the house, where she believed he had murdered the child and threw it in the river abutting the property. Subsequently, Francesca ran away and was never seen again, leaving Kaltrina at risk with their father.

One day after a fight and believing her life to be in danger, Kaltrina ran away and entered a shelter. When I first spoke to her I was trying to determine whether the father had abused her too. Kaltrina, whose teenage figure showed she had started to shed away the baby fat of earlier years, looked at me with dark brown eyes and shook her head, a mop of brown hair. Despite what she had experienced, she still had a smile for me, which came through sweetly from her round face. There was still a bit of hope left in her. It was the spirit of a seventeen-year-old who believed there was good out there.

What can I do to help her hold on to the belief that there was a fighting chance in this world for her?

Living at the shelter kept Kaltrina safe, but it was not a long-term solution. There were no set schedule, educational activities, or employment opportunities that could have kept her busy. Not surprisingly, her other relatives were either missing or unreachable. As far as I could tell, she only had her father, sister, and two brothers in Kosovo.

"I want to go to Germany, Jade," she kept saying in her accented English.

Kaltrina kept talking about going to Germany to join her mother. When I asked when they last spoke, she said it was about four years ago. Apparently, her parents were divorced and her mother had remarried in Germany.

I saw quickly that something must be done for Kaltrina but did not come across any programs that addressed a minor's need for a safe home and stability. So I went to talk to some of the Americans I knew at the U.S. Office, an office that performed the functions of an American embassy before one could be established. As Kaltrina was still at risk and the U.S.

Office was walking distance to the World Vision shelter where she was staying, I figured it would be safer if she found a job there.

I asked anyone and everyone if they had a paid job for a teen-ager. Though it wasn't part of my normal duties, this girl needed stability. Almost everyone I had spoken to shook their heads and went about their business, not giving my question a second thought. A few even berated me for going this far.

Finally, one colleague, who actually thought about things, suggested I try the cleaning department. Perhaps it could use a helping hand.

The cleaning department was in charge of tidying up the U.S. Office and its sister buildings, including residences of the American employ-ees. Mrs. Emini, a tall, large, fiftyish Albanian lady whose facial wrinkles showed she had endured hard times, was in charge.

When I told Mrs. Emini about Kaltrina, she immediately waved her hand at me.

"No! I can't hire such a girl!" she screeched. "I don't want to deal with her scary father coming here and bothering us. He sounds danger-ous! You don't know Albanians!"

She looked at me like I was a clueless American. Perhaps I was. But I was not going to give up that easily. Other than Vera and a few local staff-ers at my office, nobody seemed to care what was to become of Kaltrina.

I took a deep breath and simply asked Mrs. Emini to give the girl a chance, at the very least to give her an interview.

Mrs. Emini agreed.

Miraculously, after the interview Kaltrina was hired. The two women, speaking a common language and coming from the same background, had shared loss and sympathy.

Though I had helped Kaltrina solve a temporary problem, I was troubled by the response I had received from fellow Americans. It seemed that many of those I spoke to were busily running around with their proj-ects and deadlines. It was always a rush, rush, rush. Some even had the audacity to talk about their next country of assignment. Understandably, these people had meetings to go to, programs to design, money to give out, and Kosovars to save. But the style of approach was often reactive as opposed to proactive. Few appeared to be able to stop, think ahead, and see the bigger picture.

Kaltrina was a minor whose only parent in Kosovo was allegedly dangerous. She needed help—right away. Though she could stay at the World Vision shelter at no charge, it was unclear how long she would be able to do so. Rather than wait for disaster to happen, I decided that if she had some income she would be less vulnerable to a forced return to her father. If she was in America, public assistance in the form of child protective services would immediately step in and focus on her safety, housing, health, and education. But she was here in Prishtina where, ironically, this kind of service was nonexistent, though she was surrounded daily by countless international entities, millions of dollars of aid, and thousands of humanitarian workers.

One day, the dangerous Mr. Baliqi did find us.

And I experienced how essential local staff were.

We were in our office, discussing a case, when suddenly one of my employees ran in shouting, "Kaltrina's father is here! He is here!"

It was early afternoon. Most people were still at lunch. There probably weren't more than a handful of employees in the office, all of whom were Albanians.

We all looked at each other, not knowing what to do. Thankfully, Frederik Gezim, the tallest and the strongest-looking of my local staff, stood up and said, "I'll talk to him."

Out of the corner of my eye, I saw Frederik walk over to the entrance where Mr. Baliqi stood, looking grumpy and annoyed. Baliqi had his hands in his coat pockets and paced around impatiently. He was a short, fat, bald, and smug man with an ugly birthmark on his forehead.

Frederik said a few words, shook his head, and pointed toward the door. Mr. Baliqi shook his head also and raised his voice. At one point I saw Baliqi turn and look directly at me. His eyes narrowed. Frederik said a few more words and pointed to the door again. Baliqi shook his head and walked out.

"Baliqi is demanding you turn over his daughter," Frederik said to me after Kaltrina's father had left. "I told him to go away. I told him the police have her now and he must deal with them."

I refused to speak with Baliqi directly. We didn't have a common language anyway. He came back every couple of days, yelling and directing threats. In the back of my mind I saw the immediate danger he presented.

He could have a weapon on him at any time. We alerted the security officers in our building and the United Nations Mission in Kosovo Police (UNMIK-P), which was made up of police officers from the international community. The biggest problem was that rule of law had not been established, and though UNMIK-P could arrest someone, it could not hold him for long. Furthermore, since Kosovo's justice system was not up and running, trials were close to nonexistent.

I could see right away that Kaltrina and those of us helping her were in danger.

A few weeks later an American police officer named Chuck Smith came to my office. He was a stocky, muscular, tattooed man from Chicago on temporary police duty with UNMIK-P. He and his team informed me they were investigating Kaltrina's case and wanted to speak to her. Because he was American, easy to talk to, and shared my views on Kosovo, we hit it off right away. A few days later Officer Smith's team interviewed Kaltrina. She gave them her story and also told them she wanted to go home to retrieve a few things.

It was a cold day when Officer Smith, his men, Kaltrina, and I returned to her father's house. We had a clear, ice blue sky. As I boarded our Land Rover, a quick thought in the back of my mind brought me chills. What would we run into today? Would there be danger?

We drove about two hours south and arrived at her home village near Ferizaj in the southern part of Kosovo. Though the village was small with mostly shabby, one-story, gray concrete buildings, the snow seemed to give the whole place a softening effect. It covered all the filth on the roads, streets, and in the gutters like a clean white blanket. As we turned and walked down a street, Kaltrina pointed to her house. At a distance, the single-story, brown house draped in snow with a wooden front porch seemed normal, almost friendly, with trees surrounding it and a bit of forest behind. But as we got closer, the chills down my spine reappeared. I could only think of what had gone on inside. I gave Kaltrina a side glance. On the surface, she exuded no signs of fear.

At the front gate we met her younger brother who had just exited the house. He looked to be about twelve years old, was wearing jeans, and carrying a book bag over one shoulder. Kaltrina seemed surprised to see him. He greeted his sister, but she only stared back at him.

The officers started questioning the young man.

"Who's in there? Who is in the house?!" Officer Smith demanded.

The boy looked down at the ground and mumbled something in Albanian. He was clearly afraid of the officers. His words were quickly translated to mean that no one was at home and that the front door was unlocked. Apparently, Mr. Baliqi was out.

I was not sure whether one of Officer Smith's men detained the boy while we walked toward the house. The boy did not follow us and there was no further interaction between brother and sister.

When we approached the front door, I was nervous. Upon a closer look, the dwelling had broken windows and chipped paint. Since we were not trained to enter an unsecured house, Kaltrina and I stood a few feet away. A few of the officers entered the house first. After these men had cleared the inside, she and I slowly walked in. It was cold, quiet, and eerie. Things were in shambles. Tables, chairs, and drawers had been turned upside down and papers were strewn all over the place. There was even broken glass on the living room floor. What happened? I looked at Kaltrina. She looked distraught.

"My room is this way," she pointed nervously.

Kaltrina led an officer and I down a dark hall. When we entered her room, I saw it was simple and bright with a small bed, chest of drawers, and a broken window. There were trash and bits of paper all over the floor. Kaltrina quickly took a few things from inside a drawer and exited the house.

Minutes later, I found her standing on the front porch and fingering an old picture of her mother, a mother she had not seen for many years.

Then she broke out in sobs, "My house is really bad, Jade! Really, really bad!"

She grabbed my shoulders and cried uncontrollably. We stood this way for long time while the officers continued to comb the property. I felt there were many things she wanted to tell me but couldn't due to her limited English. Sympathy, anger, fear, and a great desire to help all hit me at once.

Then, as Kaltrina quieted down, I could hear the river behind the house. Its "peaceful" noise had an unsettling effect.

"Is this the river you told me about?" I asked.

She nodded.

"This is where your father threw in the baby's body?" I asked.

She nodded again.

At this point Officer Smith and a few of his men were walking around the outside of the house.

We walked up to them and Smith said, "Jade, my men were down here a few weeks ago. We had divers go into the river but could not find anything. We'll keep looking."

I walked over to the river and looked at it. It was narrow, but its current ran swiftly. I could not imagine a small, decaying body being easily found, especially after the passage of so many weeks.

Days after the visit to her father's house, Kaltrina had moved into an apartment in Prishtina with friends and was happily working for Mrs. Emini. Yet she revealed she was still afraid that her father would find her. I asked her what she wanted to do next.

"I want to go to Germany," she said again.

She wanted to join her mother. She said she had just spoken to her mother the week before and gave us the phone number. I thought it was time our office contacted Kaltrina's mother. With the help of an Albanian staffer and with Kaltrina's consent, we called.

It was a chilly February afternoon when Juliana and I sat down next to the telephone. Kaltrina was at work. Juliana, my Albanian staffer, was the one who would do the actual talking as she spoke Albanian. Neither one of us knew what the outcome would be. When we had Kaltrina's mother on the phone, she told Juliana that she was remarried in Germany and had a new family. Strangely, the mother sounded less than enthusiastic about Kaltrina joining her, offering that should her daughter arrive she would help put her in a shelter. The mother offered no more than that.

After the phone call, Juliana and I looked at each other. Juliana, a pretty Kosovar in her twenties, mumbled that this was not normal behavior for an Albanian woman. I sighed. Was Kaltrina really going to be better off as a public charge in a country where she did not speak the language? Would her unenthusiastic mother even bother to see her? Were there any friends or relatives in Germany who could support her financially and emotionally? Would the German government even want to take her?

So much for a mother's "love."

Later that day, Juliana and I went to see Kaltrina. As always she welcomed me with a huge smile. I felt great sympathy for her. She was a sweet girl who needed someone to care for her. Unfortunately, her mother left her behind in unsafe circumstances. Even now, when her mother had the chance again, she failed to reach out to Kaltrina in a way that a mother should.

Kaltrina looked bravely at Juliana and me. We told her what her mother had said. She acknowledged this was what her mother had told her last week. Then she became quiet.

I stepped forward and said, "If you still want to go to Germany, I will try to help you get a travel document. I can't promise anything else."

Kaltrina said she wanted the travel document.

Subsequently, I went to see the Office of the United Nations High Commissioner for Refugees (UNHCR) about this. This entity, which had its headquarters in Switzerland, had hundreds of internationals working in Kosovo. It had the mandate to protect and resettle refugees and also had the power to issue a travel document called a laissez-passer, which served as a passport. The evening I sat down with Damon, the UNHCR representative I knew through Chia, things did not look promising.

Damon was a tall Croatian with a big head and a booming voice. He had a wide face and gray eyes that never seemed to smile. When he spoke, it was as if his words were law. He hardly ever laughed, nor did he seem open to opinions different from his.

I told Damon about Kaltrina's plight, her desire to go to Germany, and the fact that she was still at risk. I suggested we act now since she was a minor and could be moved to the front of the line in getting a laissez-passer. Instead of arguing with me over whether Kaltrina was a refugee covered under UNHCR, he focused on her age. Damon insisted that Kaltrina should wait a year or so until she turned eighteen, then apply for the travel document herself. That way she could be certain that it was what she really wanted.

I looked at him, pleaded for Kaltrina again, but it appeared we were not getting anywhere.

My meeting with Damon ended without achieving anything. I could see that he failed to see that Kaltrina was still in danger. It didn't matter that she was a minor who had no helpful parent, guidance, or protection. With a temporary place to live and a job, what else could she wish for? Perhaps the German government would not even welcome her. Moreover, lots of Kosovars were displaced and in need of stability. She was only one of many.

Damon had bigger fish to fry.

Interestingly, Damon did not stop me from starting the application process for Kaltrina's laissez-passer. Several weeks later I managed to obtain preliminary documents for her from UNHCR. I gave these to her and told her that she could do whatever she wanted with them. She took them from my hand and thanked me. For the rest of my time in Kosovo, Kaltrina remained at her job at the U.S. Office. There were many reasons for her to stay, and the lack of warmth from her mother had a lot to do with her not going to Germany.

◆ ◆ ◆

Thousands of Albanians who had fled Kosovo were now returning from nearby countries, among them Switzerland, Germany, and Italy. When they fled years ago, their houses were either taken over by squatters or destroyed by eruptions of violence with the Serbs. Families were split apart in the exodus and members went missing or dead. Now, upon return, these people were in desperate need of housing, food, medical services, transportation, employment, education, financial assistance, and information. Moreover, the government they had known no longer existed.

In the middle of trying to solve these crises it became apparent how ill-equipped the international community really was. The more I looked around the more I saw how very few of us, including me, had a good understanding of the region's history, the basis for its disputes, and the extent of its deep-seated divisions, which were all essential to forming viable solutions. Yet this lack of knowledge did not stop the hordes of international entities continually trickling in. Many were given huge budgets and, day after day, rushed to put out fires big and small, often tripping over each other in the process: a family in Gjilan needs shelter, a young victim of human trafficking needs protection, a group of Albanians was dumped back at the Macedonia-Kosovo border, a child from Lipjan needs serious medical attention . . .

Every now and then a group of friends, all Americans, and I would go out to dinner, to talk, laugh, relax, and share the week's frustrations. It would usually be at one of the many restaurants that had sprung up in Prishtina recently, catering to the international community. These were the places to be and to be seen.

On one such evening we all met at the Parliament Restaurant in Dragodan near the U.S. Office. This restaurant had just opened its doors when the U.S. Office was setting up. American, British, French, Italian, and Swedish clientele were among its many constants. With a menu featuring cordon bleu, gourmet pizzas, Mediterranean salads, and tiramisu, the flow of internationals through its front door was nonstop. Many would enter, look around, say hello to everyone they knew, and then plop down to gaze at an exotic wine list.

As we sat there and chatted, leaning over a smooth white table cloth dotted by two small candles, I could hear bits of conversation from the other tables. Like many of its sister establishments, it was apparent that the Parliament Restaurant was not only a place where internationals came to eat but to network, politic, socialize, and look for a mate.

"Who's that curvy blond?" one man asked his friend, gesturing at an attractive young woman across the room.

"Oh, she's the new coordinator for Mercy Corps—."

"She's hot," the man said, raising his glass of wine. "I think I'll go over and say hi." He winked as he gulped down his drink and stood up.

Another conversation, between two women, was going on to my right.

"That meeting we had this morning was so pointless. What a waste of time!" one of women exclaimed, frustrated.

Her companion nodded sympathetically over mouthfuls of salad.

"Did you see how the donor stepped in and just interrupted me? He just doesn't like me. I think I'm going to have to sidestep around him from now on. I can't afford to lose his support, but I can't get anything done with him."

Then one of my colleagues leaned toward me.

"See that woman over there in the red shirt talking to the man with his back toward us?" he whispered.

I nodded.

"Well, she's the new Protection Officer at UNHCR. She replaced Terry. We're going to have to kiss up to her from now on."

I frowned. Our organization had a UNHCR contract and we were often running around, doing things at its command.

These conversations went on and on.

Though the atmosphere was relaxed, friendly, and even rowdy when too much wine flowed, it did not include the local staff of these entities. The people present, except for the wait staff, were almost always foreigners. Basically, the foreign community got together, laughed, flirted, exchanged information, and sought advice from one another, failing to see that consulting with Kosovars just as often was equally, and likely more, important.

"The locals here are peasants, just peasants," an American UNHCR representative told me later, shaking her head disgustedly. "They remind me of the villagers in China to whom I used to teach English."

I grimaced and looked away.

◆ ◆ ◆

As in Kaltrina's case, other situations arose that tested the international community's capabilities—often irksomely highlighting its limits and its shallow understanding of the local culture.

One day, while in my office, I received a radio call that there was someone I needed to visit in a women's shelter. I thought it was the run-of-the-mill runaway case requiring our intervention to reunite family members. When Eduard, Juliana, and I arrived at the shelter, there was nothing "normal" about the case.

The runaway was a wife, an Albanian, whose first name was Rita. Rita was a woman in her mid-thirties with short brown hair, a gaunt face, dark circles underneath her eyes, and quiet manners. She held a small baby in her arms when she opened the door to let us in. Except for her ballooning stomach, which indicated another pregnancy, she was very thin. As I edged closer, I saw the bruises on her face. They were the first signs of deeper problems. I waited for her to speak.

Through translation, I came to understand that Rita had run away from her husband and her mother-in-law. She said that her husband had beaten her at the direction of his mother. When I asked her what she wanted to do, she stated she wanted to return to her husband but only if a need was met. She asked us to build her a wall.

A wall?

I didn't understand this and asked her to repeat herself. She repeated it: a wall. Yes, she wanted us to build her a wall inside the house she shared with her husband and mother-in-law. Apparently, Rita was living in the living room and had no privacy. She believed that if there was a wall that encased her in a room of her own, the other occupants of the house would leave her alone.

I scratched my head. I told her that our nonprofit existed mainly to deliver emergency supplies and information to displaced Kosovars. We did not build walls. We were not a construction company.

She looked at me pleadingly. She was depressed and had no place to go. She emphasized she was not running away from her husband but wanted to return. She only needed this permanent physical partition in their house.

We all spoke to her and told her that this wall was not the solution. Her husband and his mother could still abuse her, even if a wall existed. Did she still want to live with them? Was there another relative she could go to?

There wasn't, or so she said. Given the massive population displacement of Kosovars, she did not know where her other relatives were or if any of them were even alive. Then I looked at Rita's belly. I asked her when she expected to give birth. She answered that it would be in about two months.

At this point Juliana pulled me aside. Always alert and perceptive, she asked if I knew that our nonprofit had a water sanitation division. I said I did but did not know much about it. Juliana revealed that sometimes the water sanitation department also did small construction projects. Perhaps it would be willing to help us with this one.

We told Rita that we would need to visit her husband's house. We made no promises. We would be in touch.

Days later I went with Eduard and Juliana to the house Rita shared with her husband and mother-in-law. Rita remained behind at the shelter with her baby. When we arrived, her husband Agim and his mother were present. They allowed us into their one-story house, which looked fairly neat on the surface. But I could sense tensions underneath. Agim, a round man with a dark mustache and a balding head, was nervous. His eyes kept darting back and forth while he spoke and his right knee would not stop twitching. His mother was a thin, unsmiling, gray-haired matron who projected a veneer of calmness that barely concealed her iron-fisted tendencies underneath. Silently, she put up with our meeting but looked at us with narrowed eyes. It was as though we were intruding into her rightful space.

We spoke with them about Rita and what she wanted.

Not surprisingly, Agim and his mother denied ever abusing Rita. Surprisingly, they seemed nonchalant about the wall request. The only thing Agim expressed was that he wanted Rita and the baby to come home.

Somehow I didn't believe Agim and his mother's story. Something wasn't right with their version of events. I did not want Rita to return to them at this stage, but she did not have a place to go. The shelter was filled with people and taking more in each day. It was unable to provide any special treatment for a pregnant woman who was also taking care of a baby.

So I went to find Mike Hanson, the head of our organization's water sanitation division.

Mike was from England. A handsome man in his fifties with wisps of white hair over his temples, he and I first met on my original flight into Kosovo. There had been an empty seat next to me. I remembered this tall Briton walking up and saying with a sexy accent, "May I sit here?"

I looked up. He was wearing a black leather jacket, jeans, and leather shoes. Very stylish, I thought.

"Sure," I said, shrugging, and returned back to my reading.

During the flight, Mike told me that he was an engineer and had worked in other developing countries. He had given me a few tips about looking for a job in Kosovo, but little did we know we would end up working for the same nonprofit organization.

I told Mike now about Rita's plight and asked him if the wall was a possibility.

"Yes we can do it," Mike answered. He had the workmen and the materials for it.

The only problem was that Mike had looked upon me with prurient interest, conveying his message with flirty remarks and gifts of chocolate. I now remembered why I had stayed away from his department.

My dilemma was that I needed to make sure he was going to build this wall, even while I rejected his advances. He assured me he would and in several weeks the project was done. Rita returned to her husband's house with the baby.

Shortly after this incident, the chief of mission of our organization became ill and returned to his home country New Zealand. I remember when I was informed that Mike would be the new acting chief of mission. I was leaving the building when one of my coworkers told me. Mike happened to be standing outside as I walked out to the street.

"So you've heard," he said.

I nodded.

His eyes gleamed. He leaned over and said, "Let me take you to dinner tonight."

I was uncomfortable. He was my boss now.

"Mike, I can't go to dinner with you. It wouldn't look right," I answered.

He smiled suavely, whispering, "We'll make it a working dinner. I'll come by around six and pick you up."

By this time, I was living in a house in downtown Prishtina that was rented by the organization. I shared it with two coworkers of the same rank. At 6:00 p.m. Mike was walking up to our front door.

"What is *he* doing here?" one of my housemates said looking out the window.

He was her boss too.

"Uh—he's here to take me to dinner. We have a project to discuss," I nervously threw in.

My two housemates looked at each other.

We went to a restaurant that night and on the whole, the evening passed with little incident. As Mike drove me back to my house he revealed that when he initially met me on the plane it was no accident that he came to sit next to me.

"I think you are really pretty," he said. "You remind me of my former girlfriend."

I gulped. I didn't care to remind *anyone* of a former girlfriend. I told Mike I had a boyfriend. Mike looked at me and his expression showed little concern.

I got out of the car and said goodnight. My housemates were in their rooms. The next day in the office, one of my housemates gave me a wink. Then another coworker did the same. Gossip traveled. This wasn't going to be easy.

For the next little bit, I did my best to avoid him. But our offices were small and there was no getting around it. Often I would have to speak to him about something work related. Every time I was present, I would get a gleaming smile. But his smile was not as sunny as I would have liked. There was something unholy about it.

Then he asked me again. "How about dinner tonight?"

Before I had a chance to say anything he added, "We'll talk about one of the projects."

I said I didn't need to talk about any projects. But he insisted. I *insisted* if we were going to have a working dinner, I should be able to bring my deputy Bill Nate. Mike sighed. I could bring Bill if I wanted to.

Bill was a smart, no-nonsense native of South Africa. He was organized, articulate, and hard to intimidate. Apparently, he had already heard about Mike's interest in me. So when I went to inform him about dinner he rolled his eyes.

"Do I have to be dragged into this too?" Bill groaned, looking at me.

I told him that it was for proper appearances and a personal favor to me.

That evening Bill, Mike, and I went to dinner at the New Era Restaurant. It was one of those snazzy restaurants that catered to the international community. With its state-of-the-art techno lighting, sleek stainless steel chairs and tables, and sexy dance music, it was the place to be. The three of us laughed over salads and a gourmet pizza. Mike drank quite a bit of wine and seemed very happy. We ended up not discussing any projects. When it was time to go, Mike dropped Bill off first.

Then Mike and I were alone in the car. Suddenly, he turned off on a quiet road and stopped the car.

I wasn't expecting this.

His hands and lips were visibly shaking. I hadn't noticed this about him before. Was this a medical condition or too much wine? He had switched off the headlights and turned the motor off. Now it was almost completely dark.

"You are very different from all the others," he said nervously.

I looked at him. Why was he nervous? What did he want to do?

Strangely, I did not feel threatened. The whole incident was just awkward.

"You don't want me, do you?" he asked, looking at me.

"No, I don't," I answered, shaking my head.

He let out a long sigh, turned the engine back on, and drove me home. As I climbed the steps to my room that night, I felt the increasing discomfort of my situation. With the endless challenges we daily faced, the numerous management problems our organization had, and now a sexually charged chief of mission at the helm, I knew what I had to do. I had to finish my contract and go instead of renewing it for another term as I had earlier intended.

The next morning, Bill came running into my office breathless.

"Rita had her baby!" he exclaimed.

My staff and I gathered around and talked excitedly. The Albanian social worker on staff who had been working with Rita's family relayed the news. She told us that Rita had given birth to a baby girl in that secluded room we had built for her. Sadly, Rita was alone during the birth. Neither her husband nor mother-in-law was there to help.

That was mixed news to me.

How could Rita be healthy or happy? Did she receive the medical care she needed? Where were her husband and mother-in-law?

Our social worker assured us that medical attention had been arranged for Rita. However, the new mother wasn't happy. The old problems resurfaced as we had predicted. But there was nothing we could do. Our organization was here to provide emergency supplies and information only. We were not a permanent office or a family counseling center.

As I returned to my desk, I thought about cases like Rita's, Kaltrina's, and others that had no easy solution. These Kosovars and their families had received short-term fixes for deep-seated, reoccurring problems when, ideally, they should have been referred to comprehensive programs with long-term goals. Like Kaltrina's, Rita's family needed more than what we were able to assist with. It needed counseling, anger management courses, and, perhaps, a criminal investigation on her husband and his mother. Beyond this, even had we had these services in place there was still an uphill battle with the local culture whose family unit was tight. Unlike the West, people here were not used to participating in social programs and finding solutions through them.

Looking around the international community, it was frustrating to see how many entities were "solving" problems but offering little in terms of longstanding solutions and even fewer that were culturally relevant. It was as though Kosovo was just the "flavor of the month" to the world's do-gooders in the year 2000.

Still, was it realistic to expect that age-old disputes between the Albanians and Serbians could be resolved by a sudden swarm of foreigners, most of whom had never focused on the area and its inhabitants until now? Many of the local ethnic disagreements had roots that predated 1400!

Ultimately, *who* had the responsibility to "fix" Kosovo's problems? Was it the West? If the international community continued to hand out assistance, how and when will the Kosovars have the motivation to design, fund, and implement their own programs?

Another foreign-run program that did not work well was the Come and See Project. As the Albanian-Serbian crisis gained speed in 1996 and 1997, many Kosovars fled their homes to nearby countries. Now, years later, with the help and incentives from international entities, many of these Kosovars were given a free round trip to "come and see" Kosovo to ascertain if and how they might rebuild their lives here.

On a cold winter afternoon in Prishtina, a UNHCR representative and two nonprofit aid workers, I was one, were asked to speak to such a group—freshly flown in from Switzerland. It was an audience of several hundred and we were just three people on the stage. When I looked out into the sea of faces, it was apparent these Kosovars were better off than their counterparts who had stayed in Kosovo. They might not be legal in their country of refuge, but they certainly looked cleaner, better fed, and less fatigued.

As I spoke a few words along with the other two, I began to wonder why I was there to encourage a group of people to return permanently when they had found a comparatively better life elsewhere. Understandably, the Swiss government did not want them. However, what incentive could there be for these people to return? Wouldn't they just be adding to the many social problems already facing Kosovo?

Moreover, what did I know about war or being a victim of one? The three of us on stage were all in our early thirties. I could only imagine what the audience truly thought as they listened to three foreigners, all fresh-faced, with permanent homes in peaceful countries advising them on the "joys" of returning.

In the end most of these Kosovars returned to their country of refuge. They had had a taste of a better life elsewhere and even "sweeteners" like money were not enough to convince them to stay.

This was a classic case of minimal success when a program was foreign-initiated and had little local buy-in.

15

Dicey Meeting

In early March 2000, I heard that two of our Serbian staff working in Lipjan, about an hour south of Prishtina, felt unsafe going to work. In 1999 after the North Atlantic Treaty Organization (NATO) had stepped in and forced Serbian forces to withdraw, the Albanian population had taken control of Prishtina. Consequently, most Serbs went into hiding in their own villages, and thus many of our Serbian staff did not work out of our main office but in satellite offices near their respective homes. One, a young woman, had sent me a message that she needed to talk. I decided to pay a visit to her house. I had heard that another armed skirmish had taken place between a group of Albanians and Serbians near her village.

The day we set out Eduard seemed nervous. I had asked him what was wrong. He mumbled something about having to go to a Serbian village. I knew he was Albanian, but he would remain in the vehicle. I did not require him to get out and walk around with me. I only needed his driving skills.

I should have been more sensitive to his concerns.

When we arrived at the Serbian village near Lipjan, Eduard said, "I'll drop you and go, okay?"

I didn't quite focus on what he meant. I was distracted by what I saw. Heavy snow was falling. We had entered an area that had paved roads and all the streets were organized as a grid. There was no one walking around and all the houses appeared boarded up. Even so, compared to the Albanian villages I had visited with their broken sidewalks, potholes, and messy spirals of streets, this community was peaceful, clean, and neat. On the surface it appeared that things were in order, but I wondered what had happened and why my employee needed to see me. I looked at the houses again and wondered if any were occupied. The high chain-link fence around each yard had a locked gate so one had to climb the fence to get to the front door.

We found the house of Adrijana, my Serbian employee, with a high fence around it. The front door appeared boarded up. I looked at Eduard.

"Do you think she is in there?" I asked.

He nodded in the affirmative.

"Well, it looks like I am going to have to climb that fence," I mumbled.

He shrugged.

As I got out of the car I told him, "Park wherever you feel safe and stay hidden. When you see me come out, drive up."

As soon I stepped out into the snow, Eduard zoomed off. Not a soul was around. It seemed as if the whole village was deserted.

I looked at the fence and wondered how I was going to scale it. It looked delicate and might collapse under my weight.

I started climbing it. It was difficult. I couldn't gain any height and the fence was weak, wobbling all around. The heavy snow wasn't helping either.

Suddenly, I heard an odd noise to my right. With my feet and hands trying to gain traction and my clothes very wet from the snow, I slowly turned my head. There, out of nowhere, was a military tank heading my way.

Who's that?

Wobbling, I fell off the fence and landed flat on my back in the snow. I cursed. I was wet. I was alone. I had no weapons. The tank was coming.

I got up. There was no escape. I might as well face *it*, whoever *it* was. I walked over to the side of the road and watched the tank. It stopped near me. After a few moments of silence, the top popped open and a blonde guy bobbed his head out.

"Hello there!" he shouted in a European accent.

I waved.

"What are you doing?" the blonde guy asked.

I pointed at Adrijana's house.

By this time, he had climbed out of the tank and was standing in front of me. He was over six feet tall and wearing a camouflage uniform.

"I need to talk to my employee in that house," I said, brushing snow off my sleeve.

He looked at Adrijana's house and then back at me. His blue eyes sparkled with amusement.

"I'm with the Finnish army," he said. "We're patrolling the place. *You* shouldn't be here alone. It isn't safe."

Thus I learned the Finnish contingent of NATO, the intergovernmental military alliance, patrolled this village. They were here to keep order and peace. I was going to be okay.

In several minutes, the Finn climbed the fence and managed to get to the other side. Once inside the yard he was able to click open the gate. I walked in and he escorted me to the front door. There was movement inside the house as I saw the front curtains wiggle. Adrijana and her parents had apparently been watching from inside but hadn't felt safe enough to come out. As soon as they saw me approach, they opened the door.

"I'll wait for you out here," the Finnish soldier said.

I nodded as I stepped inside. The first thing I noticed was that the house was very cold, though not as chilly as the outside. There was no carpeting but plain white floor tiles. The furniture, though not new, was clean and neat. There was a dining room and a sitting room with a great deal of space between each large piece of furniture. Nothing was congested in the house—not the bookshelves, walls, or on tables. Apparently, the family did not believe in overcrowding anything.

Seeing me shiver, Adrijana and her parents led me to the dining room table where it was slightly warmer. I looked at my host, hostess, and their daughter. All three were bundled up in layers of old sweaters. Adrijana's father, a heavy aging man in his fifties with crooked yellow front teeth, nodded to me and excused himself. Meanwhile, her mother, a dowdy middle-aged woman with a smoker's voice and many wrinkles on her face, asked if I wanted coffee. Adrijana herself sat down next to me. She was a slim young lady in her twenties with a cute pixie haircut.

For the next hour or so, I spoke with Adrijana and her mother. As we were short on Serbian-English translators, I was unable bring one. But Adrijana knew enough English to communicate with me. Apparently, her mother wanted her to give up the job with our nonprofit organization. Though the family needed the money, her mother did not want her to be a target for anyone, particularly Albanians. There had been skirmishes, and people got injured or killed. The matron, looking at me, said that if I were a mother I would understand.

"You! You a mother?!" she inquired, pointing a wrinkled finger at me.

"No," I shook my head, feeling a bit ashamed.

I was in a quandary. Kosovo was a mess. Good local employees were hard to come by. Even harder to find were those who could speak English well enough to communicate with the international community. In my organization alone, we employed approximately thirty local staff. More than half were Albanians with the remaining ones Serbs. Almost all international entities employed both groups and needed to. It was a way to reach out to both ethnicities, have them be part of the rebuilding of Kosovo, and to keep the peace.

I looked at Adrijana. I could sense she wanted to keep her job. She was young, full of life, and wanted to be part of the action. She was a good worker and always attended to the emergency needs of the Serbs in her area. Understandably, she did not wish to be in danger, but that came with the job.

I did not want to lose her.

In the end I simply stated that it was up to Adrijana. I was not going to pressure anyone to do a job that she was uncomfortable with. Adrijana looked at me and said she enjoyed what she was doing. Her mother ultimately relented.

The family gave me another cup of hot coffee before I went back out into the snow. I was touched by the warmth I felt in this Serbian home.

As I left, Adrijana and her mother locked up their house again. The Finnish soldier was waiting for me, but this time, instead of a tank, he was sitting in what looked like a Humvee. A second Finnish soldier, also in camouflage uniform and just as blonde, was with him. Eduard was nowhere in sight. Though I had a walkie-talkie radio, Eduard did not. This was one of the weaknesses in our program. There was no way I could reach him.

"Coming?" my tall Finn asked.

I hopped in. The three of us headed back to Prishtina. On the way, I explained to the soldiers what had happened during the visit. They chuckled. They were amused. They didn't approve of this Asian American girl being alone in a Serbian village. I was an odd specimen they had picked up on their patrol, which made the whole morning more interesting than usual.

Since I had too much Turkish coffee at Adrijana's house, I really needed a pit stop. It was going to be at least another forty minutes of driving and we were passing a small forest. There were no shops or gas stations around. I looked at my Finns and wondered whether I should ask them to stop on the side of the road. This was one of the female humanitarian's many predicaments.

Finally, I cleared my throat, "Ahem. I really need to use the restroom. Do you know where one is?"

Both Finns looked at me and then burst out laughing. I didn't see what was so funny.

"Okay, I know where a restroom is," the driver said in his accented English. "Just hold on—."

He continued to giggle. Apparently, a girl needing to urinate was something comical.

Within minutes we were pulling into a military base. The soldiers told me that this was one of their bases. As we passed the gates, they waved to the guards who waved back and we zoomed right through. In not too long we were pulling up to a line of port-o-johns. They pointed to one with the female symbol on it.

"You go in *there*," my driver directed as if I didn't know which one to enter.

I went in. Minutes later I emerged. I must have had a goofy look on my face because both soldiers waiting for me burst out laughing again. This was one of the most unromantic moments I ever had in front of two horribly cute guys: coming out of a primitive toilet with hands unwashed.

"You feel better now?" the driver asked with an amused look.

Before I could answer, he and his comrade high-fived each other and roared with laughter again.

That afternoon, the Finnish soldiers drove me back to my office in the city. They didn't have to but they did, and I was grateful for their assistance. I thanked them at the door and waved good-bye. That was the last time I ever saw them.

As I headed toward my desk, the first person to walk by was Eduard. He seemed relieved that I was back but had an uncomfortable look on his face. I didn't know what to say to him. On the one hand, I should apologize for being so insensitive to his fears. It was not uncommon for foreigners not to see things the same way locals did. But on the other hand, I felt he should have told me if he felt so strongly about not going to a Serbian village.

I saw very quickly that communication, particularly between people of different cultures, was key. If I could so easily have misunderstood my driver over a simple matter, what hope was there for complex communication at higher levels between countries when things were tense? Was the West able to communicate clearly to Kosovo and vice versa?

Even with all the aid we had poured in, NATO's presence, and the communication we had with the Kosovars, things were not changing as quickly as we would have liked. Old scores and old ways of doing things between the Albanians and Serbians were not going away.

I looked at Eduard, waved my hand, and said, "Just forget about it. Things worked out. Next time tell me if you don't feel safe going."

He nodded.

16

Showdown in a Salon

As I was nearing the end of my contract, an incident happened that gave me a deeper view of the local people and how some of them saw us, the foreigners.

It was late March and the weather was getting warmer. As I passed the window of a café one day, I saw my reflection and noticed my hair was getting long. Too long. I needed to find a hairdresser. I asked Juliana if she could recommend an inexpensive salon.

"Yes," she said, "I know just the place."

The salon she recommended wasn't far from our office. Juliana told me that she needed a haircut too. I looked at her honey-colored locks. They were straight and shoulder-length, about the same texture and length as mine. When we arrived at the salon, she said something to the female stylist who was cutting another woman's hair. The stylist looked at me and answered back in Albanian.

"The haircuts will be ten deutschmarks each," Juliana translated.

"Fine," I said.

At that time, the euro had not yet been introduced in Kosovo so the German deutschmark was the most commonly accepted currency though francs, liras, and U.S. dollars were also used.

The stylist attended to Juliana first. I sat nearby and flipped through a magazine. When Juliana was done, she pulled out a ten deutschmark bill and gave it to the lady. Then the stylist motioned for me to come forward. I walked up, sat down on the chair as directed, and Juliana translated how I wanted my hair cut. It was exactly the same way she had hers done.

When the stylist was finished, I pulled out a twenty deutschmark bill because I did not have anything smaller. I gave it to the stylist who took it to the back of the store. She was gone for a good five minutes. I waited.

When she returned, she noticed I was still there.

"Okay. Bye," she said gesturing that we were finished.

"What about my change? I want my change," I said.

The stylist began to mumble in Albanian to Juliana. Juliana's eyes widened and she answered back angrily in Albanian. The stylist, who could not look me in the eye, looked down at the floor.

"It's not my store," she said in my direction.

By this time a few more customers had entered and a second stylist came out from the back room.

"I still want my change. You owe me ten deutschmarks," I demanded.

The stylist shook her head and mumbled something more in Albanian to Juliana. Juliana's face was red now. I believed she was embarrassed for her own people. Everyone in the room had now caught on to what was happening and knew things could escalate at any moment.

It was one of the few times overseas where I weighed the consequences for "losing" my temper in front of everyone. I was angry. It wasn't the amount of money stolen so much as it was the outright taking of it. Ten deutschmarks was equivalent to about five U.S. dollars. Up until this point, no matter how poor the Malawians were or how big a bill I gave them, they never cheated me this way. Moreover, Malawi never received half as much international aid or attention as Kosovo did. The stylists in this metropolitan salon were far better off than most Malawians I met. If these Albanians wanted to charge me a higher price for their services, they should have stated so up front. They should not have taken my change, particularly when I was told a clear price beforehand.

Still angrier, I remembered the main reason why I was in Kosovo. Was it really for my benefit? This job was neither comfortable nor the path to riches. I was working for a nonprofit organization during the coldest of winters where even electricity and running water were luxuries. I took chances with my own health, security, and well-being to help these people. Though I did not expect special treatment by virtue of being a foreigner, I certainly did not care for the treatment I did receive.

I was fuming.

So I stepped forward and in front of all the stylists, customers, and Juliana, I began to shout loudly and sternly.

"Do you know *why* I am in this country?!" I asked. "Do you know *what* I have been doing for the last several months?! It is to help your people! *Your* people!"

I went on. I reminded them that Kosovo was dependent on the international community's goodwill and resources, and that they should not abuse the hard-earned good relations Kosovars have with foreigners. I told them to take a good look at themselves in the mirror and there were many mirrors in this salon.

Everyone in the room stopped what they were doing. They looked appalled. They must have understood. The stylist who took my money kept her gaze at the floor.

"It's not my store," she said again lamely.

Juliana's face was completely crimson by now.

I turned, walked out, and let the door slam behind me.

This incident still has a bad taste in my mouth whenever I remember it.

That afternoon back at the office, I sat quietly working at my desk. Mike no longer came by to bother me. I believe he now understood where he was with me. From a distance, I could hear several local staffers whispering to each other. Every once in a while, they would glance my way. Finally, Chia came over and said she had heard what happened at the salon.

"Yes, it was unfortunate that my money was taken," I confirmed.

At that moment, several of the local staffers looked down at their shoes. I could see they felt bad. One of them admitted that she had heard what happened too.

"We are sorry it happened to you," this woman said apologetically.

It touched me that they were concerned. I expressed my appreciation and went back to work.

That evening I mulled things over. If corruption could happen at the local level, on such a small scale, what about at higher levels on a larger scale? It was no secret that the interim government of Kosovo was accused of corruption. I could only imagine a foreign entity or person doing business here and getting cheated in a similar way. This would discourage any future business transactions or investments, not to mention give the country and its people a bad name.

Why didn't these Kosovars think ahead? Were they really just "peasants" as my UNHCR colleague had dubbed them? If they thought ahead, they would see that defrauding foreigners wasn't in their best interest. Besides, was it really worth the money, in my case, a few deutschmarks? Even on a grander scale, was it worth it? Ultimately, Kosovo was dependent on outside intervention and investment for political stability and economic growth.

I fell asleep, trying not to think too much of the day's incident. As in other cases, one should not associate an unpleasant event with an entire group of people, but separating the two was difficult.

◆ ◆ ◆

The morning of my departure from Kosovo was not without drama. I was to travel by surface to Skopje, Macedonia, to board an international flight. The Skopje International Airport was often used by the international community as the Prishtina Airport was not fully functioning. As I still had friends at the U.S. Office and one of its employees would be driven to Skopje for the same flight, the Office kindly agreed to take me as well.

At 4:00 a.m. I was the first to be picked up. It was a cold, dark morning. As we passed through a residential area in Prishtina to fetch the other passenger, one of our tires blew. This caused our driver, who was driving fast, to swerve through the darkness haphazardly. We ended up in a gutter on a street without lights. Pushing open his door, the driver, an Albanian, stepped out to look at the mess.

I sighed.

Seconds later he peeked in at me, his warm breath fogging up the window.

"The parking lot with other U.S. Office cars is not far from here. I have the keys. You wait," he said.

He ran off. I saw his shadow disappear into the darkness. I sat alone in the quiet, wondering about my time in this country and my less-than-grand exit from it.

About thirty minutes later, the same driver drove up in a different vehicle. I could see why the U.S. Office had hired him. He was a responsible man. He motioned for me to get in. After picking up the other party, we raced down to the Skopje airport, barely making it in time for our flight.

After checking in, I was able to breathe easier. As the gate area was small I was able to walk the entirety of it. Passing near the restrooms, a pungent smell of sewage came through. Entering the women's, I saw large heaps of human waste on the floor. Predatory flies buzzed on the waste, walls, and everywhere. It reminded me again that I was in a part of the world where the standards for sanitation and the quality of life were lower.

But then, I wondered, with all the money and interaction the foreign community had shared with this part of Europe why was Skopje International Airport, Macedonia's "face" to the world, like this? Some private businesses in Skopje I had visited, like the Aleksander Palace and the Rose Diplomatique hotels, reflected class and competence. People here were capable of achieving high standards. Yet somehow in public entities and programs, foreign assistance made little difference. The corruption, mismanagement, and incompetence were nonstop.

And still millions of dollars of aid, countless programs, and humanitarians were trickling in.

The Kosovo chapter in my life had come to a close, but the problems plaguing this part of world continued. Just like in Malawi, I wrestled with the acknowledgment that foreign presence did not necessarily equate to development, nor did throwing more money at problems arrive at solutions. I knew that I had only touched the tip of the iceberg when it came to the greater complexities of U.S. foreign assistance. But like in Malawi, I wasn't ready to give up. I still believed that things on the ground could improve.

I just wasn't ready for the surprise I would find next.

Surprise in Iraq

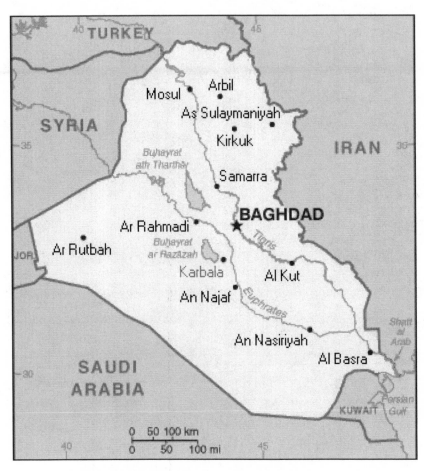

Map of Iraq courtesy of Wikimedia Commons.
https://commons.wikimedia.org/wiki/File:Iraq_map_karbala.png.
Image is in the public domain. No part of it was altered.

Flashback Three

Our plane had landed at the Baghdad International Airport. The temperature outside was oppressively hot. One by one, we passengers entered the immigration area and noticed its lack of air-conditioning. Wiping the sweat from my brow, I took out my U.S. passport, turned to the page with my Iraqi visa, and got in line. As I approached the desk, I handed my passport to the Iraqi immigration official. He took my documentation, looked at me, looked down at my passport, and something changed in his face. Instead of gesturing for me to pass like he did with other passengers, he said something in Arabic that I did not understand. When I pleaded, "Excuse me, sir, I don't speak Arabic—" He pointed at me and shouted, "You! Out!" Alarmed, I did not know what to do. When I turned my head, two Iraqi officers were coming my way. Within seconds they escorted me out of the line and down toward a dark hall.

17

Ultimate Rejection

"Case dismissed!" the judge exclaimed as he slammed down his gavel.

My client was ecstatic. He had been charged with assault. He was a macho young man with tattoos on both arms. The prosecutor had pictures of the victim, my client's girlfriend, bleeding heavily from her nose right down to her white blouse.

But we were lucky that day. The prosecutor, a smart smug redhead, had made only a partial disclosure of the police report. My client had the right to the entire copy, which we had asked for several times to no avail. Finally, at this hearing, the no-nonsense judge, who did not like his time wasted, dismissed the case.

Exiting the courthouse that morning and saying good-bye to my client, I felt the pang of something missing hit me again. It had been hitting me on and off for years.

After Kosovo, I had returned to southern California and entered law school. When that was completed, I became a prosecutor and then eventually a civil litigator and criminal defense attorney. Representing clients who had been accused of committing some really heinous crimes, I tried to see the better side of things. I tried to be convinced that I was *helping* the people in my community.

But it wasn't enough.

I missed working abroad. I missed the excitement of going into a new place, a new culture, and helping to rebuild people's lives.

By May 2010 I had already moved back to Arlington, Virginia. Looking for a job in overseas development, I saw an ad for a teaching position in Baghdad, Iraq. I could do that, I said to myself.

Saddam Hussein had been tried, convicted, and executed a few years earlier. His reign was no more. There was chaos in Iraq as American and other international entities struggled with the aftermath of war. Each day countless foreign contractors ran around inside Baghdad's International Zone (IZ), also known as the Green Zone, and beyond, implementing various peace-building, reconstruction, and stabilization programs. Little did I know what I was getting into.

Looking closer at the ad, I was amused to find that the address of this potential employer was only two blocks from my apartment. Instead of the usual approach of emailing my resume, I just picked up the phone.

Once the employer was on, I told him who I was and why I was qualified for the job. I also added that I lived two blocks away and would be happy to walk over in person to meet him should he have time. He had time. We met and I got the job.

I was now working for a small company that contracted with the U.S. government to implement programs abroad.

Within days I attended a pre-deployment orientation at the company's office. Here I met the other two employees who were hired for the same program. The three of us, Cathy Seimsen, Alicia Stans, and I, made up the team going to Baghdad. Cathy was a young African American graduate student from Pennsylvania. Though she had long dreadlocks that seemed to weigh down her face, she was lively and energetic. She told us that she had recently returned from the Caribbean where she had gathered data for her dissertation. Alicia, by contrast, was a middle-aged school teacher from Colorado. Though her appearance was neat—her hair dyed brown to hide the gray—and she was well-spoken, there was an artificiality about her manner that cautioned me not to take her words at face value. She smiled at Cathy and me, revealing that this would be her fourth contract in Iraq, having previously been there on other U.S. government–funded programs.

Within minutes of sitting down in the orientation room, I was surprised by a nudge on my arm.

"Do you have a pen and a piece of paper?" Alicia whispered at me. "I didn't bring anything."

I looked at her. Prior to this meeting, all three of us were told to come prepared for a long orientation that would include a number of important details. While I had pen and paper and shared them with her,

I was aghast at how someone could purport to be a professional, ready to go to a war zone, but attend a vital meeting unprepared.

First impressions were hard to erase.

For the next several hours, we were informed of the details to our program. The three of us were to teach business English for three months to Iraqi government employees from the prime minister's office. We were told that these Iraqis spoke the language but needed to brush up on their speaking and writing skills due to frequent contact with the international community.

A few days later we departed Washington, D.C., for Baghdad. It was June 2010. After thirteen hours of sitting on an airplane, we landed in Amman, Jordan, our transit point where we would spend one night. As our taxi drove down a multilane highway to our hotel, I rolled down the window. The red-colored desert, the locals wearing long tunics while walking their camels, and the bluish-colored mountains in the distance all fascinated me. Even the smell in the air was right. It was a pleasant mixture of earth, flowers, and life. I had a good feeling about Amman. It was a place where I could see myself living.

Early the next morning, with our luggage in tow, we headed for Baghdad. The flight to Iraq was only ninety minutes. Soon after a light breakfast on the plane, the pilot announced we were descending into Baghdad International Airport. My adrenaline was pumping.

I looked out the window. In sharp contrast to Prishtina's cold and gray appearance, I saw sunlight, dirt, and dust. It seemed like I was looking into unending stretches of desert. When the plane finally landed and I disembarked, the heat was even more intense than that which I had experienced in Malawi.

Things seemed uneventful as we bumped along in an old beat-up shuttle to a dilapidated airport building. The tarmac had potholes everywhere. Many of the passengers were fanning themselves as there was no air-conditioning inside the shuttle. A few people pulled out their cell phones and made calls in Arabic.

When we entered the airport building, the immigration area was filled with a group of women from Iran. They were covered from head to toe in black. All I could see of them were their eyes. Just looking at them made me sweat.

"It's hot in here," I mumbled to Alicia, wiping the sweat off my brow.

It must have been over 100 degrees Fahrenheit in the room. I was uncomfortably warm wearing just a t-shirt and slacks. With no fans and no air-conditioning, I could only imagine the perspiration and suffocation these women were enduring.

As I got into the long immigration line, Cathy and Alicia were right behind me. American military and civilians, Europeans, Japanese, Southeast Asians, and, of course, Iraqis all stood in it too. Things appeared to be going smoothly.

Then I got up to the immigration desk.

The officer who took my U.S. passport was a serious, unsmiling man who had the classic Iraqi features I saw on CNN: tanned skin, dark eyes, and dark hair, the same coloring as Saddam Hussein.

Then suddenly, without warning, he mumbled something in Arabic. When I inquired further, he shouted.

"You! Out!" he said loudly, pointing at me.

I was aghast.

What did he mean by "out"? There must be some mistake!

I pointed to the Iraqi visa in my passport and told him I was part of an English teaching program. But he shook his head, hollered for his fellow airport officials, and within seconds they were heading my way.

In a flash I was unceremoniously escorted out of the line and into another direction, away from the other passengers. The officials looked very intimidating in their grayish-green uniforms and dark boots, almost like policemen who were here to round me up. With trembling hands, I showed them my Iraqi visa again. They shook their heads. We were heading down a dark, dusty hall. What was this?

"Wait! Wait! Where are we going?" I asked in alarm.

One of the officials yelled at me in Arabic. I had no idea what he was saying. Anxiously, I turned my head and looked behind. Cathy, Alicia, and two male passengers had been rejected too. I saw Cathy desperately trying to explain something to one of the officials who shouted back in Arabic. All four had alarmed looks. They were being escorted down my direction.

I began to grab at any foreigner who passed me. I knew I needed to make a phone call without delay. A Briton passed me and I hung on to his arm. Quickly, I told him it was an emergency and he handed me his cell phone. With the Iraqi officials frowning, I made a call to our employer in Washington, D.C. There was no answer. Time difference was another enemy.

"Go! Go!" one official barked, forcing me down a hall.

Before I knew it, we were in the baggage area. Under tight supervision, the officials ordered us to retrieve our luggage. We were then shooed down another hall, then up a dusty flight of stairs in a roundabout way to the departure lounge. Our e-tickets were taken from us and ripped up. We were unnerved.

There were no payphones or foreigners around. After what seemed like an hour of standing and waiting desperately for the unknown, we were ushered through security and to a departure gate. Soon I realized we were going to board the same plane on which we had arrived two hours earlier.

As we boarded the same beat-up bus from the gate to the plane, I pulled at another man's arm. He allowed me to use his cell phone. I quickly called the security officers who were supposed to pick us up at this airport, who told me they helplessly watched behind a glass wall as we were escorted away from the baggage area. Sadly, we were inaccessible to them. The phone call had so much static that the security officer at the other end, who sounded American, was screaming at the top of his lungs.

"Tell the Iraqis to let you—in!" he yelled.

"We've already told them!" I shouted desperately. "They've rejected us! They're throwing us out!"

"What?" the security officer shouted back. "I—I can barely hear you!"

Being an experienced traveler, I had more phone numbers on me. The next call I made was to the duty officer at the U.S. Embassy in Amman since it was quite clear that we were going back to Jordan. I called and told the officer, an American woman, what had happened and that we needed assistance although, still shaken, I wasn't able to articulate what kind.

"When you arrive in Amman get yourself to an ATM and then call your employer," she said, sounding annoyed, as though I was bothering her on a Saturday morning.

"Can't you do anything?" I asked desperately. "The three of us are Americans citizens and we need help getting into Iraq. We're here to teach English."

"No, I can't," she said unsympathetically.

And with a don't-bother-me tone, she hung up.

I looked at Cathy and Alicia. It was apparent they had caught on to my conversations. The three of us were visibly shaken.

With phone calls eliciting no relief we, the rejects, climbed the steps back onto the Royal Jordanian plane. The minute we entered, the stewardess recognized us and gasped. I nodded my head in gloom. I asked her if this denial of entry was common. She said it happened sometimes.

"I'm sorry," she said, handing me a glass of water.

I sipped it and closed my eyes. I had no idea what was going to happen to us. Of all the dangerous places I had ever been to, I had never been this afraid. I wondered what would happen once we reached Amman. Would there be more trouble at the airport? Had the Iraqis communicated something negative to the Jordanians about us? *Who* could help us?

During the flight, Alicia, Cathy, and I tried to form a plan. It was obvious we needed to reach our employer and find a place to stay. But for how long? Would we try to reenter Baghdad? Our first day of class was fast approaching. What if we did not enter Iraq on time?

As these anxious thoughts flashed through my mind, we landed in Amman. When we came before the Jordanian immigration officials, we could not help but relate what happened. We were shaken up and could not stop talking about it.

"*You* are welcomed in *my* country," an official said, looking at me sympathetically as he stamped my passport and let me pass.

I was never more grateful to hear those words.

When the three of us entered the arrival area, there was a man holding a sign, "Mr. Jade Wu." I whispered to Alicia and Cathy that this must be for us. We approached him and he said that he was here to drive us back to the Holiday Inn Amman, the hotel we had stayed at earlier. Either our employer had gotten my phone message or the helpless security officers waiting to pick us up in Baghdad had been in contact with him.

An hour later, upon entering my room, I collapsed into bed. I could not believe what had just occurred that morning. *I was rejected by a sovereign nation.* Wasn't I there to *help* Iraq? Why did *it* not want me?

I had never known such rejection before. Even repudiation by a previous boyfriend did not come close.

That evening, after a long three-way conference call with our employer in D.C. and his office in Baghdad, we received new Iraqi visas and roundtrip plane tickets. We were to fly back to Baghdad early the next morning—as if nothing happened.

Early the next morning, we flew back to Baghdad International Airport. The sight was familiar, but the feeling was different. Instead of excitement, we were tense. When we entered the immigration area, we were all on edge. As I turned my head I saw the same Iraqi official who had rejected us the previous day. He was sitting by the door in his grayish-green uniform and dark boots, watching as the passengers walked pass. When he saw the three of us, he signaled for us to approach him. There was no smile. I did not know what was happening, but it was clear this was not standard procedure.

"Come here," he commanded, leading the way.

We were led to a desk off to the side. After waiting for some time, we were told to present our new Iraqi visas. Upon showing them, we were told these were no good. There was some mumbling between the immigration officers in Arabic that we did not understand. Our U.S. passports were then taken and we were unceremoniously led again to the baggage area.

My mind was whirling a thousand miles per minute. We were in a worse situation than we were in yesterday. Our passports had been taken. Seeing the security detail waiting to pick us up behind the secure glass wall again, I felt completely helpless and frustrated. They were inaccessible. They could see us, but they could not do anything. As I grabbed my luggage, I wanted to scream! We were denied entry *again*! Our passports were taken!

But they could not hear us.

This time, as we boarded our Royal Jordanian deportation flight back to Amman, we were escorted by four Iraqi men. We were not told what their roles were, but one of them must have had our passports because we would not have been allowed to board without documentation.

All three of us were immensely ill at ease throughout the flight. Alicia, especially, was visibly shaking.

"No, no, not again," she mumbled, shaking her head.

Leaning forward with her head faced down on her lap, she looked like she was going to have a meltdown. I asked her if anything like this had happened on her previous flights into Iraq. She shook her head. I began to weigh my options. I wondered how much it was going to cost to get out of this mess, if we would be able to exit the Amman airport with minimal hassle, and if our teaching jobs would ever come to fruition. As these dark thoughts passed through my mind, I could hear my colleagues talking loudly and nervously. I gestured at them to lower their voices. I didn't want them to say anything that pointed to fault or responsibility. We did not know who was listening and what would be done with our statements.

Arriving in Amman *again*, we were emotionally and physically exhausted. But at this airport a new surprise awaited me. The previous day, when we were rejected by Iraq, the cost of our return flights to Amman was simply taken out from our original roundtrip e-tickets. That was why our employer had to buy another set of roundtrip tickets for us to fly back to Iraq.

This time, prior to reaching the immigration counter, we were led to the Royal Jordanian Airline desk. A balding clerk, speaking limited English, checked all three of our new e-tickets, making sure this return flight from Baghdad to Amman was properly accounted for. Alicia and Cathy were handed back their U.S. passports, which apparently the Iraqis had given to Royal Jordanian. Then he looked at me. Something appeared wrong with my e-ticket.

"You owe $509.00 dollars, please," the clerk said matter-of-factly.

I was aghast.

"This is my e-ticket number and here is the confirmation code. You can take this return flight out of my round trip," I said desperately pointing at the numbers.

The clerk shook his head.

For some reason, he either did not know how to read my e-ticket or the numbers were confused. I had to be escorted to a nearby bookshop inside the airport to buy a phone card so that I could call my employer to sort this out.

I was so anxious over the string of events I felt faint. Not only was my job not being realized but I was about to be out five hundred plus dollars! This was ridiculous.

Wasn't I here to *help* Iraq?

For the next hour, due to phone static and time difference, I tried to call my employer in D.C., his office in Baghdad, and the ticket agent in the U.S. who issued this e-ticket. The only one who picked up was the ticket agent. I told her what had happened and she read me my e-ticket number. I jotted this down and handed it to the Royal Jordanian clerk. He verified it and finally handed me my passport.

I almost collapsed.

Breathing a sigh of relief, I glanced at my e-ticket again when we were waiting for our luggage. The ticket number this agent gave me was exactly the same number on the ticket itself, the one I handed to the clerk originally.

Had there really been something wrong with my ticket or was the clerk in need of new glasses?

Back at the Holiday Inn Amman, the three of us felt ill. Fortunately, our employer had again booked us rooms and we collapsed into our beds. Psychologically shaken and emotionally exhausted, I fell asleep that afternoon and did not wake up until 9:00 a.m. the next day. Golden sunlight streamed through the window and a breeze fluttered the curtains. All was quiet as I sat up and wondered what to do next.

The last two days were not dreams. They were real-life nightmares.

Following a conference call that afternoon with our employer, Alicia, Cathy, and I sat in the business center of the Holiday Inn staring at the floor. We were still in shock. Alicia was very emotional. She broke down sobbing, saying she needed this job.

"You don't understand, I need the money," she wailed. "I haven't worked in a while."

I said we all did. Yet I was less trusting than my two colleagues. I did not want to attempt a third entry into Iraq and fail again. It wasn't just the denial of entry I was afraid of but the fact that the Iraqi officials could detain us. I had visions of rotting for days in a rat-infested cell without anyone knowing.

As we pondered why the Iraqi government denied us entry, Cathy, the calmest of us all, made a surprising announcement. She said that she was going on a date that evening. She had met a man in one of the hotel's bars and he asked her out. I could not believe that after what had happened she could focus on a date. I guess people do respond to crisis in different ways. My only concern was that she proceed carefully. After all the three of us had been through in the last forty-eight hours, we could not deal with another mishap.

It was agreed we would fly back to Iraq in a few days after our employer obtained new airline tickets and visas for us. Until then we were to relax. It was time to recover, sunbathe, and swim.

The Holiday Inn had a nice size swimming pool. The next day I wanted to give it a try. Yet I noticed that there were no women at the pool in bikinis and the only swimwear I had brought was a two-piece. Not wanting to offend and risk even more trouble, I called down to the concierge and asked whether I could wear mine to the pool.

"I—I'm not sure. Can you hold please?" the concierge asked.

He put me on hold and went to get his supervisor. While holding, I wondered how serious this issue was. From what I had seen around town, Amman was a nice combination of East and West. It had some familiar fast food restaurants, such as McDonald's and Kentucky Fried Chicken, but also kept its Middle Eastern flavor. The city had open-air bazaars, mosques, malls, and big-name banks. Most women wore head scarves and long dresses. Surely with this mix of East and West, the hotel would allow me to wear my two-piece bathing suit to its pool?

Finally, after waiting for several minutes, a supervisor came on the phone.

"Madame, you can go swimming. No problem," the supervisor said confidently, not answering my question.

At this point I was so fed up waiting that I thanked the man and went swimming. No one gave me any trouble. After all, I had asked.

The day came for us to attempt a third entry into Iraq. I knew that if this trip was unsuccessful, we would be going home.

When our plane finally landed at Baghdad International Airport, I took a deep breath. I peeked out the window. The same tarmac, beat-up bus, and dilapidated airport building were all there. Their reappearance mocked me.

As the aircraft doors opened and we descended the stairs, an unexpected minivan drove up. An Iraqi man hopped out from the driver's seat and asked if we were Jade, Cathy, and Alicia. After verification, he drove us to the doorstep of the airport. We saw the same immigration officers walking around in their familiar grayish-green uniforms and it was difficult not to have our hopes dashed.

We were told to proceed to a nearby desk instead of standing in line. At this desk, the same officer who had rejected us twice before now smiled. *It was the first time I saw his teeth.* He said something in Arabic that sounded welcoming. We were asked to fill out paperwork and pay a small fee for an emergency visa.

Why weren't we allowed this option before?

Relieved that we got through, I could not help but think of all the unnecessary costs of the last several days. My blood pressure rose as I knew what was going to happen. In the industry of peace-building, stabilization, and reconstruction contracts, these expenses were going to be passed back to the U.S. government, as our employer was a government contractor, and eventually on to the American taxpayers.

I was angry.

I couldn't help but wonder. If the Iraqi government had really wanted American skills, knowledge, and materials, why did it not expedite their smooth entry? What was the purpose to have us fly back and forth, wasting time and resources? Moreover, were top people in Washington and American program directors in Iraq working to resolve this? Didn't the U.S. have the bigger muscle since it was providing millions in aid?

Talking to various people in the last several days, it was frustrating to know that we weren't the first to be denied access for no apparent reason.

Retrieving our luggage and following our security detail to the parking lot, we saw three armored vehicles waiting. Interestingly, each of us three was told to ride in a separate vehicle. As I sat down in one and fastened my seatbelt, the driver and an armed guard sitting in the front gave me an orientation. Neither was taking any chances. They wanted me to know where the valves, switches, and radios were should they become incapacitated. The reality that things could get very nasty began to kick in.

As we drove down a long paved highway toward the IZ, I saw how dry the outskirts of Baghdad were. The sun was high and the stretches of smooth desert seemed never-ending, spotted only here and there with clumps of concrete buildings. There was not even a shrub around. Everywhere I looked it was dust and dirt. Dust was in the air, on the houses, on the roads, and even on the few people walking during the heat of the day alongside the highway.

I was also surprised at how many checkpoints we had to go through to reach the IZ. Each time we came upon one, the Iraqi soldiers manning it would peer into our vehicle, look at us, look at our documentation, and look at me again before allowing us to pass. Surely, I thought, with more checkpoints to go, we were going to run into a glitch somewhere.

But we didn't.

Finally arriving at the IZ, which had high walls and a huge gate, we cleared our last checkpoint and were in.

But what I saw inside was less than ideal. Though Saddam Hussein's Hands of Victory monument was a sight to behold with two huge swords crossed to make an arc for cars to pass under, the paved roads were not well maintained. Armored SUVs, military vehicles, and dusty sedans bumped along after one another. Heaps of garbage and overturned trashcans appeared at almost every intersection. Sickly looking dogs, thin as rails and without owners, scoured the streets looking for food.

When our vehicle made a right turn, I saw another set of high walls topped with barb wire and a guarded entrance, indicating a foreign-operated compound. As we continued down the dusty street, there were more of these. Along the way, situated here and there, were small Iraqi convenience stores, high-rise apartment buildings with faded exteriors, and even a mosque.

It occurred to me then that the area inside the IZ was and still is a part of Baghdad city.

"How big is the IZ?" I asked my driver.

"Oh, about four square miles," he said. "It's big enough to hold a couple of Saddam's palaces, government buildings, a number of foreign compounds, the U.S. Embassy, and these apartment buildings." He pointed to ones we were passing.

Other than a few locals I saw coming in and out of stores, there were no other pedestrians. I commented on the lack of people walking around.

"It's not safe here," my driver said. "There have been kidnappings. Foreigners have been forced into cars at gunpoint."

The guard in the passenger seat nodded.

With our vehicle making a final right turn, we drove into a small compound where we would be living and working for the duration of our contract. TONI compound was a little over an acre. It had a two-story concrete building that contained classrooms, sleeping rooms, and offices, a tiny grass-covered courtyard, and a string of rectangular trailers used as more sleeping rooms. The entire compound housed about forty-five men and five women, most of whom were American subcontractors.

Showing me to my trailer, a seasoned TONI female pulled me aside.

"You should stick close to your room and the office," she said quietly. "Don't wander down other walkways. Those rooms are all occupied by men and they haven't seen their wives in a while."

Surprised by that comment and still absorbing all that had happened in the last few days, I entered my trailer and set my suitcase down. It was one room with a desk, chair, bed, small closet, and TV. A bathroom with a shower and toilet adjoined. Nothing in the trailer was there for decoration. Everything in it was functional.

Even before I had a chance to change my shirt, comb my hair, or settle down for a few minutes, there was a knock on my door. I was told it was time to meet the Iraqi students I was going to teach.

After a quick staff meeting with Alicia and Cathy where we decided they would teach the large Intermediate class together and I would teach the smaller Intermediate and Advanced classes alone, we were ready to enter our respective classrooms. As we had arrived days behind schedule, the classes had begun. Substitutes, other Americans working in the IZ who had a connection with TONI, had been hired to teach temporarily. That afternoon Alicia, Cathy, and I began by "shadowing" our substitutes. It was an absurd situation.

Other than at the airport, I had had very little contact with Iraqis. When I opened the door to my classroom that afternoon, I saw one group of my students for the first time: ten men and one woman. They were all seated around a huge oblong table with paper, pens, and books in front of them. The substitute, a plump but pleasant woman named May, was teaching the definite and indefinite articles.

"The door, the table, the keys," May said, referring to each item.

"Da door, da dable, da keys," the students repeated with a heavy accent.

The students appeared to be in their thirties or early forties and sported the classic features of Iraqis: dark hair, dark eyes, tanned skin, and stocky build. Almost all of them wore suits and looked very serious, almost formidable. They were government employees from the prime minister's office, a no-nonsense bunch.

I stepped forward and smiled.

When they saw me their eyes widened in surprise.

Perhaps they had expected a blond, blue-eyed Caucasian to walk through the door. Instead, a dainty Asian American girl, who had just blown into their country with hair uncombed, shirt wrinkled, and a deer-in-the-headlights look, stood right in front of them.

A moment of silence took place as each side sized the other up.

What did *they* think of me?

Figure 17.1. My trailer, TONI compound, Baghdad, 2010

Figure 17.2. TONI compound's walls. View from inside the International Zone, Baghdad, 2010

Figure 17.3. Trash piled inside the International Zone, Baghdad, 2010

18

Embarrassing America

During the first week of teaching, my students were very quiet and somewhat distant. There were about eleven people, including one woman in each of my two classes. Whenever they were in my presence, the students were always professional and acted with decorum. The men mainly wore suits while the women wore long dresses and head scarves. Usually on time and prepared, they all spoke some English, although the verb tenses and word order were often confused.

By the second week, each student had looked me over and proceeded to ask questions cautiously. Little by little the ice was broken. After a few more days, they were two of the warmest groups I had ever met.

They were curious about the American culture and how our university system worked. They wondered how a female like me could work in foreign countries without an accompanying husband. They told me about their own struggles before and during the fall of Saddam Hussein. It appeared that all of them had jobs that involved communicating with the international community, though they did not reveal their actual positions. They had accepted change that came with technology but seemed reticent to embrace the full tray of Western values.

"How much does four-year university cost in U.S.?" Iyad asked during class one day, scratching his sideburns.

His colleagues looked up at me in anticipation.

"Well, it depends on whether the school is public or private, and whether the student is living on or off campus," I answered.

My students looked confused. Slowly, I explained the differences and what I read was the average cost of a private four-year university education in recent years.

"Private is too much!" Iyad exclaimed, making his calculations quickly.

Before I knew it, another student had scribbled on paper what the cost was converted into Iraqi dinars. Everyone gasped. I was amazed. Their minds worked terribly fast.

Then Abdul, always impeccably dressed, told the class about some of his humorous experiences as a student at the University of Basra in southern Iraq when he had to share a house with ten guys.

"Ten men in house!" Abdul exclaimed, holding out both hands to show ten fingers. "Only two bathrooms. Big problem. Big—problem!"

We all laughed. We felt comfortable with each other and I saw that my students respected me. Everything seemed to be going well.

A few days later I entered the classroom as usual, greeted the students, and began my lesson. Because the air-conditioning in the room was broken, I left the door open to the hallway.

Suddenly, in the middle of our lesson, loud shouting came from the hall.

"You fucking cunt!" a man roared. "You're fucking useless! I don't know why this is not fucking possible! You're so fucked up! Just so fucked up! Do you hear me?! You're a fucking cunt!"

My face turned beet red.

His rage went on.

I peered down the hall. A tall, big-muscled American named Michael, who had been hired to provide martial arts training at the U.S. Embassy's gym, was screaming at Brenda, an American woman. His language was so foul that I winced as my students heard every word.

We all stopped what we were doing. Everyone within earshot was shocked. Brenda did not say a word. She was a small woman with frizzy blond hair and there was nowhere to run. She just stood frozen.

I stood frozen too.

Unable to look my students in the eye, I slowly made it to a chair and sat down. I wanted to hide. After the shouting had stopped, there were several minutes of heavy silence. It became so quiet one could hear a pin drop. No apology or action by me would be sufficient to erase this embarrassment on behalf of America.

My students all stared at me. They were from the prime minister's office.

Finally, one of the men stood up.

"You are a woman too," he said gravely to me. "I must apologize for him because he has insulted *all* women." He then turned and looked at his female colleague as well.

All the male students nodded in agreement.

Struggling with shame, I whispered a thank-you. As I did so, Michael walked past our room in a huff and out the building, letting the door slam behind him. I looked down at the floor. What was he doing here? He wasn't fit to be in Iraq. *He wasn't fit to represent our country overseas.*

I cringed. I could not believe that a graceful Iraqi man had to apologize on behalf of a crude American. Weren't we Americans here to teach, advise, share skills, and set an example?

Now the people we were "teaching" were actually teaching us.

My eyes remained downcast for the rest of the day.

Figure 18.1. Students and me (*front row, center*), International Zone, Baghdad, 2010

19

Behold Iraqi Americans

TONI compound was an interesting place. Surrounded by high walls topped with barbed wire, the inhabitants were relatively safe, though every so often we could hear rockets flying through the air and crashing in the distance. On the other side of the walls was a dumpy, trash-ridden street of the IZ, not far from an old government building of Saddam Hussein. With the English classes onsite, there was a lot of commotion daily as students arrived and many of the Americans left for work to other locations. Almost every American on TONI was a subcontractor and a number of them were Iraqis who had fled to the U.S. years ago.

Sitting in its small cafeteria one morning, I noticed something. It was subtle and had been happening for some time, but this morning it was readily apparent. I was at the breakfast table with a few of our local staff, the Iraqis hired to be program assistants, grounds maintenance and cleaners, when suddenly a fellow American walked in.

Paul, a short, stocky program advisor from Arizona, headed straight for the coffee dispenser. When he saw me, he said good morning and I nodded back. After grabbing a cup of coffee and a piece of toast, he walked right out of the room, never glancing at the others at the table.

I digested the scene.

Paul was an Iraqi who had left Iraq in the eighties to escape Saddam Hussein's regime. He was a Chaldean Christian who went through Greece, working in odd jobs, and eventually made it to the U.S., where he was able to obtain American citizenship. Now, years later, very proud of his accomplishments and the fact that he owned his house in Arizona, he returned to his birth country to earn a high salary and to use his language skills, vetting Iraqis for translator jobs in U.S. government programs.

Paul never sat at the dining table when the local staff was there.

Another Iraqi American on TONI who had a similar history was Steve. Steve, who also vetted locals for translator jobs, would come into the dining room, get his food, sit down, and nod to everyone. But he usually only spoke to the other Americans at the table. In fact, the only time I heard him speak to a local staffer was when he was yelling at the kitchen staff in Arabic, telling them the bread basket was empty.

Sitting down to lunch with Steve one afternoon, we talked about our lives back in the U.S. Within earshot of the local staff, he let it be known he owned a house in Virginia and was building a second one. He then related he had just returned from vacation in Italy and how, while there, he took the opportunity to buy clothes by the designer Brioni.

"Brioni, you know the brand?" he asked, looking at me. "It's expensive. It's what James Bond wears."

I listened politely and then changed the topic. When I told him how much I liked swimming and hoped to resume it after my job in Iraq, Steve immediately interrupted. He revealed that he had just bought a pair of designer goggles: they were over $200.00.

Mark, an Iraqi American who had fled Iraq and previously worked in Saudi Arabia, had an even softer approach. During mealtimes, he would sit at the table with everyone, say hello, eat, and converse. But before too many minutes had passed, it was clear Mark was only talking to his fellow Americans. Moreover, he would "lament" about the construction workers who were building his second house in Minnesota and how much money he had spent calling his wife and his lead man on the project. The subject was repeated again and again at different meals.

In a time of national uncertainty and welfare, I wondered what our local staff truly thought about these conversations.

Walking around TONI I never did see Iraqi Americans laughing and joking with the local staff. There were a few Americans of Iraqi descent on the compound, however, who were polite and spoke professionally to the locals. One would have surmised, given all the international money and aid coming in, that Iraqi Americans who spoke the language and understood the culture would take the lead in rebuilding Iraq. But no, it was as if those who had left the country years ago and had "made it" in America wanted to keep a distance, a defined line between themselves and those who had remained behind, showing a "superiority" over the latter.

Talking to Brenda about these subtle but troubling dynamics made things clearer. Brenda, who had braved the unfortunate outburst from Michael, was a German American who worked on TONI as its camp manager. She was alert, smart, and had seen many subcontractors come and go.

"You have to remember, Jade, that not all Iraqis are the same religion, tribe, or mindset," she said.

I nodded. Though I knew there were different religions and tribes within Iraq, I didn't expect these dynamics to be on TONI compound. I didn't expect that the *Iraqi Americans* would be adding to the complication. Things on the ground were certainly more complex than that which met the eye.

"There are Sunnis, Shiites, Chaldean Christians, and a few other groups," Brenda went on. "They don't all see things the same way you know."

I came to learn that many of our local staff were Shiites, while many of our Iraqi Americans were Chaldean Christians. Given these two groups' unhappy history with each other with the Muslims suppressing the Christians, old scores, differences in wealth, and status in the community only added to the greater divide—instead of closing the gap.

I took a deep sigh. I felt I had only come upon the tip of an immense iceberg.

But then, weren't all of us here on this compound working toward a common goal? Weren't we supposed to be rebuilding Iraq?

It seemed as though "rebuilding Iraq" was only the label, the title, or the cover many used as their reason for being here. Most were here for a job, an income. For many Iraqis, American citizens or not, memories from the past were fresh and not going away.

If prejudice and troubling dynamics could happen in a small compound with so few Iraqis, couldn't it happen elsewhere and at all levels? I could well imagine these Iraqi American subcontractors who were vetting locals for jobs giving preferences to those in their own tribes and religion—and many of us non-Iraqis would not even know the difference.

Beyond that, who is to say these preferences were not done at higher levels, say, at the U.S. ambassador's office or even in Washington, D.C.?

Brenda took a deep breath.

"It's complicated," she said, shaking her head. "It's a lot more complicated than you and I can fathom."

I looked down and shook my head too. All this was not rebuilding the country but slowing the process down.

20

He-whore or Husband?

Life inside the IZ was not easy. Navigating the challenges of security, a different culture, language, and religion, many people were stressed all the time. But this did not prevent Americans and other foreigners from having fun. Every weekend there was time spent socializing and drinking, with Baghdaddy's bar inside the U.S. Embassy being a favorite hangout. The uneven ratio of men to women made everything more interesting. With far fewer women than men, the heat was on. Extramarital affairs took place whenever desire and opportunity allowed. Susceptible females were catered to and given favors by men. Some took advantage of their sexual power and used it to the detriment of others. Two on our compound repeatedly allowed unauthorized male guests to stay overnight, compromising everyone's security.

On a sunny afternoon Alicia asked me to come to her trailer. She wanted me to meet her Iraqi boyfriend. He had just arrived from Sulaimaniya, a major town in the Kurdish part of northern Iraq.

I was curious. When I had first heard about him, I didn't know whether this was a serious relationship. She had told me she met him in Iraq a few years ago when she was on another contract. Then I wondered about all the checkpoints he would have to go through to get here. How would he do it? Did he have a pass?

It turned out he did not have a pass, but Alicia, who had friends in the U.S. Embassy, managed to get him through the IZ's gates and eventually into our compound. I thought about what this said for the "tightness" of our security.

He was now inside her trailer to eat, sleep, and, according to Alicia, copulate for the next several days.

When I knocked on her door that afternoon, she opened it with a big smile. Within seconds I was being introduced to Ali Ahmed, her boyfriend. He was wearing a collared t-shirt and slacks. His English was elementary and heavily accented. He seemed quite a bit younger than she: about forty to her sixty. With a full head of dark hair, dark eyes, and stocky build, he looked just like any other Iraqi man I had seen on CNN. I wouldn't be able to pick him out of a crowd of locals. Giving me a forced smile, he went over and sat down on a chair in the room. I could sense he was uncomfortable with my presence—uncomfortable to have me see him in her room. For the next hour or so, she and I carried on a conversation while he nodded politely. Alicia seemed very happy.

Walking back to my room later, I was lost in deep thought. Was Ali the reason why Alicia kept returning to Iraq? How was this relationship going to work? I had noticed two thick dictionaries in her trailer: one English to Arabic and the other Arabic to English. Was this the way they communicated?

A week passed with Alicia focusing her energy on Ali while Cathy did more of the teaching. Ali, who was not authorized to be on TONI, never left Alicia's room.

Heading to class one afternoon I ran into Alicia, who sported a big smile.

"I just hope," she giggled, "that Joe wasn't disturbed by our lovemaking last night." Her eyes twinkled, referring to her neighbor.

I winced. I didn't need to know about her amorous activities.

Days later, after Ali had left, Alicia explained that she planned to marry him. She had even brought from home a Mikimoto pearl necklace to wear at the ceremony. While my jaw dropped, she told me that she had also brought $6,000.00 in cash, withdrawn from her own account prior to departing the U.S. There were many hurdles to overcome in an Iraqi man marrying a foreigner in Baghdad and she was prepared to help him financially engineer it.

Alicia said she had given Ali the $6,000.00 to use, if needed, in persuading a local judge to permit the marriage. He was supposedly on his way to meet that magistrate and would call her in a few days.

I was shocked. Inwardly, I had so many questions. Was he married already? Did he have children? How was Alicia going to check on his background? What did his family say about this match? What did hers say?

I kept silent, not wishing to seem hostile. Alicia was a middle-aged divorcée with grown children from her previous marriages. Ali, according to Alicia, was also divorced with two adolescent daughters.

One of the documents Ali had shown me prior to his departure were his divorce papers translated into English. But he didn't tell me why were they in English or whom was he going to take them to.

Two quiet weeks passed. We went about our teaching. Suddenly, one afternoon Alicia approached my room breathless. She said she had received a phone call from Ali. He was back in northern Iraq. He had just had a fight with his father about marrying a foreigner. The old patriarch would not approve of it. Ali had allegedly left the family home and checked into a nearby motel to cool down.

Apparently Ali, his two daughters, and the patriarch were all living together in Sulaimaniya.

"I want to bring him and his daughters to Colorado with me," she said determinedly. "They will have a much better life there."

She seemed so sure he wanted this too.

I was less hopeful. I did not know Ali well. From my outsider's perspective, there were many downsides to their union. He was Muslim. She was not, nor did she wish to convert. He was twenty years her junior. This would raise some eyebrows even in the U.S. He also spoke very little English and she spoke almost no Arabic. How would they communicate on the big things or anything? Given the lack of popular support for U.S. involvement in Iraq, Ali could well have trouble being welcomed in some American communities. Was Alicia ready to face that?

A few days later I found Alicia in her room with red eyes. She was very upset.

"What happened?" I asked. "Is Ali okay?"

"We broke up," she said, her voice shaking.

She did not tell me how it happened, but she was in the middle of writing a letter demanding the $6,000.00 back. She said she would have an Iraqi friend translate the letter into Arabic and make arrangements to deliver it to Ali.

I was quiet. I didn't know what to say. All I could do was let her cry on my shoulder.

That night I thought about Alicia's plight. It was so easy for the few foreign women in a war zone to fall prey to men's flattery. Even an average-looking American woman, who would not normally get a second glance from a man in a Walmart, had a number of admirers. Sometimes these "artificial" relationships led to hurt feelings, unwanted pregnancies, and even divorces. Other times, they resulted in favoritism, lack of professionalism, and security breaches. Many of these men and women who had spouses in the U.S. defined themselves as "geographically single" and "available." It was as though these unions were an unhealthy side effect of our transient lives in conflict zones.

But Alicia had taken it a step further. She had become involved with a local. This by itself brought on an additional set of complications. Due to the security problems, Americans had limited movement in the country. Most Americans did not travel in the same social circles as Iraqis. Most never visited Iraqi homes, schools, or social gatherings. Consequently, Alicia did not have access to the full picture of who Ali was and what life was like for the Ahmed family. She might have had to fill in blanks where there were ones to fill. Moreover, since she did not share a common language, culture, or religion with Ali, what she saw in him might be only one-tenth of who he really was.

As for Ali, what were his motivations? Did he really love Alicia? Was he ready to uproot his daughters, leave his father behind, and move to the U.S., a corrupt Western country in his eyes? Perhaps he simply enjoyed Alicia's company and the benefits of her money. Whatever his intentions, they were difficult to decipher due to the cultural, political, religious, and linguistic barriers.

In the days following the breakup, Alicia resorted to drinking and missed a class or two. Luckily, Cathy was there to step in.

One morning, Brenda approached me.

"I don't know what is happening to Alicia," she said, looking directly at me. "I walked by her this morning and she smelled of alcohol."

I looked away, not able to meet Brenda's gaze.

"She told me it was the astringent on her face but I know better," Brenda continued. She was no-nonsense.

Taking a deep breath, I went to find Alicia that afternoon and told her that she needed to watch her step. We were all here to a do a job and were paid well to do it. We needed to keep our eyes on the ball.

But her eyes, still red, only focused on the floor.

For the rest of our time in Iraq, though Alicia resumed teaching, her spirits were low and a bottle of liquor was never far away. Moreover, none of us ever saw Ali or heard about the $6,000.00 again.

21

Eye-openers 1–?

One day my student Mohammad Hassan wanted me to meet his supervisor from the prime minister's office. Mohammad was a bright, tall, young man who perfectly fit the word gentleman. He dressed immaculately in a suit, held open the door for others, and always greeted everyone upon entering the room.

"She's coming to TONI compound today," he said excitedly.

This piqued my interest as I had no idea why his supervisor was coming. Shortly after class that afternoon, I saw an elegantly dressed Iraqi woman alight from a car and walk toward our main entrance. Mohammad stepped forward and introduced me.

Mrs. Masri, a lady in her fifties who exuded dignity and grace, spoke fluent English. When I saw her she was wearing a head scarf, a business jacket, and a long skirt, all coordinated. As we sat down, she told me what a wonderful job I was doing with her employees. Surprised, I thanked her and told her that my students had taught me a great deal too. We chatted a bit and she invited me to her house for dinner in the coming weeks. Apparently, she had two daughters coming home from London for the summer where they had been studying.

"I really want them to meet you," Mrs. Masri said.

I told her that I looked forward to making their acquaintance.

Before leaving, Mrs. Masri gave me a large chocolate cake as a sign of appreciation. I was really surprised and touched. The warmth I felt from her and my students was a far cry from that which I had experienced at the airport.

The next day in class, several of my students asked if there was anything I wanted to do in Baghdad before my time here was over. Though my last day was still weeks away, there were a number of things I wanted to do but could not due to security problems.

Then suddenly I had a request. I said that before I leave, I would like to go to a mosque with one of them and observe prayers.

"Is that possible?" I asked, looking around the room.

My students looked at each other. They knew I wasn't Muslim. But to my surprise, they were very opened-minded. For the next few minutes they talked among themselves about how to make this a reality.

Then Noor, my female student whose name means "light," spoke up.

"I pray at a mosque not too far from here," she said. "Let me speak to my imam and get back to you."

Noor was a Shiite, as were the majority of my students. Conservative, she usually wore a head scarf and a long dark dress that covered everything to the ankles. Judging her by her clothes, one might assume she was quiet, cold, and standoffish. Surprisingly, she was anything but that. She was warm, level-headed, and professional, an eye-opener for me to the Shiite women of the world.

Sure enough, in a few days, with the blessing of my security office and the consent of her imam, Noor and I drove to her mosque. It was one of the ones inside the IZ. Upon her advice, I wore a long-sleeve shirt, slacks, and a head scarf—anything that covered me from head to toe. As we arrived, I saw that the mosque was a large, newish-looking building with a huge dome and a visible minaret. When we parked the car and stepped out, the imam, wearing a gown of complete white, came out to greet me.

"Are you our visitor today?" he asked in very good English.

Surprised, I nodded. I was not expecting to be met by the imam nor was I expecting him to speak English.

"You are most welcome," he continued, smiling. "Please follow me."

We followed him up the steps to the entrance, took off our shoes, and went inside. Once in the mosque, the imam gave me a short history of the place and told me that if I had a camera I was welcomed to take any number of pictures I wanted, even during prayer. He then gave me a CD.

"Listen to it at home," he said smiling. "It talks about Islam in English."

I felt at ease as I walked through the mosque. There was a feeling of peace. It wasn't fancy but there was wall-to-wall carpeting, clean walls, and a few windows. There were no tables or chairs but a water dispenser at one end with glasses beside it. I brought a glass of water to Noor. The temperature outside was boiling and inside it wasn't much better, although we had fans.

Within minutes the imam took his post. Prayer was about to begin.

A number of local men and women had entered. The men lined themselves up in the front of the room all facing one way, while the women gathered in the back of the room, facing the same direction as the men. Almost all the men wore t-shirts and slacks, while the women dressed like Noor. I was the only foreigner present.

Hearing the call to prayer, Noor turned to me.

"Jade, we're women," she whispered. "We *have* to pray in the back."

I followed her to the back rows where the women were. Then prayer started.

I looked in front of me and saw rows of men praying. They stood, knelt, and bent forward while their foreheads touched the ground. Then they stood again, knelt again, and bent forward again, going through each step over and over.

I looked around. The women were doing the same thing too.

After watching this scene for several minutes, I, being the equal-opportunity American, turned to Noor.

"Why are the men in the front?" I asked. "Why can't the women be in the front? We're all praying."

I was completely expecting her to give me cultural and religious reasons. Instead she turned to me and called my attention to *how* the men and women were praying.

"Look! Do you see what they are doing?" she demanded. "They stand! They kneel! They lean forward! Their foreheads touch the ground! Their behinds go straight up into the air! Do you think it would be a *good idea* for the women to be in the front? And the men in the back staring at rows of women's behinds? The men won't be able to concentrate! You need to think! You need to be practical!"

My eyes were opened.

She had put me in my place. Though I had seen Muslims praying on TV, this thought about modesty never occurred to me. It had never

Figure 21.1. Mosque I prayed in, Baghdad, 2010

occurred to me that there was a practical reason on top of religious and cultural ones—but an Iraqi woman pointed this out.

We Americans really needed to open our eyes and look at things differently.

◆ ◆ ◆

Weeks after my arrival in Baghdad another American joined us on TONI. His name was Stan Smith. Stan was a bright young computer programmer from Oregon. He was blond, fit, and had the physique of a bodybuilder. With his military background and IT skills, he was hired to do administrative tasks for the compound. As it happened, Stan was given the largest office on TONI.

When I walked by his office one afternoon, I found Stan, with arms crossed, standing in the hallway staring off into space. Puzzled, I asked Stan what he was doing. He rolled his eyes and pointed toward his office.

I peeked in. Several Iraqi staffers were in the room with their mats out praying. Apparently, Stan's window and balcony provided an unobstructed view in the direction of Mecca.

Prior to his arrival, few of the Americans had focused on the fact that this room had a view facing Mecca and that some of the local employees prayed here several times a day. Before Stan, the room had been mainly used for storage.

Now Stan was inconvenienced. He told me that he was constantly interrupted throughout the day by prayers. He said he had been polite enough to accommodate the first week, but this was beginning to affect his work.

"This is *so* annoying," he mumbled, shaking his head. "I have deadlines to meet, reports to write, phone calls to return—and then there is *this*," he said gesturing toward the Iraqis who were praying.

I sighed.

"I wish they would just hurry up!" Stan shouted rudely into the room.

I was appalled. Several of those praying turned and looked at him. Obviously, they had heard him but they went right back to praying.

As I quietly tiptoed away, I thought about what it meant to be culturally sensitive. This concept had been raised on and off throughout my time overseas, but no one had actually defined it. Was it Stan who wasn't or was it the Iraqis who weren't? After all, this was an American-built compound, funded by American money, and the office had been given to Stan. It was his workplace. Surely, the Iraqis could have gone somewhere else to pray? Indeed, several of their colleagues prayed elsewhere. They could face Mecca even if a room did not.

Still, shouldn't Stan recognize he was in an Islamic country? What did he expect coming to Iraq? Was it reasonable for him to assume that his office here would operate like one in the U.S.?

Or does being culturally sensitive really mean that both sides find a compromise as each recognizes and accepts the other's differences?

◆ ◆ ◆

On a quiet Friday afternoon, while eating lunch at TONI, a fellow American introduced me to two young women who were guests at our table. Michelle and Karen, both with the Foreign Agricultural Service in the U.S. Department of Agriculture, told me they had been working in Iraq for more than a year. Michelle, with brown hair and a small frame, had a smattering of freckles on her face that seemed to stretch as she smiled and talked. She said she enjoyed working in Baghdad and was sorry that her tour was ending in two months. She had an apartment in northern Virginia and would return to her D.C. office after leaving Iraq. Karen, equally friendly and sociable, was tall, big-boned, and athletic. She was from Washington State and would return there at the end of the summer.

As we chatted, it transpired that the three of us were runners. I expressed my frustration over the lack of a gym and running path on TONI. Happily, they invited me to run with them the next morning on another compound.

"We'll take you to Liberty," Karen said, between bites of salad. "It has a nice running path inside its perimeter."

At 4:30 a.m. the next day, Michelle and Karen picked me up in their SUV. As we headed to Forward Operating Base Liberty (FOB Liberty), I asked why we had to be so early. Karen explained that she needed to be in her office by 7:30 a.m.

A few kilometers from TONI, FOB Liberty was not a base I had ever visited before. As we pulled into it, I saw the hauntingly beautiful palace that Saddam Hussein's family had built. "Uday's palace" was what Michelle unofficially called it since it was believed that Saddam's son Uday had spent a great deal of time there. It reminded me of a medieval crusader castle with its tall, vertical turrets allowing occupants an unobstructed view of Baghdad. Parking the car, Karen said that as with other palaces in the IZ, this one was now used as office space for the Americans.

Then she winked at me.

"I'll take you inside once we're done running," Karen whispered.

I salivated in anticipation.

The three of us ran the inside perimeter of FOB Liberty for a good forty minutes. Just as on the extensive grounds of the U.S. Embassy Baghdad, this FOB had crates of imported water bottles available for anyone who was thirsty. In the middle of our run both running mates stopped, grabbed a new bottle of water each, broke open the seals, drank several gulps, and threw the rest on the ground. As these almost-full, 1.5-liter bottles rolled away with water pouring into the ground, I commented on the waste. The two ladies just looked at me, shrugged, and ran on.

This bothered me.

I had seen this kind of waste before at the embassy. Lots of people did it. Just like the expenses of my multiple trips between Jordan and Iraq, it irked me that the cost of these supplies would be borne by the U.S. government and eventually the unknowing American taxpayers. Since many of our supplies were costlier than usual as they had to be flown in, I felt that the administrator of each compound should have had better controls over their distribution.

But they didn't.

When our run was over, Karen did as she had promised. We headed over to the palace.

It was shortly after 6:00 a.m. No one was around. We entered through an unlocked side door and immediately had access to several rooms that had been turned into offices. In addition to computers, desks, and chairs, I saw file folders, calendars, Styrofoam cups, and three-ring binders. In a smaller adjacent room, there was a coffeemaker, microwave, and an almost-finished Snickers bar in a wastebasket showing that indeed Americans had been here. Walking into the main foyer, I noticed the high ceiling, the grand staircase, a fancy carpet hanging, and a few worn but ornate armchairs—all indicating this was once a place of decadence.

I sighed, taking it all in.

"There's something else I want to show you," Karen said pointing upstairs.

As the three of us agilely climbed the staircase, my curiosity and wonder increased. I could hardly believe I was in a palace of the Hussein family. Arriving on an upper floor, we passed several more offices and then reached a dark corridor. With no windows nearby to shed light, the corridor had a gloomy, haunting feel about it. It was eerie to think that Saddam Hussein had once walked through this place himself.

Following Karen and Michelle through the dark space, I saw there was a dimly lit room at the other end. Once inside, Karen pointed to my right. Taking up the entire wall a huge bas relief depicted planes, with American flags on them, dropping bombs onto Iraqi women and children.

It was very clear that the Americans were the aggressors and the victims were the Iraqis.

"Saddam had this piece commissioned years ago to show his visitors what he claimed the U.S. was doing," Karen explained.

I stared. The bas relief was horrible. What it depicted was despicable. Suddenly, the whole palace had an unsettling effect to me.

Then another thought ran through my mind. Was this piece mere anti-American propaganda or did it show an actual event where the U.S. military hurt Iraqi women and children?

The three of us stood there silently for several minutes.

Afterward we went up another flight of stairs and out onto a large balcony. Now, from an upper floor of the palace, we looked beyond the IZ walls to the city of Baghdad and its huge mosque. Stretching for blocks, it was bigger and grander than any mosque I had ever seen. In contrast to its magnificence, a large number of shabby, stand-alone smaller buildings littered the city. Some were covered with grime, others had war damage, and more had been reduced to rubble. Though early, a film of pollution had lined the air. Its nondiscriminatory particles covered everything.

As I took in the breathless view of beauty and destruction before me, I wondered how much good, if any, the war on Iraq did for its people. It had removed a dictator, but what did Iraq have instead? Security? Stability? A better quality of life for its masses?

Moreover, I wondered if the war did anything for U.S. national security. The instability in the new Iraqi government and fragmentation within its society worried many countries. Without stability, the future of Iraq remained uncertain and this affected the balance of power in the region and the world.

Unable to come up with answers, I took a deep breath and gazed into the panorama again. Not everyone, even in Baghdad, had the chance to stand on this balcony and see the stark comparison between good and evil, the contrast between the untouched and the destroyed. They existed together side by side and, somehow, there was something extraordinary in it.

Then I recalled the movie *Braveheart* in which William Wallace told his army that every man dies but not every man lives.

I really felt I was *living*.

◆ ◆ ◆

As it was not possible for me to run with Karen and Michelle every day, I would frequently accompany a fellow American from TONI who had access to the U.S. Embassy. We would meet in TONI's lobby in the late afternoons and drive half a kilometer to the embassy compound to use its state-of-the-art gym.

I remember the first time I laid eyes on its grounds. The embassy had high walls, and covered a massive area. No other compound within miles came close to its jaw-dropping size. Once inside this fortress, it was a different world. It no longer felt like Baghdad: the roads were paved, the buildings were modern and sleek, the gym was first-rate, and the swimming pool was Olympic size. It was as though I was in a large, contemporary, well-heeled college campus. All I had to do was twirl around and see it was money, money, money everywhere.

"Isn't this place neat?" Cathy said smiling as we headed toward the gym.

"Yeah, it's another world," I answered, taking it all in.

As I visited the embassy more and more, it was difficult not to notice the waste. Frequently, there were the abandoned half-full water bottles lying around, plates of food taken but barely touched in the cafeterias, mists of water freely spraying from building perimeters, and lights left on continuously in office buildings. Even the ambassador's residence, which was located on a grassy lawn inside the grounds, was palatial.

It was difficult to forget that all these luxuries existed, in a desert, within blocks of local people toiling to make ends meet, to whom consistent electricity and running water were rare comforts.

As one of the most repugnant things about Saddam Hussein was his lavish lifestyle while his people struggled, it was ironic that within the IZ the most extravagant constructions were built by him and the U.S. government. Equally disturbing, now that Hussein's regime had been overthrown, was that Americans, temporarily or otherwise, occupied many of his palaces.

"We're just making use of the space," Karen told me once.

Though there were certainly practical reasons for the U.S. to have a large, fortified embassy and to use Hussein's past residences for office space, the symbolism was not ideal. I wondered how much thought, discussion, and debate there had been about these matters at any level of our government before decisions were made. Were any of our policymakers sensitive to the fact that these arrangements and their symbolism could have an adverse impact on our efforts in Iraq? What happened to the minority voices raised in objection?

I took a deep sigh. As I entered the gym, I couldn't help but wonder what our Iraqi neighbors in the IZ truly thought of us Americans.

◆ ◆ ◆

On a hot July day, Noor invited me to her office. As she worked for the prime minister, her building was inside the IZ. It was lumped together with a number of other government buildings, outdated in style, institutional-looking, and surrounded by Iraqi security guards.

Since Alicia and Cathy had not been invited by their students, I went alone in an armored car with a driver. When we pulled up to the government buildings, I could hardly contain my excitement. Going through the security checkpoint, a female Iraqi officer asked to hold my ID. From past experience in other countries, I knew it was a bad idea to give one's passport as it may not be returned. I offered my Virginia driver's license instead and was quickly ushered through. Surprised at not being patted down, I walked through the gate and met Noor who was waiting on the other side.

"Glad you made it. Let me introduce my husband, Hassan," she said smiling.

It turned out Noor's husband was also a government employee. He was an older man of large girth with grayish curly hair, dressed in a dark suit and leaning on a cane. When I walked up to him, he greeted me with warmth.

"Noor has told me a great deal about you," he said in perfect English, smiling.

The three of us walked down a large hall and into a spacious room where a colorful oil painting depicting a local market scene dominated one wall. This receiving room, though not elaborate, was well swept and presentable. The furniture, a sofa, several leather armchairs, and two coffee tables, was comfortable and functional. Noor had prearranged a plate of fruit for us that was laid out upon my arrival. The three of us sat down, chatted, and ate as I gazed around, taking in everything.

"I wish I could go to an open-air market like that," I said, pointing to the painting.

Hassan shook his head.

"For us it is easier to do all our shopping in supermarkets," he volunteered. "One could find everything one needs in a store."

I smiled. I had heard from the Iraqi Americans on TONI that my students did their shopping mainly in supermarkets, buying prepackaged foods like we did in the U.S. I was surprised at first as I had naively assumed that most people here bought their groceries from open-air markets. I suspected my students did this because they needed the convenience and could afford to—which many in the larger population could not.

Then the conversation turned to where Noor and her husband lived.

"This past weekend was too hot," Noor said, fanning herself with a piece of paper.

"Yes it was," I said, remembering that I had to turn up the air-conditioning in my trailer.

"You know," Noor went on, "we live here in an apartment inside the IZ and the electricity is always being cut! In the entire building! Appliances can't work and the air-conditioning stops. This goes on for days. It's unbearable."

Hassan nodded his head gloomily.

"When this happens," Noor continued, "we pack our bags, grab our son, and go to my in-laws."

"Where do they live?" I inquired, curious.

"In another part of the city, far out from the IZ," Noor answered waving her hand.

I looked at the couple. Compared to the majority of Iraqis, these two were, what I considered, high-powered. They were literate and had good jobs in Maliki's office. Yet somehow their living conditions were still lacking, even after the many years the West has poured in millions.

After a few more minutes of polite conversation in which neither Hassan nor Noor said much about their work, Noor took me to the offices of my other students. I spoke with Mrs. Masri, who again invited me to dinner, and visited with the others who stood up from their desks to greet me.

Each office I walked through that afternoon appeared well organized with computers on most desks. The furnishings were presentable but not expensive. Most of the desks, chairs, and bookshelves reminded me of the quality I had seen in low-end furniture stores in the U.S. There was no indication of opulence as there had been in the palace on FOB Liberty nor any of the high-tech snobbery I had seen at the U.S. Embassy. The entire building was clean, well-lighted, and air-conditioned. Almost all the employees, even the few women with their head scarves on, wore suits. Many were at their desks working.

I had heard it was not easy to get a job in Prime Minister Maliki's office. Beyond merit, one had to be well connected. As I chatted with my students, I pondered who they were, what their connections were, and the significance this had on the future of the country.

When it was time to leave, Noor accompanied me to the security lounge. As I retrieved my driver's license, I related my surprise at not being patted down upon entry.

"I arranged for you to be given VIP status," she explained, smiling.

VIP status?

I was surprised. Yet this was the thing about Iraq. One never knew what was around the corner. In a matter of weeks, I had gone from being a two-time deportee to a VIP.

◆ ◆ ◆

Soon thereafter Alicia, Cathy, and I were called into a meeting at TONI by our program director because some of our students wanted fewer days for English classes. Currently, we were teaching four hours a day five days a week.

Now some students wanted to have the English lessons squeezed into four days or even three. Several said it had to do with their work schedules—they all went to work for several hours before coming to class—and others said it had to do with their children's schedules. A few just wanted to explore whether they could learn the same amount of information in fewer days.

Sitting in the meeting room, I could see there was a problem. Our employer was open to change provided we were each teaching at least twenty hours a week, it was a unanimous decision among the students, and there was no objection from the U.S. Department of State, our funding agency.

"We could do it," Alicia said confidently. "We could teach five, six, or even seven hours of English a day."

I frowned and looked around the room. Cathy said nothing. She hardly ever did when it appeared that there was going to be a disagreement. Yes, we *could* teach five, six, seven, or even eight hours a day, but would that benefit the students? Would it mean that they actually learned more and could speak English better? What was the point of this program anyway?

"I don't agree," I said. "I'm happy to accommodate students' schedules, but I don't see that stuffing in so many hours a day of a language helps the students."

"We can do it," Alicia stated again, impervious to the downsides. "If they want seven hours of English a day or more, we'll do it."

Alicia seemed more concerned about preserving and prolonging her job than the welfare of the students. She didn't want to offer an opinion that was against what students were proposing lest it had an adverse effect on the existence of the program.

Yet in a few days' time, we saw that our meeting had been pointless. Our students were unable to agree on a new schedule. They were unable to present us with a unanimous decision, showing agreement and cooperation with each other. Our discussions didn't even make it to whether the new schedule would benefit their learning or whether the Department of State would object.

Taking a stroll around the compound, I sighed. If this small, innocuous program had so many problems coming to an agreement on a schedule, what about the decision-making for larger, more expensive and complex projects with many stakeholders? It was frustrating enough to watch how a colleague was ready to do just about anything, even if it was not in the best interests of the recipients, to preserve her job. Equally disturbing was how some students pushed for a change, without taking their colleagues' needs into consideration.

Was this an echo of the self-interest that was so pervasive at every level and that seemed to drive many of the foreign-funded programs?

I had an uneasy feeling it was.

Ultimately, what were we Americans really doing in Iraq? Were we rebuilding the country or merely building up our bank accounts?

◆ ◆ ◆

The night I was to go to Mrs. Masri's for dinner I was very excited. I actually had a dinner date in Baghdad! When my armored car drove up a residential street in the IZ, I saw a plain but clean, one-story apartment building. As we stopped, I stepped out and walked up to her front door. When I got there a huge white cloth had been draped over her open doorway.

This was interesting.

As there was no doorbell, I knocked on the wall beside the entrance. The cloth was made of such material that a person inside the apartment could see the visitor standing outside but not vice versa. I did not know it but Mrs. Masri was already observing me through this cloth. Within seconds, she pushed the material aside and welcomed me into her home. I was again touched by her warmth. This gesture was such a huge contrast to the "welcome" I had received from the airport officials.

Once inside, I was introduced to Mrs. Masri's friends and her two daughters. Noor was there too. Except for me, everyone was Iraqi. It turned out this was a women-only gathering so none, except for Noor, had their head scarves on. I hadn't realized that if men were not present, Muslim women did not need to cover their hair. For the first time, I saw Mrs. Masri without her head scarf. I couldn't help but stare. She looked so different showing her shoulder-length honey-colored locks, round face, and smooth forehead.

"Did you think I didn't have hair?" she asked, sensing my surprise.

We all laughed.

Then Mrs. Masri's daughters began to tell me about their lives in London. Both were university students. The younger, Jana, was wearing a tank top and jeans. She was thin with long brown hair and dark eyes. I could have easily mistaken her for a Calvin Klein model. Her elder sister, Yasmin, was more demure. She had fuller curves, a sweet smile, and wore a long lilac dress that went down to her ankles. Falling into comfortable conversation with both, I asked if they covered their hair in London.

"Oh yes," Yasmin said nodding. "Whenever we go out we are always covered good and proper."

Then I asked what nationality they were.

"We're British Iraqi," Yasmin answered smiling.

Apparently, the Masri family had dual citizenship, which was interesting given Mrs. Masri's position at the prime minister's office.

I found both daughters easy to talk to and we slipped into a banter about the British royals. One even offered her opinion of Camilla, Duchess of Cornwall.

During dinner, the women were really curious about my true opinion of Iraqis.

"So Jade," Mrs. Masri began slowly, "now that you've been here a while, what do you think of Iraqis?"

All the women turned their eyes toward me.

Being a guest, I had to be diplomatic. Nevertheless, I told my hostess and her friends about my tense moments at the Baghdad International Airport and how that affected my initial opinion of the people. My audience listened attentively, nodded in sympathy but did not express surprise.

Apparently, they were aware of such incidents.

Then several of them began sharing their individual stories about surviving the war.

"I got off work one night, was walking to my car when several men jumped out and attacked me," Sina began. She had a business-like air.

"Why?" I asked. "What did they want?"

"I don't know," Sina said shrugging. "I fought back, but my friend was there too and they shot her right in front of me."

"Did you call for help—the police, anybody?" I asked, jaw dropping.

Sina shook her head. She said that calling the police wouldn't do any good.

"But what about the next day?" I continued. "Did you go to a doctor? Get medical help?"

Sina shook her head again.

"I wasn't injured," she said, "only a little bruised. I returned to work the next day. What was there to do?"

I was quiet. She was telling me she had no choice. Life went on.

It was amazing. I was sitting among a group of educated females who were speaking their minds. Who, despite the hardships of war, the burdens of family and cultural restrictions, still pursued a profession. They exuded enormous emotional strength, something our American media failed to focus on. In the U.S. we speak of successful women who are wives, mothers, and career professionals all at once. What about Iraqi women who are all these things *and* war survivors?

Then I zoomed in on what one of these women wore. While most in the room wore long tops covering their torsos and trousers, this woman, in addition, wore about ten gold bangles on each arm. The gold looked to be the yellowish 22-karat kind. I was told that these bangles were a sign of wealth, beauty, and femininity. But given the hardships these people endured, I suspected that those who had anything of value wanted to keep it close to them. The gold was portable and could be a basis for starting life anew elsewhere.

Toward the end of the evening, Jana wanted us to get together for a picture. Even before the cameras were pulled out, the women started putting on their head scarves.

"Wait! Wait!" Yasmin exclaimed, quickly pinning on her head scarf.

It was an automatic reaction. They were happy to take the picture but only if properly covered as the photo might be seen by an unrelated male. After the photo was taken, the women began to relax again, automatically removing their head coverings.

Later there was a knock at the door. The husband of one of the guests arrived to fetch her. Before he could come in, he was told to wait behind the white cloth until all the women, except for his wife and me, had covered their hair. When the women were ready, they called out to him to enter.

It was a fascinating culture sprinkled with bits of femininity and demureness.

When my armored car pulled away from Mrs. Masri's that night, I thought about how much this evening humanized Iraqi women. They expressed their opinions but, at the same time, gave me time to state mine. They appreciated some Western influences such as technology, chocolates, and bits of fashion, but they also held on to their cultural values. They did not complain about women's rights to me, but they certainly valued their ability to be heard and to work. Many of their personal stories reflected intelligence, thought, and logic.

These were hardly the characteristics that we Americans associated with Iraqi women.

Most of our news focused on the bombs, the killings, and other horrors of Iraq. When it came to the women, the news usually showed them running around, covered from head to toe, railing about their dead sons and husbands. Few outlets focused on the educated females, what they had to say about their lives, their future and the West.

For the rest of my time in Baghdad, I did not see any of my American colleagues on TONI venture out to spend time with locals outside of work. Due to security problems this was understandable. However, many of them did go out of their way to spend time with each other and other foreigners. This was an unfortunate reality within the international community.

Given these troubling dynamics, were we Americans best suited to rebuild the country?

◆ ◆ ◆

It was August 2010, toward the end of our stay in Baghdad. Our students got together to throw Alicia, Cathy, and me a going-away party. They organized a potluck lunch and brought plates of cooked food, fresh fruit, and soft drinks. I was touched by their generosity.

At the party, I sat down with my students and laughed at some of the antics that happened in our class over the last few months. Then suddenly Iyad started to lament about his marriage.

"I had a fight with my wife last night," he said, looking at me.

I was surprised. Iyad, who was usually a quiet man with gentle manners, was sharing *this* with *me*?

"My wife was angry with me," he continued. "I came home late because I had to work but she didn't believe me. She thought I was out somewhere. I slept on the couch." He looked down at his food like a dejected husband.

I blinked. His words gave me another bird's-eye view into the personal lives of these locals. Unlike the action-packed horror we saw on CNN about life in Baghdad, these men's lives seemed so normal to me.

Then another student jumped in.

"Me," Abdul said as he chomped on a cookie, "I'm afraid of my wife too."

I stifled a laugh and asked why.

"She controls everything," he explained, throwing his hands up in the air. "From the minute I wake up she decides what I eat for breakfast and what clothes I wear. If I say no she gets mad. She shouts!"

Several of us sitting next to him chuckled. I said that this sort of relationship happened in the U.S. as well.

I was amazed at how frank these men were. Nothing I had read in American newspapers talked about the friendliness and frankness of Iraqi men, particularly when it came to men-women relationships. Now these men were discussing intimate issues with me, an outsider and a non-Muslim. It was as though the "distance" between an Iraqi and an American had been temporarily overcome.

The last day of class arrived. I was morose. My students felt it too and they knew what I was thinking: would we ever be able see each other again? How would our friendship be affected by the future relationship between our two countries?

As we began class, the whole room was solemn. Toward the end, one of my students stood up and said the class had something to give me. I was surprised. He handed me a small box. It was a jewel case. I opened it and there was a beautiful gold necklace with a gold sphere as a pendant. Excited, I immediately put it on. The students told me they knew I would always travel, always explore further lands, and because of this the pendant represented the world.

I was touched.

Later as we all headed down the hallway for a last handshake, one student, Mustafa, quietly handed me a small package.

"You must not open this while I am here," he whispered.

I was so excited to receive the gift that I opened it immediately. The gift was another jewel box and inside was another gold chain with a pendant. This time the pendant was shaped like the country of Iraq. While I was admiring the gift Mustafa thoroughly blushed. This was from him. I guess as a single man in his early thirties who was giving jewelry to a female teacher he felt a bit shy. Nevertheless, I told him how happy I was with the necklace and that I would always treasure it.

The last few minutes with my students had arrived. I escorted them all to TONI's parking lot. One by one they drove away. I stood and watched sadly until their cars were like specks of dust in a distance, none of us knowing what the future would hold.

22

Fredericks of Baghdad

On my last morning at TONI, there was a knock on my door. I was packing and thought it might be the driver, ready to take me to the airport. When I went to open it I was surprised to find a group of Iraqi women instead. I knew them of course. They were our administrative, kitchen, and cleaning staff. Wearing jeans, buttoned-down shirts, and no head scarves, they smiled up at me. But for their accented English, they could have been mistaken for women in the U.S.

"Can we come in, Jade?" they asked. "We want to say good-bye."

I nodded. They came in, sat on my bed, and giggled.

"We have a gift for you!" one of them said excitedly. "But we must prepare it. Can you step outside for a few minutes?"

"Sure," I answered.

I saw the glimmer in their eyes and heard the mischievous tone in their laughter. I stepped out and waited in the heat of the August sun.

While waiting, I thought about these women. They did their jobs faithfully and never gave me any trouble. Though I saw them every day, unlike the educated women at Mrs. Masri's, very few of them talked to me about their personal lives. They would greet me, crack a joke, and then move on with their work.

After a few minutes, one of the ladies opened the door.

"You can come in now," she said giggling.

When I reentered my trailer, I saw two pairs of sexy, lacy underwear laid out on my bed: one black and the other nude. Gasping, my face turned crimson. I hadn't expected this. Was this for me? Why would *they* give *me* lingerie? Where in war-torn Baghdad did they find these?

They all saw the look on my face and roared with laughter.

Finally, one of them managed to speak.

"Yes, these are for you," she said, still giggling. "We are giving them to you because we know you are engaged. You will be married soon. You must wear these on your wedding night. You *must* make your husband happy!"

My eyes went big. I recalled telling one of these women months ago that I had a fiancé but I did not expect her to remember. Moreover, I was not expecting racy gifts from women we Americans failed to see as sexual objects.

As I looked around, it was amazing to see these women laugh, bat their eyelashes, and talk excitedly like it was a bachelorette party. These women exuded a sexy, sensual side I had never seen.

American media often depicted Iraqi women as conservative, religious, serious, and downtrodden. To look for a smile from them, much less hear them gush about the opposite sex, was beyond imagination. Had someone pulled out a crystal ball before I departed Washington, D.C., for Baghdad and prophesied that I would return one day with lingerie, compliments of Iraqi women, I would have asked what kind of drug he was on.

What did we know about Iraqi women anyway? Did we even think they wore lingerie?

And wasn't understanding Iraqis key to our efforts in their country?

Treasuring these unusual insights, warmth, and gifts, I flew out of the country without incident. My Iraq experience had not been what I had expected. On the one hand, I was surprised to have found local people who were down-to-earth, discerning, funny, and kind. On the other hand, I was disturbed to see that things on the ground were more complicated, fluid, and unpredictable than what was often reported. Beyond that, the behavior and attitudes many Americans displayed here were disconcerting. Many had their own agendas and rebuilding the country was not at the top of their lists. Moreover, few were sensitive to how their speech and behavior affected local perceptions of us and our country.

As I landed at Reagan National Airport, I wondered how informed top people in our government were. Were they aware that Americans had been denied entry into Iraq? Though this might appear insignificant on the surface, the political implications and the costs were certainly indications of more serious matters.

Equally troubling was the U.S.'s purported policy of cost-effective management of its overseas programs. Was the handling of pricey resources and the building of expensive constructions in Baghdad part of this goal? If not, whose responsibility was it to speak up and make appropriate changes? It was disheartening to see how much American money and resources went into Iraq to be used so freely and with little accountability when the U.S. economy hobbled through a recession.

With these realizations, I picked up my luggage and headed back into D.C. U.S. foreign assistance was a lot trickier and more complicated than I had ever imagined. It seemed that the givers were no better than the receivers.

IV

Numbers in Afghanistan

Map of Afghanistan courtesy of Wikimedia Commons.
https://commons.wikimedia/org/wiki/File:CIA_map_of_Afghanistan_in_2007.gif.
Image is in the public domain. No part of it was altered.
Note: Kondoz is also spelled Kunduz.

Flashback Four

It was early evening in Kunduz. The temperature had dropped so I wore my long coat and mittens. I exited my trailer to begin a walk inside the Kunduz Regional Training Center. As soon as the male Afghan police trainees saw me, they started to gather, whisper, and stare. At first I made my way past them, looking directly at them. Several of the men leered at me. I wondered what was so fascinating to them about me. These men have lived on this compound as long as I have and have seen me on a daily basis. Yet with each round, what began as a small crowd became more and more numerous. It was akin to a scene in Alfred Hitchcock's movie, The Birds, in which each time Tippi Hedren turned and looked, the number of crows increased dramatically. Soon my Afghan audience was in the hundreds, crowding the sidelines of my path, almost blocking it. They gazed, gestured, and said unsavory things. As they inched closer, my heart beat faster and I began to weigh my options.

23

AK-47 as an Accessory

"Watch out!" someone shouted.

In a flash of several seconds, I saw the colleague in front of me lose her balance. Wobbling helplessly with her loaded AK-47 in her hands, she went crashing to the ground.

Crash!

Everyone's heart, including mine, stopped.

Luckily, her rifle did not go off.

It was February 2011 and the snow all around had turned into ice. We were at a shooting range just outside of Dulles, Virginia, learning how to use a pistol and a rifle and drive in a convoy. It was all part of our pre-deployment exercise prior to going to Afghanistan.

"Position! Aim! Fire!" our instructor barked.

The day was cold and the temperature was still dropping. Practicing with an AK-47 was pure hell. Due to its weight, I had to strain to get it up to a level where my aim was even close. Moreover, the motion of the rifle was intense. Each time I pulled the trigger, it would fire and recoil, bruising my right shoulder.

I glanced around. Several colleagues were fumbling with their AK-47s too.

But this was what one had to do if one wanted to go to Afghanistan on a U.S. government contract.

Even before my Iraqi sojourn, I had heard about a rule of law program the U.S. Department of State was funding. Since I was a seasoned lawyer who had development experience in several countries, I thought it was a good way to combine my legal and overseas experience.

But it was not easy to get in.

I knew that with some variations, Congress appropriated money for peace-building, reconstruction, and stabilization efforts in Afghanistan. The money usually went through a federal agency for a particular program. That agency would either execute the project in the field using its own employees or hire a contractor to do so. If a contractor was used, it would usually hire subcontractors to be the actual implementers in the host country.

Though this string of relationships sounded simple on the surface, in actuality it was not. There were layers of people at every level and in between. It was a complicated web of connections where many could claim successes, or point fingers, but few would own up to the failures.

Still, complications and cut-throat competition did not discourage anyone. Big and small, there were many contractors in this industry: Dyn-Corp, Academi, Halliburton, Northrop Grumman, and Bechtel, to name a few. The competition was stiff. Money was big and so was greed. Many contractors hired lobbyists to run around Washington, push the company's agenda, and land million-dollar, sometimes billion-dollar, contracts. There was no stop to this whirlwind of activity.

In 2007 I started interviewing with a number of entities in D.C. that had received U.S. government money to do rule of law in Afghanistan. Nothing came of it. But I pursued this in 2008, 2009, and in December 2010 the interview seemed to stick.

Now I was standing in a shooting range, gritting my teeth in the cold. I had to laugh. I was this metropolitan lawyer who normally wore pearls, dry-clean-only clothes, and heels to work. Suddenly, those items were switched out and in their places were a sweater, thick leggings, muddy boots, and an AK-47. The difference couldn't be starker. But I wanted to do rule of law and this was a hoop I had to jump through.

There were other hoops, of course, including passing a background check, obtaining a medical clearance, proving U.S. citizenship, and even attending a mandatory meeting with a psychologist.

Reentering a large meeting room at the Holiday Inn Dulles where all the candidates invited to this training had gathered after the shooting range, I mingled around. Many were sharing their stories about convoy driving and shooting, and others were just glad to be back in a warm room. There must have been about a hundred or so people, but only a handful were lawyers—and only two of them were women. I was one. Other candidates were program administrators, correction facilities officers, and security personnel. Most were in their forties and fifties and from all over the U.S. Surprisingly, many did not have overseas work experience. A few did and for them, like me, Afghanistan was going to be another notch on the belt.

As our orientation week passed, everyone traded information, joked, and laughed off the nervousness of heading to a war-torn country. At one dinner, some of us agreed that parts of the training, which were mostly PowerPoint sessions, were long and tedious, while other parts had very little relevance to what we would be doing. Curiously, many of the trainers had not been to Afghanistan themselves and for those few who had, it was not in recent years.

In one session, a woman asked what the average ratio was of men to women on a compound. My ears perked up. The trainer answered that it was about three to four hundred men to about eight to ten women. Though this was disconcerting, it sounded right from what I had seen in Iraq.

Toward the end of the week, another trainer, who had been to Afghanistan himself, volunteered an interesting suggestion. He told us to write down our salary on a yellow Post-it and stick it on our computer monitors.

"When things get rough in Afghanistan," he advised, "just look at that Post-it."

I heard him. We all did. It made me wonder how many people in the room were mainly in it for the money and how this would affect the U.S. effort in the host country.

◆ ◆ ◆

It was a sweltering July day in 2011 when I departed for Afghanistan. Standing on the tarmac at Regional Southwest Airport in Fort Myers, Florida, my point of departure, I wiped the sweat off my brow as I reviewed my itinerary again. I had to change planes in Dulles to get to Dubai, where

I would spend one night before continuing on to Afghanistan. As things turned out, my Florida flight was so delayed that I almost missed my connecting flight in Dulles.

"Hurry! Hurry!" I mumbled to myself. Desperately dragging my carry-on, running and cursing down the terminal, I was one of the last passengers to board the aircraft at Dulles International Airport. Finally arriving at its entrance, I showed my ticket and jumped onto the plane as the doors shut behind me!

I was going to Afghanistan.

Two of my colleagues, Nancy Stiles and Leonard Sims, were already on board. I had met Leonard at the pre-deployment orientation and he was expecting me on this flight. In his fifties, tall, Nordic, and handsome, Leonard had an elegant gruffness about him. He was polite but had strong opinions. He wasn't someone one could push around. He had been a public defender for more than thirty years in Arizona, which likely added to his strength of character.

With my hair disheveled, I hurriedly scooted down the crammed aisle, tripping over and stepping on other passengers' feet. In a distance, I saw Leonard wave.

"You barely made it!" he exclaimed, greeting me.

I nodded, still breathless from all the running and rushing. This was going to be a *long* flight to Dubai and the pilot just announced overhead that we should all take our seats.

After thirteen hours of uneventful sitting, we arrived in Dubai, United Arab Emirates. I had never been to this country before. As I followed fellow passengers to the immigration lines, I observed how first-rate the airport was. It was modern, spacious, and sleek and possessed all the state-of-the-art monitors one could hope for.

Subsequent to retrieving our luggage, Leonard and I stood outside waiting for our transportation. Apparently, Nancy had gone on ahead to the hotel alone. Standing silently, I took in everything around me: the lights, the noise, the people. Dubai seemed new, strange, and wonderful. The women were stylish yet covered. The men were handsome yet mysterious. In contrast to what I had seen of Iraqis in person and of Afghans on TV, these Emiratis were rich! Their roads were paved, their cars were fancy, their jewels were large, and their buildings were skyscrapers.

Is this what a developed Muslim country should look like? Did some in our American leadership envision the new Iraq or the new Afghanistan as looking like this?

We arrived at our hotel. The night passed and the next morning arrived. But there was an unnerving surprise right before our departure. As I waited in the hotel lobby for our airport shuttle, I happened to glance at the coffee table in front of me. There, spread out, was the Dubai newspaper for the day. On its front page was an article about the assassination of Ahmed Wali Karzai, the president of Afghanistan's brother, just the day before.

President Karzai's brother was shot?!

One would have thought that the security around this man was top notch. But no, he had been shot by a trusted confidante in Kandahar. The violence was nonstop and I was going to *that* country—today. I folded the newspaper quietly as Leonard and Nancy approached. This was not encouraging news as the three of us headed out.

Inside the SAFI airplane the cabin was extremely hot and stuffy. Unable to bear it, Leonard signaled the flight attendant.

"Miss, can you turn on the air-conditioning, please?" Leonard asked politely, removing his jacket.

She mumbled something and answered that they would do so *after* the plane had taken off. I had never been inside an airplane cabin this warm before. It was as though the closer we got to the host country, the more things broke down or failed to work.

Sitting by the window for three hours, I finally saw land in the distance. We were getting close to Kabul International Airport (KIA). When we approached, the pollution and the long stretches of undeveloped land, dotted here and there by clusters of rural houses, told me that we were indeed in Afghanistan.

Exiting the plane, I saw the mountains of Kabul surrounded by a beautiful lavender haze. Their peaceful presence had a calming effect. Then I turned and saw the immigration area and immediately broke into a cold sweat. I had been thrown out twice by an Islamic country and could not have it happen again.

Wearing a head scarf and a long black shirt that covered my torso, I tried to do everything possible not to be offensive to the Afghan airport officials. As we inched our way toward the immigration desk, I purposely sandwiched myself between Nancy and Leonard.

"If anything happens," I told them nervously. "You need to call someone. Call the U.S. Embassy, our employer, President Obama. Call someone!"

I was nervous.

When I finally stood before an Afghan immigration official, he gave me a cold stare. I held my breath. He didn't shout. He didn't point. He just stared. I wondered whether he thought I was related to the Hazaras, a downtrodden Afghan tribe centered in Bamyan Province whose members had East Asian features.

Before I knew it I was admitted.

Breathing at last, I headed toward the baggage claim. But it was a lesson in chaos. Suitcases were everywhere: on the moving belt and on the floor. Groups of passengers were walking around trying to sort out which bags belonged to whom. The whole room left much to be desired. It needed new paint, new carousels, mopped floors, and, I thought, cleaner-looking bag handlers. My cultural imperialism was rising.

Luggage in tow, the three of us headed toward the exit. Once outside there was more confusion. No signs or directions about where to go appeared. Afghans and foreigners were walking in all directions. The air was thick, the temperature was warm, and the sidewalks were choppy. Yanking our suitcases along, we all noticed that KIA was a far cry from Dubai International Airport.

Luckily Sara, an American coworker, was there to greet us. We had met her at the pre-deployment orientation months before. She had entered Afghanistan soon thereafter and was kind enough to email me tips about KIA. It was a relief to see a familiar face.

"So good to see you again," Sara said, giving me a hug.

"Thanks for being here," I mumbled gratefully. "This airport is a mess. It took me a while to find my suitcase."

Sara nodded sympathetically.

Wearing a pastel head scarf and dark clothing that covered her from neck to toe, Sara led us to our armored car where a driver was waiting. An old Afghan man with a gray beard, pretending to be a bag carrier, approached out of nowhere and began harassing Leonard. The man kept sticking his hand out, asking for money. Leonard had carried his own bags, but this old man was very insistent. He would not go away.

Once inside the vehicle, we all looked at each other. Soon another harasser came to my window and stuck his hand out. He, too, had provided no service. I was beginning to wonder about this game. It reminded me of other impoverished countries where foreigners were seen as an easy target.

Without wasting another moment, Sara gave our Afghan driver the signal to drive. If I had thought the streets of downtown Baghdad were worn-out, dusty, and chaotic, the streets of Kabul were worse. With potholes everywhere and only one traffic light working in this congested city, our vehicle bumped along haphazardly, squeezing through intersections whenever possible. As we sped along, I saw small mud shacks, rundown buildings, broken sidewalks, and dust-covered women in black burkas begging for money in the street.

After twenty minutes our driver made a sudden right turn and we were in the driveway of a large compound surrounded by high walls. Newport. At its huge gate, our vehicle stopped. The hood was opened and several Afghan security officers, each padded with a bulletproof vest and carrying a rifle, walked around our car, inspecting. Sara told us this was where we would be staying until further notice.

Newport was around ten acres and spacious. There was a cluster of easy-to-erect Quonset huts that served as offices and storage space, another cluster of two-story concrete buildings used as residences, and a few one-story buildings used as classrooms, dining halls, and other facilities. The rest of the area was open space with a huge parking lot for armored SUVs. The first thing I noticed was that the roads inside were all unpaved. Unevenly shaped rocks, each about the size of a three-ounce soap bar, covered the dirt roads. This made it difficult for anyone to walk or run with any speed.

Then there were the large trenches surrounding the outside perimeter of every building. They were about two feet wide and three feet deep. I had never seen anything like them before. They had to do with drainage—which struck me as strange in a dry country. The only problem was that one had to mindfully step over a trench each time entering and exiting a building.

Stepping over a trench that afternoon to enter my residential hall, I kept chuckling, "Mind the gap! Mind the gap!" as I thought of the London Underground. Little did I know I would use this motto later to refer to the greater divide between the Afghans and the Americans.

Entering the room I was assigned, I was pleasantly surprised. It was the same size and construction as Leonard's and Nancy's. But unlike in Iraq, it wasn't a trailer. It was inside a two-story concrete building and though small, it had its own bed, bathroom, desk, chair, TV, and refrigerator.

Then I stepped into my adjoining bathroom.

The shower bar was very high, probably seven or eight feet off the ground, but the shower curtain ended two feet above ground. There was no bathtub or shower door so I could predict water was going to splash out. Then on top of a rack, just as high as the shower bar, several rolls of toilet paper were stacked. I looked down at the dispenser. It was empty. I looked up at the toilet paper again, I could not reach it.

My life in Kabul had begun.

Figure 23.1. View of Kabul mountains from Newport. Note the guard towers and the barbed wire, 2011

Figure 23.2. Quonset hut office buildings inside Newport, 2011

24

Not Here to Question!

Our first week at Newport was strange. We were not given any sort of welcome packet, schedule, or map. There was no introduction to who's who or briefings about security, compound procedures, or do's and don'ts. In fact, the first night, we had to ask an American sergeant, T. James, to show us the way to the dining hall. Subsequently, we learned that another company managed Newport and that the compound housed approximately 150 Americans from several American entities, including the U.S. Army Corps of Engineers. Our company had a small office on the grounds, but its main office was on another compound in Wazir Akbar Khan, downtown Kabul, where the bulk of its employees worked and lived.

As the days passed, Leonard, who knew someone in the downtown office, was able to jump into a specific position there. Meanwhile, Nancy and I, after initially informing our main office that we had arrived, were told to wait for an appointment with our respective managers.

After days of meaningless television watching, eating in the cafeterias, internet surfing, and staring at walls, I took the initiative and contacted program management again. I finally got an appointment. It was on an early afternoon when I had my first meeting.

An armored vehicle drove up in Newport to take us to the downtown office where the meetings would be held. Nancy had an appointment too. She was going to be on the administrative side of things: processing vouchers and helping employees with their medical reimbursements. I looked at her. She was a tall, confident African American who exuded a quiet dignity. She had been in Iraq as well. I liked her.

As the Afghan driver stopped the car, hopped out, and looked at the two of us, we got a surprise.

"No vests?" he asked, gesturing with his hands.

He explained that we were supposed to be wearing bulletproof vests prior to entering the vehicle. I had no idea where to find these or that we were even supposed to have them that day.

Nancy and I looked at each other, turned back to the driver, and shook our heads. He motioned for us to board anyway. Soon we were passing through downtown. It was a hot day as I looked out onto the dirt-ridden streets, broken sidewalks, women in burkas, beggars sticking their hands out, and mud-built shacks—all within several minutes.

Just like the day we arrived, the traffic was horrible. There seemed to be no rules. Cars, motorcycles, trucks, and pedestrians came and went whenever they could squeeze through. When our vehicle halted, I saw a donkey-pulled cart to my right, a man-pulled wagon to my left, and a dusty old truck behind us. The assortment of transportation was beyond belief.

I saw groups of schoolgirls with their head scarves on and books in hand, walking to school. If I had not been otherwise aware of the extreme gender inequality in the country, this scene might have fooled me into believing that things were better than what the press had reported.

Nearing our downtown office, my mind raced through all that I had just seen. It was fascinating how inside a war zone people still managed to carry on something akin to normalcy. It was as though within the eye of a deadly "storm," the city still teemed with life.

Then our vehicle made an abrupt turn and pulled into a compound containing several large houses, each at least three-stories tall, with garish exteriors. A mixture of dark green, light blue, muted red, and beige made up the colors of the facades. Many windows were large with ornate trim. Satellite dishes poked out here and there. On the upper floor of one of the houses was an extensive balcony with lawn chairs. Inside these walls were our main offices and more sleeping rooms. Unlike Newport, the whole compound was only about three acres with patches of grass and paved sidewalks between each building.

As I walked into a house, there was a dank smell. The carpet was a dirty dark red and all the rooms on the first floor had been turned into offices, each with a piece of paper taped on the door indicating the name of the department. Ascending a narrow metal staircase, I arrived at the second landing and immediately saw a large copy machine, cases of Xerox paper, and several desks with Afghans sitting behind them. Apparently, this house did not have enough office space.

Climbing another set of steps to the third floor, I was told to wait here for Fred Olsin, my new manager. After a good fifteen minutes of standing around, nodding my head to the Afghan staffers passing by, and listening to various phone conversations from nearby rooms, a short, stocky unsmiling man walked quickly toward me. Within seconds of meeting Fred, I sensed he would not be easy to get along with. Though his words greeted me, his body language communicated he had better things to do. Clean-shaven with even features, his dark eyes looked me over briefly before they darted back to surveying others in the room. There was an impatience about him. After a limp handshake, he motioned for me to sit down.

Without further ado, we spent the next two and half hours going through a handout, a set of rules on how to communicate by email with our funding agency, the U.S. Department of State.

"Look at the next page. It is really important," Fred emphasized, his jaw tense. "I want you to know this."

We flipped to the next page. Though on the surface, this could have been interpreted as mere formality from a prickly funding source, I had a feeling it was more. This handout basically discouraged communication directly with our funding agency, lest we reveal some potentially damaging details.

"You are here to do as you're told," Fred said firmly, looking at me. "Not here to question! No one cares what you think. You are here to do."

I was appalled. I hadn't even said a word.

I wondered if Fred's boss back at headquarters in the U.S. knew he spoke this way. I felt sure that if headquarters knew, corrections would be made. Lawyers were paid to think, analyze, argue, and advocate. So were advisors. If we were truly here to "advise" the country on issues of law, don't we need to ask questions? Don't we need to *think*?

As the meeting ended, there was still no mention about my specific assignment.

I waited for several minutes. I finally had to ask, "Do you know where I will be assigned?"

"That will be discussed later," Fred answered curtly, shooting me an irritated look.

As I slowly gathered my handout and put it in my tote bag, I thought about waste. I thought about the half-full water bottles in Baghdad, the expensive but culturally irrelevant programs in Kosovo, and the lazy Peace Corps volunteers in Malawi. In fact, I had seen waste in every foreign country I had had the privilege to work in. Waste seemed part and parcel of overseas programs funded by U.S. taxpayers. It was part of the mentality, the development culture, and the way things "worked." Worse was when the program administrators themselves failed to recognize it when they were supposed to be watching the company's, or more pointedly, America's resources.

Now waste was here again. I had already spent days waiting at Newport with nothing to do but get paid. Even when I asked, no, *begged* for an assignment, there was no decision. Was I just a warm body, a number in Afghanistan to fulfill a contractual term?

Wasn't I trying to do my job?

Was Fred?

I had heard that in this industry, contractors were compensated for the number of people on the ground as opposed to what each person produced. Unfortunately, my experience thus far validated this theory.

Finally, after a few more days of nothingness, which I understood from colleagues was the norm, I was told to find Gerry, another advisor who lived and worked in Newport where I had been staying all this time. It was bizarre that I had not been told about him before.

Gerry was a large man and with a big booming voice. Although he liked to joke and laugh, he was one of those men who could intimidate with his girth and height. He wore gold-framed glasses and large, starched white shirts with colorful ties. Looking at him, I knew he was well over a foot taller than me.

When he saw me approaching, he bellowed out with a laugh, "Hello Jade! Good to meet you. We don't have anything for you yet but, here, you can read these."

He handed me several heavy white binders. I must have had a deer-in-the-headlights look. He explained a few things about the program, informing me there were about sixty international staff, most being Americans. Many of the lawyers and judges were spread out around the country. The greatest number was concentrated here in Kabul where each advisor had a special task of teaching, coordinating classes, or working with a particular Afghan government office.

Then Gerry had to go to a meeting.

As I was not given an office, I wobbled back to my room, carrying the heavy reading material. Is this what being a rule of law advisor was about? When was I actually going to be part of the program?

I spent the next several days reviewing the big binders. They contained pages and pages of lesson plans. I assumed, as no one was guiding me, that these were courses that would be or had been taught to Afghans in the legal community. At a quick glance they seemed the regular kind of class one would give to legal professionals anywhere: constitutional law, human rights, gender equality, legal writing, and so forth.

But as I zoomed in on one lesson, I could not help but notice that quotations had been inserted as the lead-in. It began by quoting Franklin D. Roosevelt and Winston Churchill.

I stopped for a moment.

While these two famous men stood for democracy and freedom in the West, what did they stand for in Afghanistan? Did our students even know who they were? Even if a few did recognize these names, should Roosevelt's and Churchill's words be given the same prominence here?

Since neither Churchill nor Roosevelt played a large role in Afghanistan, I wondered why the lesson didn't begin with quotes by famous figures from this side of the world. Hadn't the lesson planners studied Afghan history?

Then I kicked myself for not having read more on the history of Afghanistan. If I had been better informed, I would have understood whom our students likely respected. I tried to imagine myself in an America that, somehow due to a crisis, was occupied by foreigners. These invaders entered and dominated our infrastructure, telling us they are helping to rebuild our country. During this time, they are involved with many aspects of our government, including law, finance, health, education, and defense. Yet as time passed, it became apparent how little these invaders understood us, our culture, history, and values. I imagined myself, a trained professional, sitting in a classroom waiting to be taught by one of them. He or she enters, speaks in a strange tongue, and begins to quote people I didn't know or cared little about.

Visualizing Americans through Afghan eyes was sobering.

◆ ◆ ◆

Several weeks before teaching a law course, Gerry suggested I observe the ones being taught by others. Some of the classes were taught by American advisors and others by Afghan legal experts on our staff.

The first time I observed a legal seminar held at Newport, I was pleasantly surprised. A female Afghan lawyer had complete command of the class. She went through concepts, answered questions, and sparked

Figure 24.1. Locals jaywalking in Kabul, 2011

Figure 24.2. School girls, Kabul, 2011

Figure 24.3. Downtown Kabul, 2011

an animated discussion. The students, mostly men, were seasoned Afghan judges, prosecutors, defense attorneys, and police officers from the Kabul community who respected her and showed her deference.

This scene diffused some of my earlier conceptions about Afghan women's standing in society gained from American media.

"She's amazing," I said to myself.

Yet I was surprised weeks later when I was pulled aside by an American colleague.

"You know Ara?" this colleague asked, referring to the female Afghan lawyer whom I had watched teaching.

"Yes," I answered. "She's powerful."

"Well, there's a little problem," this colleague continued, whispering. "Ara has been selected to teach for a few days in another province. This involves overnighting and since her family can't go with her, can you be the chaperone?"

I had never been anyone's chaperone let alone an attorney's.

Despite her status, education, and qualifications, Ara could not travel alone because, according to local custom, that would cast a shadow on her reputation.

Astounded, my thoughts were racing. Ara seemed so impressive, so knowledgeable, and so professional in front of the classroom. Yet a small task like traveling alone was out of the question. She needed "supervision" as her culture dictated. The restrictions of Afghan society suddenly became very real.

Later, when I approached Ara to ask if she needed me to accompany her, she looked torn.

"Do you need me to go with you?" I asked, trying to sound understanding.

She let out a deep sigh.

"No. No," she said, shaking her head. "I'll take care of it."

On the one hand, she wanted to be like her male colleagues, able to step up to any task. On the other hand, she knew the cultural rules she was bound by. She looked at me sadly.

In the end I did not accompany her. I only learned that she made the trip but nothing more. Perhaps having an American woman did not meet the standards for appropriate "supervision" in the eyes of her culture.

A week later I observed another legal seminar that opened my eyes further to the gender dynamics in the country. The incident was so small and seemingly insignificant that it could easily have been missed.

A male American colleague was teaching a class of fifty Afghans at Newport. About ten of the students were women who sat together and away from the men. The afternoon was very hot and the room was terribly stuffy. During the lesson, one of the women quietly got up and headed to the room next door. In a few minutes she returned with a number of water bottles in her arms. She gave one to each of the female students and then walked all the way to the back of the room to give one to me. She skipped all the men, including the instructor.

"Thank you," I said, pleasantly surprised.

I had not asked for a bottle of water. I did not even know her name, nor did I greet her upon entering the class. But she noticed me. She saw that I was female, although my lack of a head scarf suggested I was non-Muslim. Despite this difference, she included me. This told me something about Afghan women. They reached out to foreign women over foreign men—and perhaps even Afghan men.

As teaching wasn't the only aspect of our jobs, we visited Afghan professionals in the criminal justice system and "mentored" them. This usually involved meeting with locals in the prosecutor's office, the courts, police stations, and various other justice institutions. Talking to these professionals about their jobs and exploring what trainings they needed, we were expected to champion concepts that were prevalent in many Western systems: due process, equality, fairness, transparency, and so forth.

On my first day to accompany a colleague to a mentoring session in Kabul, I took a backseat. My lead, George Maise, was a lawyer from Michigan who told me he had been in Afghanistan for a few years. He possessed a great deal of knowledge about the local culture, gained from working in several provinces. Hardworking, efficient, and no-nonsense, he, the leader of our Kabul team, always started his meetings on time and expressed great unhappiness with those who were late.

While we were in the armored vehicle, George turned his attention to where we were going and gave me a few tips. We were going to visit an Afghan judge.

"What am I supposed to say to this judge?" I asked, a bit lost.

"Don't worry. I'll do the talking," George answered reassuringly. "Just follow my lead. You'll be fine."

When our vehicle pulled up to a large government complex in downtown, I hopped out and felt the scathing heat of the summer sun. As I had on a head scarf and a bulletproof vest, which added layers, sweat seeped through my long shirt.

"Oh, it's hot," I mumbled to George as perspiration dripped from my brow.

Hundreds of Afghans were going in and out of the complex in no organized fashion. Some were wearing their long tunics and others had on shirts and slacks. Following George, I entered a huge, dimly lit, and dank smelling building where there was no air-conditioning and many locals loitered in the hallway.

They gazed at us. We were the only foreigners around. We did not even have an armed guard or weapons. An uncomfortable thought filtered through as I wondered what we would do if an insurgent suddenly emerged. There was nowhere to run.

Notifying the judge's secretary that we had arrived, we were ushered into the judge's office within minutes. As his room was on the ground floor with few windows and no lamps, the lighting was dim. Even so, I could see chipped paint on the walls and tears in the large, overstuffed sofa. Judge Abdullah rose from his chair to greet us. He was a pleasant man with short hair and no beard. To my surprise he wore a suit too, but the jacket and the slacks were uncoordinated: not the same color nor made of the same material.

After the initial greeting, George and I proceeded to remove our body armor. As a rule from the U.S. Department of State, we were to take off our bulletproof vests when meeting with a local counterpart. It was a gesture of goodwill.

Since George had been doing this for a while, he deftly removed his vest in a few seconds and sat down. I struggled with mine. Most of these heavy vests were made for men, so mine was disproportionate to my height and weight. It was a strain to take off as I had to raise it over my head. Fumbling nervously, my hands tried to catch my head scarf before it fell off and became trapped by the Velcro straps of the vest. Judge

Abdullah saw my hair and watched humorously as I, the new advisor, struggled with the realities of my job.

My face colored with embarrassment when I finally took a seat next to George. For the next half hour, we discussed training prospects for the judge's staff. The mentoring was not quite the classic definition of a master advising a protégé but a discussion about how to make the local counterpart's job better, better as in more efficient and equipped to administer due process.

"You want to do the training next month?" the judge said to George, raising an eyebrow. "I won't be here for the last half of August."

"Oh?" George responded.

"I have some health problems and will go see a doctor in India," the judge explained, rubbing his stomach. "Digestive problems."

I had heard this comment before from other Afghans. Apparently, those who could afford it went to India for medical treatment.

George and I took notes as the judge spoke. We then worked out a schedule that would fit the judge's calendar.

When it was time to leave, we thanked the judge for his time and proceeded to put on our protective gear. As I raised the heavy vest over my head again, my head scarf fell off once more. Worse, this time *my hair* became entangled in the Velcro straps. Amused, the judge walked over and reached out with his bare hands to help untangle my hair. I was surprised when I felt his cold fingers against my neck! All that I had heard about the Afghan culture indicated that unrelated men and women kept appropriate distances from each other. As an American female, perhaps I did not count as a "woman" and he felt he could touch me.

It was a startling moment indeed.

25

Who We Were

Life at Newport was interesting. In its vast space of ten acres, Newport housed offices, classrooms, residences, dining halls, laundry rooms, storage space, and a gym. As several American entities, civilian and military, shared this compound, there were people walking around daily in battle dress uniforms (BDUs) and also in civilian clothing.

I took a good look at the residents. The majority were men in their forties and fifties. Most were here on some peace-building assignment with wives back in the U.S. Some had been working in Afghanistan for years.

From the conversations I overheard, most of these men did not trust Afghans. Many thought that Afghans did not want to change, at least not in the direction the West wished. Some even believed that the locals were unable to change, unable to reason, and unable to learn. Very few had high opinions of Afghans, the local culture, religion and traditions. Many did not know enough about Afghan history, nor did they care to learn it.

"The people here don't have cognitive skills," one man said to his friend over dinner. "I was trying to explain something simple to an Afghan the other day and the guy just gave me a blank stare."

His friend nodded.

"They don't have linear reasoning," another man at the table volunteered. "Their way of thinking is just—all over the place." He gestured with his hands.

Everyone in the group laughed.

As I leaned in, more questions formed. *Why* were these Americans here in the first place?

From what I heard many had debts they needed to pay, family dynamics they wanted to escape, an adventure they wished to pursue, and bank accounts they needed to fill. Advancing American national interests or making Afghanistan a safer, more democratic country was not at the top of their lists.

And there was more.

Given the daily pressures of their jobs and the risks of being in a war zone, it was easy to feel stressed all the time. To alleviate the stress, a group of Newport occupants turned to alcohol. For those who chose this path, it was apparent they thought that rules concerning alcohol did not apply to them. I could not believe the amount consumed and the regularity with which some visibly abused liquor. One would have thought that in a dangerous Islamic country where Muslims were forbidden to drink by their religion, foreigners would have had the common sense to consume alcohol discreetly.

As we followed the Muslim work schedule, our work week was Saturday through Thursday. Friday was a holy day, a day of rest. Starting Thursday afternoons, I would hear Americans discussing how much they looked forward to drinking that evening. Yet Newport had a rule: no alcohol inside the compound. But for security reasons, no one was allowed to exit and drink on the street either.

It was then that I learned this rule, like others, was just a statement of intent while its enforcement was virtually nonexistent.

When Thursday evenings arrived, managers and subordinates alike, from several entities gathered on the rooftop of one of the residences. The laughter, chatter, and drinking started out harmless enough. Yet as the evening turned into night and the drinking continued, their obnoxious shouting and pejorative language became louder and louder, disturbing many of the residents. One colleague told me that during one such gathering, a drunken American ran to the edge of the rooftop and mimicked out loud the call to prayer.

Unable to sleep one night, I decided to take a walk. Once outside, I heard noises from above.

"Fuck! Fuck! Fuck you!" an American shouted out to the world from the rooftop.

I looked up. An unidentifiable man was on the roof, leaning over the railing. I couldn't tell if he was vomiting. Then I turned and looked about two hundred yards across our parking lot. Several Afghan guards, which Newport employed, stood at their stations taking in the whole scene. No doubt this would be shared with locals in town. I shook my head in embarrassment for America. Who were these people its taxpayers were paying to run programs, teach skills, and share values? Did they set a good example for others? Were their actions enhancing the U.S.'s image?

Did they do things instead that made Afghans abhor Americans?

As alcohol use continued in this "non-alcohol" environment, I wondered why camp management, run by a foreign company, failed to take action. I suspected it had to do with money. Every entity that rented rooms paid camp management for its services. If camp managers took a stricter stance and enforced certain rules, tenants might pull out and go elsewhere. In 2011 and 2012, there were other compounds in Kabul looking for tenants.

Adding to the negative American image that intoxication produced, other interactions between the two groups caused difficulties. One American man, no less a former surfer from Florida who liked to joke frequently and purposely in front of Afghans, replaced the word *inshallah*, which in Dari means "God willing," with the word *enchilada*.

"See you tomorrow enchilada," he said to Afghan staff who were getting ready to leave for the day.

Several of them turned to look at him, giving a forced smile. Apparently, they didn't understand his joke.

"See you tomorrow, sir, inshallah," a local staffer said, grabbing his jacket.

"Inshallah," the other Afghan staffers said, nodding their heads to the American before exiting.

"See you tomorrow enchilada," the surfer said again, chuckling.

I looked at my colleague. He obviously didn't understand that his joke wasn't funny, that it needlessly stirred up resentment in Afghans who saw it as mocking Islam, and that anything mocking Islam subtracted from our safety and success.

Then there was the disturbing segregation on Newport.

The two groups did not mix outside of work. The local staff and students, who commuted to the compound from Kabul, did not socialize with the Americans. Though these Afghans were polite and friendly in the office and classrooms, break times and lunch hours were spent only with each other. In the recreation room they played Ping-Pong and board games with one another but only when foreigners were not present.

Furthering this divide, Newport had two dining facilities (DFACs). One was the international DFAC, which always featured a buffet, and the other was the Afghan DFAC, which served only one entrée per meal. All foreigners ate in the international DFAC, which did not admit Afghans. An exception was made when high-level locals were visiting and for special events.

The Afghan DFAC was a much smaller facility. Afghans, of any rank, who worked or attended classes on the compound ate there. Foreigners were allowed entry, but rarely did any bother to go. The food was lower quality and the ambiance just wasn't the same.

Something was not right with this picture.

Americans were here to protect and advance U.S. interests. Part and parcel of that was the spread of democratic values. A core value in a democracy is equality. Where was the equality if they purposely ate apart from the Afghans on the compound? What message was sent by their actions?

More importantly, what message was undermined by them?

I went to Gerry one afternoon and asked about this curious arrangement.

"Is there a reason why our Afghan staff and students aren't allowed in our cafeteria?" I asked.

Gerry looked around and sighed.

"There are reasons but mainly it's about costs."

This was a noncommittal answer and it didn't make sense. The U.S. government was not going to pay the extra cost per head to feed each Afghan in the international DFAC, but it doled out enough money to build an entirely separate dining facility for them. Something didn't add up. Subsequently, I heard it had to do with costs, security, and differences in cuisine.

I took a deep breath.

Ironically, our government, the very same one that had required the removal of bulletproof vests in a stranger's office as a sign of goodwill, was unable to see the importance of nurturing relationships with Afghans we depended upon. These were inconsistent messages and they hurt America's image in the country.

Given the billions of dollars the U.S. has already spent on the country, why was this DFAC cost an issue? The Afghan population at Newport was around fifty, whereas the number of foreigners was at least three times that. If much of what we were doing was trying to inculcate our values and ideas, the inclusion of all people irrelevant of sex, religion, or ethnicity should preempt anything separate but "equal" from surfacing.

One day I decided to do a little experiment.

Since foreigners were allowed to go into the Afghan DFAC, I decided to give it a try. Arriving at work, I told my local staff I wanted to eat lunch with them.

They all looked up very surprised.

"Okay," Nemat said. "But you'll need to eat in the Afghan DFAC because we can't go into the other one."

"Yes, I know," I acknowledged. "I'll go with you to your DFAC."

When noon arrived, I stood up and asked our Afghan staff whether they were hungry. They nodded their heads. I then turned to my two American colleagues who were sitting quietly nearby at their desks and inquired whether *they* would like to join us. Both men said no. One even gave me a strange look.

"Ohh, you're starting something you shouldn't," he said, shaking his head after the Afghan staff had left the room.

What is that *something*? I wanted to bark back.

We proceeded to the Afghan DFAC. Entering, I saw it was a simple square room filled with a dozen cheap-looking fold-up tables and equally cheap-looking fold-up chairs. The white walls were almost bare, with a few notices tacked here and there. Several Afghans were already in a line that led up to a small window where a cook placed the same entrée on each person's tray.

We got our food and sat down. The staff seemed genuinely happy that I decided to join them.

Eating and laughing, the staff told me things about themselves that they had never mentioned in the office. One of them, a tall, gaunt former judge named Fahim, who always dressed impeccably in a suit, revealed a juicy detail about himself.

"Jade, I'm dating a Vietnamese girl online," he said, eyes twinkling.

My jaw dropped. I did not know Afghans here did online dating.

"She's in Vietnam. She's my girlfriend," he said, giving me a knowing smile.

I was intrigued. We all huddled together to listen to more juicy details. Another employee, Farhad, told me how much he loved running. He was a medical doctor, trained in Afghanistan, who had worked previously on another base as a paramedic.

"Oh, I used to run so much when I was on the other compound," he groaned. "My coworker was this American girl who loved running. We ran together almost every evening."

Then he told us about his knee problems and how he had to ease off running for a while. I laughed and shared how I was a runner, too, experiencing similar aches and pain.

Though this was only a bird's-eye view into these Afghans' lives and the first of several lunch hours I would share with them, I was amazed at the frankness and the humanness I saw. Their cares seemed so normal to me, so everyday.

Returning to the office later, I heard the noise as American colleagues came back from *their* lunch. The way many Americans excluded the Afghans from meals and recreation had an eerie echo of the civil rights era in U.S. history. Due to security issues, most internationals could not move in their staff's and students' social circles. They could not exit compounds whenever they wanted to visit restaurants, parks, schools, and homes. If they did not choose to make the effort to get to know these people now, there would be very little opportunity outside the compound.

Just as a provider of any service was more successful when he or she had in-depth knowledge of his or her customers, I believed that those offering foreign assistance needed to know their recipients better.

Looking down at my keyboard, I wondered at the many Americans in Afghanistan who failed to see what their actions communicated and sacrificed.

◆ ◆ ◆

Working with locals one could not help but see the brain drain. Just in our office alone, an Afghan-qualified lawyer and a medical doctor were working as mere translators. While it was understandable that these individuals would rather have steady, higher-paying jobs with a foreign entity than work for an Afghan employer in their own field, there was a drain on the country's intellectual resources. By having skilled individuals in jobs either not related to their professions or not fully utilizing their skills, we were slowing down the speed of Afghanistan's peace-building, stabilization, and reconstruction. Sadly, I had seen this in Kosovo and Iraq too.

"Jade, I'm planning to go to Turkey for a medical conference," Farhad told me one afternoon.

"You are?" I asked, surprised.

"Yes, I have to," he explained. "It's in March and this conference is important to my profession."

I said no more. I wasn't going to discourage him, nor was I going to ask what he would tell our employer. Farhad had been working in our office for months as a translator. He was smart, efficient, and he knew his worth. He knew that he could not let his medical training fade away. Afghanistan needed him more for that knowledge and skill than for his translation services.

Then I looked around the office.

Who were these Afghans employed by the international community anyway? What work experience did they have doing what they were hired to do now? Most were born in the seventies and eighties. Most had lived through Russian occupation, civil war, dictatorships, and now intervention by international forces. Many had a good portion of their lives disrupted by instability, war, and death. Some had even been refugees in neighboring countries for several years. All had seen governments come and go in Afghanistan with many laws changed or cancelled. For those in our program alone, few had the practical experience of living under a stable government supporting rule of law.

What did these Afghans know about stability in governance or having a democracy for that matter? How could they communicate the value of having a democratic government to their people?

Yet these were the best local employees we or anyone else had.

◆ ◆ ◆

One afternoon sitting in the shade in Newport, I mulled over a troubling incident that had taken place a few days earlier. Two colleagues had expressed divergent views. Yet it was not the difference in opinion that caught my attention but the way the conversation escalated. Shauna, a lawyer in her sixties from New York who used to have her own law office, said that she did not like how some of our students smelled, particularly the mullahs.

"I just can't stand their body odor," she said, wrinkling her nose. "It's awful, especially when they're close by. I think we should have a bathing requirement for those attending our classes."

"TS! [Tough shit] TS!" Quinten yelled, immediately jumping in. "It's not for us to decide whether they bathe! It's not our business! It's their choice! It's their culture!"

Quinten was the typical loud, brash, in-your-face lawyer most people deplored.

Mullahs, or religious men who had been trained in Islamic law, attended our seminars because many had jobs in the government and were involved with the administration of justice. When I had first entered the program, I was surprised to see them in our classrooms, wearing their traditional robes and headdress. But it made sense for them to be there. The only problem was, as Shauna said, they often brought with them an unpleasant odor.

The exchange quickly escalated into shouting. I could not believe the intensity with which both defended their views.

"They should bathe!" Shauna insisted.

"It's not your business!" Quinten screamed.

"But they're coming into an American compound!" Shauna fought back.

This went on. What started out as a difference in opinion almost became a declaration of war by both sides. I watched as my two colleagues went at each other's throat.

Yet a scene like this was something I had witnessed many times in war zones. Short fuses were brought on by the pressures of living in an unstable country and being away from family for long periods. What usually started out as a seemingly small matter easily became a huge argument.

In this case, whether the Afghans smelled or whether we could get them to bathe should have remained only a topic of discussion. Many of our students did not have the luxury of running water in their homes, so had we even required bathing, the reality of it happening was beyond our control.

Unfortunately, this incident was yet another reminder of how stressed we all were and how little we Americans, on the ground, understood the realities of life for the local people.

◆ ◆ ◆

Gerry approached me one day and told me that I was going to another province.

"You're going to Kunduz," he said smiling. "It'll likely be sometime next week."

I was to replace a man who was resigning after a short stay.

Quickly, I grabbed a map. Kunduz Province was in the northern part of the country on the border of Tajikistan, not far from the Hindu Kush Mountains. From what I had heard, it was rural, conservative and dangerous. Its illiteracy rate was high and crime-reporting was low, though plenty of crimes took place in that area.

Little did I know what I would find in Kunduz or in Kabul days prior to my departure.

Brad Bentford, a fellow lawyer who had heard about my assignment, expressed dismay at my going away.

"You know," he said looking a bit down, "I am happy for you but sad for me. I was hoping that we would have time to get to know each other."

I turned and glanced at him. His last sentence gave me pause. Brad was a tall, slender, middle-aged former prosecutor from Pennsylvania. He reminded me of a model in a Brooks Brothers commercial. Neat and clean, he always wore clothes that were ironed. Having gotten to know him a little, I could see he was a hard-working and dedicated rule of law advisor. But there was something odd about him that I couldn't quite put my finger on—just yet.

Perhaps it had to do with the way he quietly stared at me at times.

A few days prior to my departure, Brad called. He was living and working in our downtown compound and told me he planned to come to Newport that evening. He said he wanted to see me and also use the gym.

Hours before his arrival, he phoned again. He asked whether he could take a shower in my room after the gym.

Something didn't sound right. Take a shower in *my* room? My room was small and there was no privacy.

I grabbed the nearest friend, Wayne, and told him what Brad had said. Wayne was a thoughtful man with a gray beard. He stroked it slowly as he answered. He understood guy code.

"Why doesn't Brad ask one of us guys if he could use the shower in our room?" Wayne asked. "Why bother *you*! You should tell him when he gets here to use the men's showers down the hall."

The residential building that housed us also had a common men's restroom.

Brad came to Newport that evening and I saw him in the gym. Afterward he asked again about coming to my room. As we walked toward the residential building, I told him that he could leave his belongings with me but he would need to take his shower down the hall. To my relief, he obeyed.

Afterward Brad, Wayne, and I took an evening stroll inside Newport. There was a clear, starry sky. When Wayne said goodnight and Brad boarded the armored vehicle to return to his compound, I thought the evening ended well. I felt stupid for having concerns.

But a few mornings later, I received another surprise: this time on the internet. It was around 6:00 a.m. I had been expecting an email from my fiancé in the U.S. On Skype the evening before, we had been planning a vacation. I had asked him to do some research on where he would like to visit.

But there was no email from the U.S.

There was one from Brad.

It had been sent earlier that morning. I found it odd as Brad did not usually write. I clicked open Brad's email and began reading. Without much introduction, he revealed a fantasy he had about me coming out of my steamy bathroom, wearing only a blouse unbuttoned down to the breasts.

My eyes went big.

The fantasy went on. He asked if I wanted a fulfilling, intimate "in-country" relationship with him. I had not even heard of that term before. In our earlier conversations he had told me about his wife and children. I had spoken about my fiancé. What was *this*?

Thinking it best not to have a knee-jerk reaction, I went into work that day and confided in Wayne again. Wayne's blue eyes went big.

"Wow, guys are sometimes hung up on women and do strange things, but this guy did something very different," he commented.

Not knowing what to do, I did not respond to Brad for days. Finally, I thought it was best to iron things out. Even though I was slated to go to Kunduz, we could end up working together somehow. Being in a war zone by itself was complicated enough.

When I called, Brad picked up on the first ring. He asked if I had received his email. I answered yes. I then asked what he was doing prior to writing it. He answered he wasn't doing anything in particular. I wanted to know whether he had ingested any pills or drank any alcohol. He answered no. He began to sense that I was displeased.

Telling him the answer to his proposition was no, I reminded him I had a fiancé and he a wife. He acknowledged all this, but it did not stop him from revealing he *also* had a girlfriend in the U.S.

I was appalled.

"But I have no one special in Afghanistan," Brad volunteered.

My mind was spinning. As in Iraq, there were a large number of foreign men in Afghanistan. It was not surprising thus that the few foreign women present attracted attention, even a little five-foot-two person like me. Our program had very few women. In fact, when I first arrived, of the sixty or so international staff, only about a tenth were women. In this kind of environment, some females were ecstatic over the attention they received. They could not see that affairs arising out of these circumstances had little chance of succeeding, often resulting in injuries of some kind to all parties involved.

And, I believed, that which hurt the employees hurt the program.

Brad apparently thought I could be a sexual convenience. He did not think further about the consequences psychologically, emotionally, finan-cially, or professionally. When I asked whether he had ever considered his wife's feelings, he answered that he was heading for a divorce. When I asked the same question about his girlfriend's he replied, "What she doesn't know won't hurt her."

That was enough for me.

Shortly before flying out to Kunduz, I saw a very different side to men. This incident involved a memorable colleague named William. We all called him Bill. A middle-aged man from Maine with puffs of white hair on his head, Bill had been in Mazar-i-Sharif Province for over a year. He was the type of person one felt at ease with immediately. He was soft-spoken, nonjudgmental, and caring. But Bill had a principled side to him. He once told me that while practicing law in Maine, an American colonel barged into his office without an appointment and tried to bully him into taking a case. Bill did not like the man's approach and asked him to leave. When the colonel failed to comply, Bill got up and left for the evening.

Now Bill looked at me with concerned eyes. He had heard I was going to Kunduz, one of the most dangerous provinces in the country.

"Let's see your medical kit," he said.

Each one of us, upon entering the country, was issued an emergency medical kit containing band aids, scissors, creams, tourniquets, and other first aid items. Thinking nothing of it, I passed mine to him. He opened it, looked inside and without a word, reached into his own medical kit, pulled out some items and stuffed them into mine.

"What are you doing?" I asked.

Bill looked at me and said that my kit was missing critical items.

"But now yours is," I pointed out.

"No need to worry. My medic in Mazar-i-Sharif will refill it once I get there," he replied.

"But you're not in Mazar-i-Sharif," I said with concern. "You still have to travel there and something could happen on the way!"

He heard me. But Bill was an unselfish man, one of the most giving people in our program. He knew I was new, wanted me to be safe, and have the things I needed. He was protecting the newcomer.

No one in all my time in Afghanistan, Iraq, or Kosovo had ever been this kind to me.

26

Outnumbered in Kunduz

It was early on a September morning in 2011 when I boarded a small U.S. Department of State plane to Kunduz. The little aircraft had approximately fourteen seats and no bathroom. The flying time from Kabul to Kunduz was only forty minutes. At the other end, Bob Peters, my new manager was awaiting my arrival.

On the plane, I happened to sit next to a Scotsman who told me he was from Edinburgh. He wore a black jacket, jeans, and black boots. His white hair was cropped short. He looked ex-military. During the flight he told me a few things about his homeland and I enjoyed listening to his accent. He worked for a security company based in Kabul but made frequent trips to Kunduz and Mazar-i-Sharif Provinces.

"What will you be doing in Kunduz?" he asked, giving me a side glance.

It was not every day that an Asian American girl flies around Afghanistan. I told him I was a rule of law advisor and would be coordinating and teaching legal seminars.

"Which compound will you live in?" he continued.

"The Kunduz Regional Training Center," I answered.

He coughed upon hearing it. I looked at him, not knowing what he was getting at.

"Did anyone tell you there are over seven hundred men living inside that compound?" he asked, giving me another side glance. "I don't believe there are any women. *You* will be the only one."

My heart stopped. I had not known this. Not a word was said about the gender disparity by anyone in Kabul or anyone I talked to by phone in Kunduz.

"Are you sure?" I asked in disbelief. "Were there women before?"

The Scotsman thought for a moment.

"There were, but I heard they rotated out."

I was quiet. If this was true, why did the women leave? Am I going to have trouble? My traveling companion didn't know much more.

When we landed at the small Kunduz airport, the pilot nodded at me. Apparently, I was the only passenger who would be departing at this stop. The rest were flying on to Mazar-i-Sharif. I looked out the little round window. Bob, whom I had met briefly in Kabul before, was standing by with the security team near the small, one-story airport building, waiting for me to disembark.

Saying good-bye to the Scotsman, I stepped off the plane. Earlier that morning, I had decided that I was going to add a bit of color to my appearance. Everything seemed so drab in a war zone. The colors were often gray, brown, washed-out tan, or black. I decided if I was going to be assigned to one of the most dangerous regions in the country, I was going to go in style.

Descending from the plane wearing my pale pink shoes, a touch of pink lipstick, and carrying a hot pink shoulder bag, I must have been a vision of femininity for those watching. As long as I was professional, courteous, and efficient I was going to be me—even in a war-torn country. When I walked toward Bob and his team, I saw amused looks.

"Nice color," someone said.

We introduced ourselves, shook hands, and boarded the armored cars. Since this province was more dangerous, it was placed at a higher threat level. This meant that instead of traveling in one armored vehicle like we did in Kabul, we would travel in two with gunmen in each.

Kunduz was indeed rural. There were dirt roads, small shrubs, shacks, and more dirt roads. No tall buildings or the outline of a city appeared in the horizon. Nearing the Kunduz Regional Training Center (RTC), which was not far from the airport, I asked one of the men in the vehicle whether I was going to be the only female in the compound.

"Yes," he answered. "There were a few here earlier. You just missed them."

Then we pulled into the RTC.

I saw a huge gate, sand bags, and a handful of Nepalese guards. When we rolled into the camp, I saw more dirt roads, clusters of one-story buildings, and trailers. There was rust, chipped paint, and decay. Though over ten acres, it wasn't difficult to see that this compound was a lot shabbier than Newport.

Bob pointed to a stack of trailers in the distance.

"There," he said, directing my attention. "Those are our sleeping rooms and offices."

I looked. There were eight separate rectangular trailers of the same size; four on the bottom used as sleeping rooms and four stacked on top used as offices. Each reminded me of a U-Haul container about ten feet tall, eight feet wide, and twelve feet long; a stairway outside allowed access to the second level.

For the next two hours Bob took me around and introduced me to the internationals on the compound. Everywhere I went there were men, men, and more men. They were in offices, residence halls, cafeterias, the laundry room, recreational room, and gym. I quickly realized that not only did I have the challenges of living in a country with security problems and an unfamiliar culture, I now had the added complication of being the only female in an all-male camp.

It wasn't going to be easy.

My mind flashed back to our pre-deployment training in Dulles. The trainer had said that the ratio of men to women would typically be about three to four hundred men to eight to ten women. Now I was experiencing the extremity of that. Not even the numbers on TONI compound were this skewed.

Then I discerned the nationalities inside the RTC. As the general population fluctuated between 700 to 750, it appeared that only about forty or so were foreigners. The nationalities included American, Dutch, British, German, Belgian, Croatian, Russian, Fijian, Nepalese, and Filipino. A good number were former police officers, mainly subcontractors of the U.S. Department of Defense, as the RTC's main function was police training. Many of the Americans were officers from big cities like Washington, D.C., New York, and Atlanta. Most of them had huge muscles, rough manners, and language to match. There were also small groups of American and German military. The remaining hundreds of occupants were Afghans: about forty or so were our students in the rule of law program, and the rest were police trainees who had been recruited from nearby villages. About thirty Afghans commuted daily from Kunduz city: they worked as subject matter experts, program administrators, translators, and security officers inside the RTC.

Trying to digest all this, I began to unpack. Inside my trailer were a small bed, desk, chair, satellite TV, refrigerator, and bathroom. The small space took some getting used to. It was even tighter than my trailer in Baghdad. My only consolation was that I did not have to share it with anyone.

That afternoon I was asked by B, which stood for Barnabas, to drop by his office on the RTC before 3:00 p.m. B was a thirty-year-old Hispanic American from New Mexico. He was organized, professional, and the deputy head of the American security unit for our program. He said he needed some paperwork as well as a headshot of me for documentation.

Following B's directions, I headed toward the building that contained his office. When I opened the front door I saw a long hallway and heard voices but saw no one. As I looked for B's room, I noticed several doors were opened. Suddenly, several Americans, with lithe bodies wearing nothing but their colorful boxer shorts, came out of these rooms laughing.

Red with white polka dots, blue with flashes of yellow, green with pink animals . . .

They saw me and everybody gasped at once. I quickly mumbled an apology and covered my eyes with my notepad. I had not expected to walk into a male dorm and they had not expected to see a nonmale.

Then B appeared in the hallway, fully dressed, and apologized for the scene. I told him that I did not know this was the wrong building. B explained that this was the right building. His sleeping room and his office were the same room. Apparently, this was the arrangement with all the men on his team. Repeating apologies, we proceeded into his office to do the paperwork.

As I sat down on an armchair with a deep sigh, I wondered how many odd incidents like this were going to come my way—and how in the world I was going to navigate through this dicey, unexpected maze.

Figure 26.1. Main courtyard, international side, Kunduz RTC, 2011

Figure 26.2. Grounds, Kunduz RTC, 2011

Figure 26.3. U-Haul-shaped offices and residences, Kunduz RTC, 2011

♦ ♦ ♦

Bob Peters was an interesting man. He had been in the Kunduz RTC for over a year by the time I got there. In his sixties with little hair on his head, he was neat and clean and wore clothes that were surprisingly crisp given the inaccessibility to dry cleaning. His temper was even and he did not have the debilitating habits of smoking and drinking. Calling his wife and kids in Boston every morning, he seemed the ideal family man. Coming with a law office background, he seemed the ideal advisor. Always prompt, meeting deadlines, and never raising his voice, he seemed the ideal supervisor.

Yet something was missing.

One of the first assignments I accompanied Bob on was a delivery to the Kunduz police headquarters. A U.S. donor wanted to give two truckloads of new computers, keyboards, copiers, and scanners to the police. We were to deliver them and make sure that the recipient signed the inventory list—preferably with a smile.

Traveling to the police station with our security entourage, the two pickup trucks carrying the donated items bumped along behind us. As we entered the police station, which was just a few kilometers away, the Afghan policemen welcomed us. We were led into a small office to wait for the deputy.

After a few minutes Mr. Khan, the deputy police chief, entered. He was a huge Afghan man who had an air of importance about him. He wore a jacket that attempted to cover his girth and dark slacks that failed to hide the dust on his black shoes. He saw us but did not smile once. Through our interpreter we told him that we were delivering two truckloads of computers and associated items.

Mr. Khan sat down, nodded, and said that he was expecting this. Bob leaned forward and handed him the inventory list.

"We need your signature here," Bob pointed to a line.

Instead of signing, Mr. Khan reached down, opened a desk drawer, and pulled out another list. He said that *this* was his wish list from several years ago, one that he had submitted to our predecessors. It was longer than the inventory of equipment we had delivered.

"This is my list," Mr. Khan said again. "I gave it to an American years ago."

From where I was sitting I could see he was not entirely pleased. The donation was smaller than what he had asked for. Bob and I looked at each other. Someone suggested we head out to where the items had been unloaded. Mr. Khan agreed. He wanted to look over the entire donation.

As it turned out, the donation had been unloaded into a small room. Boxes were stacked on top of each other. Bob and Mr. Khan entered this tight space. I decided to wait in the hallway with our security guards.

While waiting for the men to finalize their meeting, I thought about how lucky these Afghans were to receive free equipment. There were so many schools in the U.S. that could have used these computers. Instead, the donor decided on the Kunduz police station and, with U.S. government assistance, shipped them all the way here.

Then an odd thought kicked in.

Were these Afghans required to feel grateful? Was Mr. Khan obligated to smile and be happy about any donation? Just because the U.S. decided to give something, must the Afghans thank us for it? Mr. Khan's wish list, which had presumably reflected his needs, had only been partially fulfilled.

I peeked into the room where they were. Mr. Khan was finally smiling and signing the inventory list. Bob took the picture that would be sent to the donor.

Then I had other questions.

Were these computers, copiers, and scanners configured to the right voltage? Can the police station's outlets accept their plugs? What about the monitors and the keyboards? Were they in Dari or English? And computer training? Kunduz was a rural place. Were we to assume that the Afghans at this station knew how to set up and use computers?

As we headed back to the RTC, I told Bob about my concerns. I wanted to know who was going to do the follow-up. Were we supposed to visit again in a few months to check on the equipment and its use?

To my surprise, Bob shook his head. He answered that our part was done. He indicated we were not to worry about what happened next.

"But shouldn't we follow up?" I asked.

He shook his head again.

Apparently, we were rule of law advisors and nothing more. We were not computer consultants or inventory monitors. It was not our duty to follow up.

It was not our duty to follow up.

Bob's attitude and limited interest in the outcome was disconcerting. There was a definite lack of passion and enthusiasm about how this equipment could be used to improve the functions of the police station. It was as if he knew this donation would not change anything in Kunduz and accepted it willingly. He was just simply doing what he was told: moving items from A to B.

But I saw things differently.

While we were to do rule of law and not computer consulting, common sense dictated that there was a real utility in having these computers up and running. Computers facilitated communication and the storage of information. These were two of the areas that the Afghan criminal justice system needed help with, and assisting the justice system was certainly a rule of law issue. But Bob's attitude was typical of what I had seen in many Americans abroad, particularly in the peace-building, reconstruction, and stabilization industry. In addition to their acceptance that things won't change or improve, if something was not stated in their job descriptions, even though doing it would be of obvious benefit, they had a ready-made justification for not doing it—particularly when it required more exertion.

Eerily, for the rest of my time in Kunduz, I never saw a computer when I returned to that police station. Bob said he saw one being used by an investigator, but it was unclear whether that computer was from the batch we had delivered. Moreover, we never knew if computer training had ever been offered or provided.

◆ ◆ ◆

As I got situated in the RTC, I decided it would be a good idea for me to teach. Prior to my arrival, the law seminars were mainly taught by the Afghan lawyers on our staff. Our students were professionals from the local legal community and nearby provinces. The vast majority of them were men. On a typical day, a class of forty attendees would all be male. Every now and then Afghan women attended our seminars too. Whenever they came, they always arrived in groups—never one woman alone. When I approached Bob about teaching, he said that he was open to that if I wanted to. He revealed that, as far as he knew, the other female American lawyers who had passed through this RTC never taught in its classrooms.

After some seminar observing and lesson planning, I decided to share the teaching of a Constitutional Law class with one of the Afghan lawyers. The night before the class began I spoke to our Afghan secretary and was informed that the students attending were all going to be men.

I thought for a moment how this would play out.

The students were experienced judges, lawyers, and police officers. Though professional and educated, they were still from a conservative region. The ones I had seen came to class wearing local dress, which was usually a long tunic, and spoke mainly Dari. They were always polite but never shook my hand. I had disquieting visions of their view toward females. What if they arrive the next morning, see me, and decide to walk out?

I shared my apprehension with Bob, who reiterated that I didn't have to do any of this if I didn't want to. *Yet I was getting paid.* We all were, including the students who received a small stipend for attendance and reimbursement for their travel expenses.

"I don't think anyone is going to walk out on you," Bob said, allaying my fears. "The students are not that disrespectful. Besides, they want their money so they'll be there."

Then he added, "Don't be fooled. They could stare at their shoes—and tune you out."

I went back to my room. Why was I doing this anyway? I didn't have to. I could just sit in my U-Haul-shaped office and fiddle with administrative tasks like many of my predecessors and contemporaries.

But then I knew why. It wasn't about the program, the class, my American colleagues, or even the students. *It was* about setting an example of female professional competence. Afghanistan was flooded with thousands of Afghan women empowerment projects. Why not set the example in our classes in Kunduz too? Why just have men go into classrooms to talk about these concepts with other men?

Realizing this, regardless of how the next day would turn out, I knew I needed to stand in front of the class and teach it.

The next day came. I entered the classroom with my interpreter. Some of the students had already arrived. We greeted one another and more came in. A few looked surprised to see me. As class began, I sensed it was imperative I state my qualifications up front. After I did so, we were able to move on with the lesson. The students listened and asked questions just as they did in any other class.

But I felt their eyes following me. I sensed they had questions about *me*.

Later, as we neared the end of the day, I asked if there were any more questions. One student raised his hand.

"Madame, we have been wondering all along. Did your husband give you permission to be here?" he asked.

The whole class looked at me apprehensively.

I understood where the student's question came from. His culture was one where the man ruled. The man decided whether his woman could come out of the house, go to work, and interact with other people.

"I don't have a husband so this is a non-issue," I answered.

Another hand shot up.

"What about your father?" the second student asked. "Did *he* give you permission to be in Afghanistan?"

The whole class looked at me again. They all wanted to know.

"My father knows that I am here, but I have not had to ask his permission since I am above the age of discretion," I answered. "Besides, I have already worked in other countries prior to coming here."

The students nodded as they digested the information. They accepted it as truth for me, a foreigner, but I sensed that they still had some way to go before considering such freedom for their wives and daughters.

27

Separate but "Equal"

The "segregation" of Afghans from foreigners I had seen at Newport was nothing compared to that on the Kunduz RTC. I noticed it the first day I arrived. Separate dining halls existed for foreigners and Afghans, but things went further. We had the "international side" of the camp and the "Afghan side" divided by a dirt road.

On a Friday afternoon, I was taking a walk when I came upon the basketball court. It was a day off and everyone wanted to relax. I saw foreigners with their shirts off, dribbling the ball, throwing it to their teammates, and having a great time. But none of the Afghans were playing and no one invited them to join in. Instead they were standing off to the side watching.

"Back off, man!" one sweaty American shouted when a local stepped too close to the court line.

Similarly, on another Friday, a number of police trainees were playing volleyball. As I walked past, I could see the white ball bouncing back and forth, and the Afghans shouting out commands to their teammates. But none of the foreigners were around. They weren't even standing on the sidelines cheering. It seemed odd that none of the international staff had an interest in this sport.

That was not all.

In a law seminar one morning, the concept of equality was being discussed. The students were listening intently. Then lunch hour arrived. There were three cafeterias inside the camp: two for the Afghans and one for the internationals. Though equality had just been professed minutes ago, now for lunch, foreigners and Afghans of any rank went their separate ways. All Afghan staff and students were reduced to eating in the Afghan cafeterias, which served lower-quality food, while all foreigners headed to the international dining hall to enjoy a buffet—where locals were not allowed.

It was difficult to reconcile our words with our actions.

This eating arrangement, like Newport's, eerily echoed the segregation of blacks and whites in American history. It was curious that none of us foreigners said or did anything about it. While it could easily be justified that the Afghan students, particularly the hundreds of police trainees, have their own dining hall due to rank, our local staff should have been able to eat with us.

It was clear from my conversations with the foreigners on the RTC that very few were interested in having Afghan staff eat with us. This was not a security concern. Many foreigners *wanted* to keep a distance, a barrier between themselves and those who were different.

To the international community's credit, a movement started in the winter of 2011–2012 that allowed the Afghan staff on all RTCs across the country to eat in the international dining halls. It was a snowy day when our compound management broke the news in a meeting to the foreigners.

Immediately, there were those who objected.

One man, Joe, from Kentucky, said that he did not like the Afghan sense of hygiene.

"They pick up food with their hands instead of using tongs!" he exclaimed, shaking his head.

Joe made it clear that if the Afghan staff were allowed into the international dining hall, he would stop entering it.

"If they're in there, I won't be. I will ask my wife to send me food through the APO," Joe declared.

We all looked at him. He was a defense subcontractor in his late forties. From the stories he told us about himself, it did not appear that he had traveled abroad much. The fact that he made it to Afghanistan for work was a miracle and an indication as to how high his salary was.

Another disgruntled American spoke up.

"Why do the Afghans have to be allowed into our DFAC?" Dave wailed. "Mealtimes are my *only* time to get away from these guys. For Christ's sake, I spend all day with them!"

Dave was a police trainer from Georgia. Even though he was only in his thirties, he was set in his ways. He did not want to see Afghans while he was eating.

I looked down at my shoes.

Were these reasonable concerns? If it was really true that Afghans picked up food with their hands, couldn't this be corrected? After all, we had only hired the best of the lot: educated professionals who carried themselves with decorum. Many times I believed our local staff's manners were better than that of the foreigners.

And what about spending all day with Afghans? Weren't *we all* spending the day with them? If spending time with Afghans was an issue, why did Dave and those like him bother to come to Afghanistan?

I was ashamed of my countrymen. Yes, they were brave. They took a chance with their lives, and they were presumably advancing our national interests. Yet protecting America's interests called for not having a totalitarian government in place such as the Taliban. Part of toppling the Taliban included gaining local support for democracy, democratic institutions, and values. Segregating Afghans like this wasn't helping our message. It wasn't communicating that equality was a core value in a democracy.

After the dissenters made their points, the camp manager stepped in. He said that though he heard the disquieting voices, the new policy would be implemented anyway as it was coming down from higher up.

Then he said something very interesting—as though to pacify the dissent.

He pointed out that lunch would be the only meal at issue since most of the Afghan staff commuted each day from Kunduz city. Since our international dining hall could only accommodate around fifty people at once, he would schedule two lunch periods to make room for the Afghan staff. The cafeteria would continue to remain open for lunch between 11:00 a.m. and 1:00 p.m. Foreigners would be allowed to enter the entire two hours, but the Afghan staff could only enter starting from noon. The Afghan students would still eat in the Afghan cafeterias due to their rank and those dining halls would remain open to both the international and local staff.

The new week arrived. The new policy was implemented, but I was not surprise at the outcome. At 11:00 a.m. about ninety percent of the foreigners went to lunch. By noon they had come and gone. From noon on the international dining hall had become essentially an Afghan dining hall with only a few foreigners who cared to be there.

The message was clear: the foreigners did not want to socialize with their local staff. This was not about security or costs. This was about prejudice, racism, and being uncomfortable with a culture and people who were different.

Interestingly, throughout my entire time in this international DFAC, I never did see an Afghan staffer pick up food with his hands or exhibit hygiene-deficient manners as was suggested. In fact, contrary to the rumors I had heard, it appeared that the majority of our local staff liked Western food and preferred our DFAC to the Afghan cafeterias. Even when pork was served, our Afghan staff did not run. They entered and simply chose other entrées.

28

Female Problems, Policy Implications

With a hot cup of coffee in hand one morning, I walked over to our main gate. It was early. I wanted to be there to greet our incoming staff and students. When I arrived, I saw something I hadn't noticed before. Nepalese guards were searching and wanding incoming people. While I knew this to be regular procedure, I observed that on this occasion all the guards were men. Later I was told this had been the case for some time. Apparently, our one Afghan female gate guard often failed to report to work. Thus when a local female arrived, a male guard wanded and searched her too. He would stand very close, wave his electric wand up and down the curvatures of her body, and then reach into her purse. Subsequently, the Afghan women told me they did not like this. It was hard enough for them to come out of the house, enter a male-dominated compound, and attend class. On top of which, being searched by men who were not their relatives was a complete violation of acceptable cultural norms.

And things went further.

There were no public restrooms for women on this RTC. At first I thought this was the case because I was the only woman. But as time passed, I saw that sometimes international females visited for the day to attend meetings in addition to the Afghan women who, off and on, attended our courses, commuting from the city.

Yet gender sensitivity and inclusiveness never seemed to be that important on this RTC. Pointing to the lack of female restrooms, I asked my team what had been done to address this issue in the past.

Several of the Afghan men looked at each other. One said that the Afghan women usually went into unoccupied trailers and used those restrooms—to the extent those were available.

"There was an American female advisor like you," another volunteered. "At lunch hour, she opened her private room and allowed the Afghan women to line up for her restroom. Maybe you can do this too?"

Those were the solutions?

I was appalled. The international community had poured billions of dollars into Afghanistan and *those* were the solutions for the Afghan women who attended programs inside the Kunduz RTC?

This certainly didn't add to our messages of gender equality, female empowerment, and cultural sensitivity.

I began to realize how female *unfriendly* this compound was.

I toyed with the idea about opening my private room for the Afghan women as a predecessor had. Yet this was just perpetuating gender inequality and cultural insensitivity. Arguably, due to my predecessor's actions, the management never felt a need to make further accommodations.

There were other problems with the idea. My possessions and personal information were all in my trailer. For security and sanitary reasons, I did not see my predecessor's action the best of choices. Given the resources and funding invested in this compound alone, I felt camp management should be able to do better than this.

For the time being the Afghan women attending our classes went to an unoccupied trailer to use its restroom. Luckily, one was available because an American had resigned and left. But a new colleague might arrive any day.

I went to Bob about this. He did not seem terribly concerned. He exuded the same lack of enthusiasm the day we delivered the computers. It was almost a "we'll cross that bridge when we get there" response, except that the Afghan women were already here.

I also spoke to camp management, which was the domain of another U.S. company. The camp manager, an American in his sixties who told us he had been in and out of the Kunduz RTC since its inception years ago, said that the visiting foreign women were using a small unisex restroom near the international dining hall, one that was also frequented by German soldiers.

"Your female students are welcome to use that restroom too," he stated, without further thought.

I could see we were not making headway.

Knowing the conservative nature of Afghan women, I knew they would not be able to use the unisex restroom. First, they would need to walk right into the middle of the "international" side of the camp, something they were uncomfortable doing. Second, the small unisex restroom contained a toilet next to a urinal, something many Afghan women would find offensive. Third, these women always kept an appropriate distance from men who were not their relatives. It was hard to imagine they would be able to line up with German soldiers in a queue.

Unbelievably, a problem that seemed to have a clear-cut solution was a nightmare to solve. It confirmed for me that men and women saw things very differently.

But this problem was much more than a Mars vs. Venus issue.

It was systemic. Like many other foreign compounds in Afghanistan, the Kunduz RTC was a coming together of several foreign entities. One company managed it while others rented space, each answering to its own hierarchy who was often either in Kabul or in the home country. Essentially, there was no one person that everyone on the compound answered to. With different bosses and different program objectives, decisions and policies were bound to clash—as was the case here. One company wanted to empower local women while another looked at the bottom line.

Even assuming camp management was open to building a restroom for women, there were still the layers of bureaucracy to overcome: Who would pay for it? Who would build it? How long would this take? Who had the right to use it?

One afternoon I went into the unused trailer to visit our female students who were taking a break. None of them were lawyers, but all were involved with community education of women's rights in Kunduz. When they came to class, they always appeared in groups. Each wore a head scarf and clothes that covered her from neck to ankle.

As I entered, they looked up. I could see there was something they wished to tell me. They all looked weary. Through an interpreter, they related their concerns.

236 ◆ Flash Points

"We don't want men to search us," one woman complained, referring to the gate guard. The group nodded in agreement.

"I don't like him putting his hands in my purse," another woman said, gesturing how the guard dived into her bag that morning.

"It is not good for our reputation to be seen coming into a camp full of men," a third woman stated, looking straight at me.

Usually these women were quiet and soft-spoken. The fact they had said this much told me they were indeed suffering. They were trying to better themselves by attending our courses, but in order to do so they were forced to submit to Western ways of doing things, many of which violated their cultural norms.

Troubled, I sensed they were expecting me to do something.

But what could *I* do?

I was stuck. As a woman, I heard them. I heard their needs and understood why they felt more comfortable speaking to me than to my male colleagues. Yet as an American, I knew something about the bureaucracy in the peace-building, stabilization, and reconstruction industry. There would be no quick solutions to their concerns.

"I'll see what I can do," I told these women.

Heading over to Bob's office, I related my conversation with the Afghan women. He said I could speak to the RTC's security department about the gate guard issue *if I wanted.* I did. The security office, run by a contractor to the U.S. Department of Defense, confirmed it had hired a female Afghan guard to search Afghan women. Unfortunately, she was not always on duty because she had another job.

Then the security director looked at me.

"How about you?" he gestured at me. "*You* should be out there at the gates searching the women."

What?

This was a bad idea. Daily there was news about locals sneaking bombs and other explosives into foreign camps across Afghanistan. With no training in security whatsoever and a different job to do, I was not fit for this position.

I shook my head. The security office could put more effort into recruiting an appropriate person.

Looking at the history of the Kunduz RTC, one had to wonder what happened. Was the gender insensitivity just about costs, or was it due to lack of careful observation, planning, and organization? Given the generosity of the German government, which had spent a lot of money on this RTC, it was hard to believe this was just about costs. For several years prior to my arrival, the German government had spent millions of euros building an annex to the compound. With so much money poured in, why weren't female restrooms ever built?

I never received a straight answer to this elemental question, nor was it ever made clear to me what the original purpose of this RTC was. Were the planners initially expecting to make this compound an all-male training facility? Or did they build this camp with the expectation to make it a coed police training ground but fail to understand the cultural needs and restrictions of Afghan women?

My thoughts went back to Ara, the Afghan female lawyer in Kabul who could not travel and overnight alone because that would cast a shadow on her reputation. If the RTC was built with the purpose of training and housing both Afghan men and women, it made sense that cultural inhibitions had prevented the women from training and living here. Either the lack of female trainees' attendance caused all the restrooms to be taken over by the male trainees or the builder did not envision female attendance and did not construct facilities accordingly.

Interestingly, Bob told me that a year ago an Afghan policewoman from Kunduz city came into the RTC for police training. She was working in the family unit of the Kunduz police station and wanted to improve her skills. Commuting daily from home, she gave the program a try. Alas after several weeks, she dropped out after being leered at, laughed at, and teased by the hundreds of male trainees.

With a heavy heart, I saw these problems had much larger implications. Without female-friendly facilities in a camp, the international community was essentially reinforcing the idea that women were secondary and that their needs were not as important as men's.

◆ ◆ ◆

Life was not easy for the only female living inside the camp. From sun up to sun down, I saw and dealt with men. In the laundry room, the cafeteria, the offices, the gym, the recreation room, and the grounds, men roamed. I walked into offices where guy-talk reigned, oaths were uttered, and in one room, a nude centerfold was prominently displayed. Some men were polite, courteous, and held open the door for me, while others couldn't refrain from conversations with sexual overtones. One man, a former police officer from Maryland who had received a care package from home, told me he had heard I liked sweets. Suggestively, he outlined how he was going to set a path for me using Hershey's Kisses leading up to his sleeping quarters.

"Come on, Jade," he whispered suavely. "You can follow the Kisses."

There were other scenes.

In one camp meeting where only foreigners attended, several men entered into a loud verbal altercation. Each time an expletive was used, its speaker turned to me, said my name, apologized, but immediately resumed with the swearing.

"I'm getting fucking tired of all this! Sorry, Jade. Just fucking tired! Sorry, Jade. Do you guys fucking hear me?!" one man bellowed.

It was a most surreal combination of inclusion, crudity, and propriety.

Another time I politely asked the man who hung the nude centerfold up in his office to remove it.

"Can you take that picture down?" I asked, pointing to the nudity.

"What's it to you?" he replied, annoyed. "It's *my* office."

"It's an office funded by our federal government's money and the picture makes me uncomfortable," I stated.

He stood up in a huff, showing his full height of six foot four. After rolling his eyes, he slowly walked over and covered the centerfold with a cloth.

But the foreign men on the camp weren't the only ones who caused difficulties.

No matter how conservatively I dressed or how professional my behavior, when I took my daily walk around the inside perimeter of the RTC for exercise, the police trainees would gather and stare. This usually began with a small group gawking at me. Then with each round, the group quickly grew to alarming numbers: twenty, forty, sixty, one hundred, and so on. Soon there were hundreds of Afghans watching me.

These men looked at me as if I were a strange specimen previously undiscovered, even though I had been living on the compound for months. Each time I passed they said something to me in Dari and made suggestive gestures with their tongues.

In the beginning I was disturbed but not intimidated, though I would be walking either early in the morning or early in the evening when few foreign colleagues were around. As the gawking continued for months, I grew increasingly uneasy. Why didn't they go away? Should I give up and stop walking? Our living and workspaces were confining enough as they were. Should I allow cultural and gender inhibitions to keep me from my daily exercise?

I was determined not to stop a much-needed respite. Even though I sometimes used the compound's gym, I continued to walk. Yet I noticed that whenever one of my international colleagues joined me, the Afghan audience quickly shrank. It was as if I was no longer up for grabs. I was "with" another man. All it took was for *one* foreign man to stand next to me and the Afghan trainees would back off.

As my gender challenges continued on the RTC, so did the ones for our female students. In addition to the gate guard and restroom issues, these women had another challenge. They reported to me that they could not eat in either of the Afghan cafeterias due to the leering of hundreds of police trainees. Since these women were not foreigners or local staff, they could not eat in the international dining hall either. Consequently, our employees ended up having to bring lunch to them in the unused trailer. This was a labor-intensive work-around.

One day I had a taste of what these women were talking about.

We were short on Afghan staff so I decided to help our secretary, Sameer, carry lunches to our female students. It was noon when we entered one of the Afghan dining halls to find the cook. As Sameer and I waited for the lunches to be wrapped, the police trainees began entering the dining facility. I watched as, one by one, each man used a thumbprint in place of a signature on the lunch tracking sheet. Almost all of them were illiterate and could not sign their names.

I stood quietly in the corner, hoping that none of them would see me.

The men took their food, sat down, and began eating. They looked terribly thin and appeared devoid of manners. Many picked up food with their hands and spoke with their mouths full. When one of them spotted me, he immediately signaled his friends. Within seconds the noise level in the entire room shot up. Some of them pounded on the tables with their fists, and others stood on chairs stomping, hollering, and making gestures at me. Alarmed, I motioned for the cook to hurry up. I needed to leave but there was only one door.

It was blocked by the incoming stream of trainees.

Sameer grabbed a few wrapped lunches and slipped out, thinking I was behind him. Carrying several lunches, I stood in front of the congested doorway but none of the men moved aside. The yelling and the gestures were now unbearable. Sweating profusely, my heart rate sped up. Finally, and only, when their commander stood up and blew a whistle did the men let me pass. Quickly, I slid out, breathing hard. It was a narrow escape.

I could not imagine Afghan women or *any* woman feeling comfortable in this environment.

Figure 28.1. Afghan police trainees, Kunduz RTC, 2012

◆ ◆ ◆

One quiet night, after the traumatic lunch incident, I was in my trailer reading when there was a knock on the door. It was J.T., one of the security officers hired to protect our team. He was Welsh, about thirty years old, and stocky with huge biceps. Yet despite his machismo, he was always professional with good manners and organizational skills. He came by now and then to discuss security issues I needed to be aware of.

For the first few minutes, we reviewed my appointments in the city for the coming week. Then, without intending to, the conversation routed over to me being the only female inside the camp.

"It's difficult," I told J.T., shaking my head. "Sometimes a woman needs a girlfriend to talk to."

He nodded sympathetically.

"I'm not a woman," he said, stating the obvious. "But you are welcome to talk to me anytime you need a friend."

I thanked him but then J.T. surprised me. He demonstrated he was a sensitive and perceptive man. He diplomatically pointed out that he had noticed the small convenience store on the grounds did not cater to women: it did not sell feminine hygiene products.

"Yes," I nodded. "I noticed it too."

But I had more bad news.

I had just received an email from Kabul stating our APO use had been halted indefinitely due to the abuse of the privilege by some in the American community. I would not be able to send or receive physical mail for the foreseeable future. On top of that, the week before I had heard that our access to a neighboring compound with a PX was also going to be restricted.

J.T. leaned forward.

"If you need anything," he said quietly, "I can help. I have friends. Just write down the product's name and we'll find it for you."

My eyes went big. This was an odd conversation.

I could not believe that I was sitting in a trailer near the Hindu Kush Mountains, talking to a man who was not my husband or boyfriend about feminine hygiene products. But this was the reality to being the lost, and sometimes forgotten, female in an all-male camp inside a war zone.

◆ ◆ ◆

It was January 2012. We were preparing for our upcoming gender law course. Our team was anticipating a large turnout of Afghan women from Kunduz city. As the only female advisor in the office, I had assumed I would play a visible role. Moreover, Bob was on vacation so our team was down a person.

Suddenly, a fellow advisor, Ralph, slid into my office. A fifty-year-old man with gray hair and small watchful eyes like that of a bird, he always gave me the feeling his first priority was to protect his own interests. Without further ado, he declared that, given his understanding of Afghan women and their culture, he was going to take care of everything.

"I don't need you to help with that seminar. I'll take care of everything," he stated to me.

"What?" I asked, surprised. "I thought I was going to do the—."

"All I need is for you to sit here in the office and be available," he interrupted. "You can write reports and answer questions from the other students who are finishing up the other course."

I was appalled. As the only female in this office I wasn't going to be involved with a law seminar designed for women?

Since he was temporarily in charge, it was his prerogative and he made it clear he didn't want me to plan, organize, or assist in any way during the entire seminar.

I looked at Ralph. A lawyer from California, he managed to find a job in Afghanistan a few years ago, first working with another company and then with our program. But even with his quick mind and experience with the local culture, he overlooked something. This class was for Afghan women and no matter how intelligent, cultured, or informed he was, he wasn't a *woman*.

I truly believed that in order to have any credibility holding this seminar, our office needed its women to be part and parcel of the course, even lead it if possible. At a bare minimum, any foreign women associated needed to be visible, if for nothing else as a sign of encouragement and solidarity.

But Ralph failed to see this and he wasn't the only one. Oftentimes the men running female empowerment programs forget to place their own female employees in strategic positions. Sometimes it had to do with ego and the desire to control. Other times it had to do with lack of vision and the failure to see the bigger picture—all of which ended up short-changing the recipients of the program.

After Ralph left my office, I wrote him an email copying a manager in Kabul. It was an uncomfortable thing to do, but I felt that if I truly wanted to help Afghan women, I needed to be involved. A seminar on their behalf should not be wholly run by men, whatever the men's understanding or years of experience.

Eventually, Ralph acquiesced and I became a visible player in the seminar. I even entered the classroom and spoke for a few moments in front of the students. Luckily, it was a huge success. A number of Afghan women attended, including those who had taken classes with us previously, as well as a few men.

It was one of those times where I was glad I had spoken up and did what I felt was best for the recipients of a program.

◆ ◆ ◆

One day sitting at my desk, I received a phone call from Kevin, one of our RTC's security officers.

"Can you come over?" he asked. "I want to talk to you."

Concerned, I immediately headed over to his office. Months ago I had been introduced to him by a friend who had worked with him in Mazar-i-Sharif. Kevin was a married man with a wife and children in Indiana. He told me he had been in Afghanistan for close to eight years.

When I opened the door to his office that afternoon, I saw him again. He was a huge man, sitting at a desk that seemed too small. Kevin was about six foot seven and over three hundred pounds. He reminded me of Hulk Hogan, but in khakis and a black t-shirt.

Kevin looked up and smiled. He began the conversation about security issues concerning my students. When the "business" part of the discussion was over, he put down his pen. He started to talk about his life back in the U.S. and asked me about mine. I wasn't sure where the conversation was going.

"There's something I need you to help me with," he said, his tone becoming more personal.

He chuckled and pointed toward his back. I was puzzled.

"I have a lot of hair there," Kevin whispered. "I want *you* to shave it."

I was speechless. Kevin repeated his request.

There was an Afghan barber on the RTC. The barber never attended to me, but I had seen other men go in for haircuts and shaves. I suggested that Kevin use this barber.

But he shook his head.

I suggested the other men on the compound.

He shook his head again.

"I'm homophobic you see," he said slowly. "I don't like men touching me."

I was astounded.

Kevin was a man in his fifties and bragged about having been in a war zone for years. *Who* had been shaving his back all this time?

Not having a smart retort, I said no. This was simply out of the question. Since I was the only female on the property, this "favor" would create inappropriate perceptions.

"Relax," he said suavely. "If you are concerned about me going to your room, you can come to mine."

He still did not understand.

I said no again.

"You know," he sighed. "Back when I was living in the Mazar-i-Sharif RTC, there was a nice lady who did this for me. *You* are not a nice lady."

I stood up and left.

Walking back to my office, I could not believe what had just occurred. This was supposed to be a work-related meeting. Yet too often in a war zone where there was a severe shortage of women, strange things occurred, calling into question the judgment of some who were representing American national interests.

Was I now perceived as a non-team player just because I refused to behave as some of the compound's occupants desired? I had tried my best to be professional and respectable. Even so, a place dominated by men continued to throw curve balls my way, and many times men and women just did not understand each other.

I told Bob about my incident with Kevin. To his credit, Bob offered to go speak to him. So did Ralph, subsequently. I gave it some thought but, in the end, decided against it. Why did it take other men to talk to the offender to sort this out? Why didn't *my* words count?

Weeks later, the tables turned—in a slightly different way.

My hair was getting long and *I* needed a haircut. Unlike Kevin, I did not have many options. The Afghan barber on the RTC, for cultural reasons, did not want to touch me. A German soldier on the compound told me to go find Tony, whom I had met when I arrived initially. Apparently he gave haircuts.

Approaching Tony's door, I could hear the noise of an electric clipper. Entering, I saw he was shaving the head of a bright-eyed young man.

"Hi, Tony, can you cut my hair?" I asked.

He looked up. He was wearing cut-off shorts and a white t-shirt that caught many of the stray hairs from his customer. Otherwise he was a neat and tidy young man from New Mexico who had been hired to be a security coordinator.

Both he and his customer laughed.

"Yes," Tony said to me. "But I only give one type of haircut. If this is what you want, have a seat." He gestured toward his customer who winked.

The guy was getting a crew cut.

Quietly, I walked away. I had a pair of scissors in my room. If only I could cut my own hair! My straight shoulder-length hair couldn't be that difficult of a job. But *who* could do it? Which one of these men would have the steadiest hands on the compound?

Then I had an idea.

I went to the medic's office. If this medic can close incisions and do detailed operations with small tools, his hands *must* be steady. Entering a white trailer where the medic's office was, I decided to give him a try.

"Sick?" he asked, looking up from his book. His name was Jim. He was from New Jersey, had a goatee, and wore thick gold-framed glasses. Putting his book down and getting up from his desk, he looked like a guy who spent a great deal of time reading in the library. But for his casual long-sleeve shirt and khakis, he reminded me of a professor I had in college.

"No—uh, but I have a request," I began slowly.

He looked at me.

I told Jim I needed a haircut. He burst out laughing.

"Luckily for you," he said, still chuckling, "I have a daughter age seven. I cut her hair sometimes, so I have experience." He smiled as he took the scissors from my hands.

We stood by a big mirror in his office for the next few minutes as he snipped away. When we were done, I walked out feeling new. I was grateful that there were a few men on the RTC whom I could depend on and ask for help from, even when the larger, more complicated gender issues on the compound and in the country remained unresolved.

29

Security Twists

"We just got word that another bomb exploded in town!" J.T. exclaimed, bursting into my office.

We all stopped what we were doing.

"It's not clear how many people died," he continued. "We're going into lockdown right now and will be so through tomorrow."

It meant all our appointments in Kunduz city the next day were automatically cancelled. It wasn't the first time this happened and it wouldn't be the last.

During the icy winter of 2011–2012, Kunduz Province was becoming more dangerous. There were car bombs, suicide bombs, road-side bombs, and insurgent activities in town and the surrounding areas. Many Afghans were injured or killed. Property was destroyed and roads were unsafe. Sometimes we could hear the explosions from the RTC. Other times the explosions caused vibrations that rocked the ground beneath us. A few times, instead of running to the bomb shelter, I just crawled underneath my desk and waited until the noise and the vibrations had finished.

Against this backdrop, Bob told me that he had heard our security threat level in Kunduz would be dropped and the number of our protection officers reduced.

"I just wanted to tell you because I know it's coming," Bob said helplessly. "I told Kabul that Kunduz didn't warrant a drop but—you know."

I was stunned. We were in one of the most dangerous areas and our protection would be—cut?

I never fully understood how security threat levels were decided, but I knew it was a complex mix of politics, resources, and budgets. Usually, the higher the security threat level, the more dangerous the province was. This often translated into how many armored vehicles and gunman traveled with us to our appointments outside the compound.

Without waiting for the level to drop, Bob and I both wrote our main office in Kabul, pleading that our security team would not be reduced.

We received back some emails of assurance, but soon it appeared that there were many layers to this cake. As things in the peace-building, stabilization, and reconstruction industry were often comprised of contracts on top of contracts, with different entities involved at each level, the ultimate say on the cut of our security personnel rested on the budgets and the politics of Washington—not the increasing level of danger in our province.

Despite our pleas, the number of men in our security unit was indeed reduced weeks later. Instead of riding to our appointments using two armored vehicles with more than one armed guard in each, we were now to travel in one vehicle with only one armed guard. It was a huge difference. J.T. had informed me earlier that each guard had a specific role to play en route as well as at the destination.

Bob and I protested again.

After another week, our two-vehicle arrangement was restored but not the number of guards. Bob accepted this. It was better than nothing. I felt less assured as I knew that each gunman was assigned to watch a specific area of the premises whenever I was at a local institution.

Interestingly, we had learned that, prior to our security threat level dropping, some Americans in Herat Province had complained that the "high threat" level hampered their movements. They wanted their threat level reduced so they could move about with fewer restrictions. Herat, on the west side of the country, was one of the most developed and safest places in Afghanistan. Yet somehow the three northern provinces in which we had offices, Herat, Mazar-i-Sharif, and Kunduz, were placed on the same threat level despite their great differences in terrain and level of danger.

As a result, when budgetary constraints kicked in and the political unpopularity of the Afghan war grew, the threat level was dropped equally for all three provinces. This exposed Americans in Mazar-i-Sharif and Kunduz to higher risks, which did not make sense. It was the classic case of one size did not fit all.

But politics and budgets were nothing new. I had seen their effects on development programs in Kosovo and Iraq. Many times decisions were made based on things that had nothing to do with the best interests of a program, its value to the host country, or the welfare of its implementers and recipients.

Shortly after our security officers were cut, I had to make a trip to Kabul for administrative purposes. While in Kabul I made an appointment with one of our security managers to discuss Kunduz. I thought it was better to speak to him in person as he had not paid a visit to our province since I rotated there.

Soren Willson was a short round man with a smattering of red hair, a red face, and beady little black eyes that peered out at you. I was told he had been in Afghanistan for a few years and seemed to know the ropes. But I never got the sense that he pushed for the welfare of the employees. Instead he watch out for the employer: he was a company man.

When I entered his office that afternoon, his body language indicated he was less than eager to meet with me.

"Hi, Soren," I said, acknowledging him.

He turned, gave me a brief look, said something inaudible, and turned back to his computer screen.

I walked over to his desk, pulled up a chair, and sat down. I had collected relevant information about several recent security incidents in our province. Given these problems, I argued, nothing warranted a reduction in our level of protection. Kunduz was not Herat or Kabul.

He looked at me and sighed. His large stomach bumped up against his desk. Though he worked hard and put in a great number of hours, it was clear he was caught in a quagmire of budgets and politics. As we talked, beads of sweat continuously dribbled from his brow. He was under a lot of stress.

"Here," he said, directing my attention to a typed report on his desk.

I looked. It was a report from the U.S. Embassy's Regional Security Office about Kunduz Province dated six months earlier.

Then Soren pointed at a map on his computer screen.

"The highlighted area is where you usually have your appointments in the city," he stated.

"I know, but how does that warrant a drop in the threat level?" I asked. "Kunduz is a dangerous area and—"

"I've got all the information I need," he said impatiently. "And since you are receiving danger pay, you should be able to deal with it."

I should be able to deal with it.

I was aghast. I was not even allowed to fight for my own security? Does giving out danger pay absolve American companies and the U.S. government from doing their best to protect their people?

Moreover, did Washington know that these kinds of cuts affected morale and eventually our efforts in Afghanistan?

My mind quickly flashed back to a horrible incident that took place months earlier. While in Kunduz, I was clearing my email box when a message came from Newport. Sergeant T. James, who had helped me when I first entered Kabul, had been captured by insurgents. Days later his body was found in a deserted area in Kabul.

I was shaken. Reality had kicked in. This place was dangerous and James' death was not just another casualty. James was someone I had spoken to, laughed with, and lived on the same compound with. More-over, his murder had taken place in Kabul and Kunduz was much more dangerous.

Looking at Soren, I pointed out that every American on a U.S. gov-ernment contract in Afghanistan was receiving danger pay, but not every one of these people was in Kunduz exposed to a greater threat without receiving commensurate protection.

Soren's face was crimson by now, but I could see this wasn't about me. *He* was getting pushed and pulled from all sides.

Our meeting ended but nothing had been achieved. Though the final decision may not have been up to Soren, I believed that he had the power to advocate, convince, and persuade. For the sake of us in Kunduz, I needed him to do that.

Leaving his office with my head down, I wondered whether I did the right thing by speaking up. Though several of my colleagues had complained to me about their inadequate security, I did not see or hear about any one of them approaching Soren.

Ultimately, if I did not speak up for my own good, who would do it for me?

Figure 29.1. Me at the courthouse grounds with a bulletproof vest that had no side protection panels, Kunduz, 2011

◆ ◆ ◆

Whenever security decisions were made, everyone was affected—Afghan staff too, in odd ways. From time to time, we were short of armored cars in Kunduz. This had to do with the Afghan government's very complicated and sluggish system of registering foreign vehicles in Kabul upon arrival. Therefore, if one of our vehicles in Kunduz had broken down, it could not be replaced promptly even though we had a batch of new ones sitting at the Kabul International Airport. All the paperwork had to be processed and fees paid before a new vehicle was released, a slow process that meant we would have periods of insufficient transportation. This affected our efficiency, security, and even our greater message to the Afghans.

As it happened, we were short on armored vehicles in the RTC one morning when I had to go to the Kunduz courthouse. At the pickup point,

B directed me to the armored vehicle, but when my Afghan interpreter and legal expert approached, he directed them elsewhere.

"No, no," B said to the two Afghans. "You two need to go in the soft-skin."

The "soft-skin" was the non-bulletproof car B pointed to. I saw my staff's faces. They weren't happy.

They were second-class citizens.

As this scenario was repeated over and over again, it hurt the image of Americans. Understandably, Americans needed to protect each other as we were more attractive targets for insurgents. Yet this arrangement worked against the concepts we were trying so hard to imbue. By directing only our Afghan staff into the non-bulletproof vehicles, we were essentially telling the locals their lives were worth less. They were *not* our equals, and the Afghans who worked for us were too polite to say anything. They did not want to put their jobs at risk.

This was one of American foreign policy's biggest problems in Afghanistan, trying to come to a happy medium between what it preached and what it did. Though not entirely America's fault, its definition of equality was only an ideal, and the democratic values it wanted to inculcate were difficult to demonstrate in this unpredictable and dangerous country.

30

Rocking the Boat

"I'm going to give you some advice, Jade," Matt said in a business-like tone. "Don't make waves. If you see something, just keep your head down and lie low. That's the way to keep your job."

I looked at him aghast.

It was one of my first memories of a conversation after initially landing in Kabul. Matt, whom I met at our Dulles training, had entered the country months earlier and had the privilege to work in Kabul, Herat, Kandahar, and Kunduz. When he saw that I had arrived, he quickly pulled me aside to give me this advice that turned out to be the unofficial "golden rule" among subcontractors around me. Over time I heard it repeated again and again.

Now, in Kunduz, Ralph was saying it too in his own way.

"I don't care what you do, but I'm not going to rock the boat," Ralph said determinedly as we walked out of a classroom.

It was a sunny afternoon and we had just finished a seminar. There were some things that needed improvement, but it would take some discussions with our office in Kabul and even perhaps our funding agency. Ralph didn't want to do anything that would appear to jeopardize his job.

I went back to my trailer and put down my books. Was it healthy for anyone to remain silent when something wasn't right? Was it healthy for employees to keep quiet, out of fear of backlash, when problems were visible on the job? Moreover, was it healthy to refrain from offering a suggestion out of not wanting to "rock the boat" when one saw a way to improve? As educated professionals, shouldn't we be raising issues that impacted our programs and constantly finding better ways to do things?

One of the consistent problems I saw overseas and specifically in the peace-building, stabilization, and reconstruction industry was the failure of people to speak up. Speaking up was difficult enough in everyday life. In war zones it was even harder. Many Americans in Afghanistan would complain to one another about how things were run, but rarely would issues be raised to a managerial level. In particular, contractors and subcontractors who wished their contracts renewed did not raise their voices to stimulate action or reform—out of fear of reprisal. Together with high salaries as a major motivational factor, in a field where things on the ground were constantly fluid and communication was essential, what kind of workforce do we have engaged in the expensive goal of rebuilding Afghanistan?

At the time of this writing, Islamic radicalism had infiltrated into Europe. The Paris office of *Charlie Hebdo* had been invaded and a number of people killed. Law enforcement agencies in Europe *begged* the public to keep an eye out for anyone suspicious and to alert them when one saw something abnormal.

In the U.S., watching these horrific incidents, local police emphasized the need for neighborhood watch. Even the overhead announcement in the Washington, D.C., Metro encouraged, "If you see something, say something!" These trends gave the impression that people and institutions were willing to listen and improve. But was this sentiment real? Or was it merely a reaction?

After being in the Kunduz RTC for several months, I came to realize that our offices were never locked. Day in, day out, they were left unsecured. This was strange as we had computers, printers, scanners, confidential information, and even a safe with money in it in one of the trailers. I asked Bob if there was a reason for this.

"There's no need to lock our offices," he said matter-of-factly. "We're in a guarded camp."

I pointed out that things were not secure. We lived on a property that housed not only hundreds of rowdy police trainees but also foreign military and other contracting companies, one in particular who was a stiff competitor of ours. Worse, another room at the camp in late 2011 had been broken into by the police trainees.

"We should lock all our offices," I suggested. "Things are not secure here."

I pointed to the safe that happened to be in my office.

Bob looked at me blankly and said I could ask camp maintenance about installing locks *if I wanted*.

I returned his look. The lack of passion he continually exuded was troubling. But very few wanted to make waves as the subcontractors' "golden rule" dictated. "If it ain't broke, don't fix it" was another popular saying. Once people got comfortable in their routines, they became relaxed. They forgot that danger was near and can come upon them without warning—*even in a guarded camp*.

Rather than wait for disaster, I went to camp maintenance. It acted fairly quickly. Within days, locks were installed and sets of keys made so that each American on our team would have access to all our offices.

But my activism was for naught.

Each evening after work, I tidied my desk, turned off the lights, and locked my office. I did not lock my colleagues' offices at first because sometimes they were still there and it was their responsibility. Yet as weeks passed, not only did I find that they failed to lock their offices for the night, they would sometimes unlock mine after work hours, enter it to retrieve something, and leave it unlocked.

I reminded them that the safe was in my office.

But they failed to hear me. Yet I was sure that if anything happened, fingers would readily point.

Then things became surreal.

When one of our higher-ups from Kabul arrived, I pulled her aside and related the issue about locking the offices.

"There's no company policy requiring us to lock our offices," she said, unbelievably, to me. "You can lock yours if you want but there's no requirement."

Instinctively, I knew she was wrong. There was no way that an entity that had valuable equipment, money, and confidential information in its offices—in a war zone no less—would want things left unsecured.

But since I did not have the rules in front of me, I tried to use logic. I answered that it was not about a "requirement" but common sense. All employees of any company have a duty to protect company property. In this case, it should be a team effort not a one-man crusade.

I returned to my desk disappointed. Perhaps I should have stayed silent and let things take their course. But wasn't part of my job to watch out for and protect company assets? Wasn't it part of the team's job too? If the RTC was one hundred percent safe, why had there been a break-in at one of its trailers? Moreover, there were the "green on blue" attacks. These were happening inside compounds across the country. Thieves and insurgents were everywhere and they knew we had valuable equipment inside this camp. Then there was our local staff. They were a great group of people. However, any of them could, at any time, be subject to enormous pressures from the outside to act to our detriment. This was something we had to acknowledge as a real possibility. We did not speak their language or move in their social circles. We had to be on guard.

Helplessly, I continued to lock my office after work every night. In fact, I locked everyone else's before going to bed and unlocked them again at 6:00 a.m. the next day. Yet if another teammate opened any one of them and left it unlocked for the night, I had no recourse. I had failed. I had made a suggestion to those who did not wish to listen.

Perhaps some had to experience disaster before they could improve.

◆ ◆ ◆

"I do not wish to discuss my cases today," a Kunduz prosecutor said to me.

We were sitting in his minimalist office, cold as an ice box, and trying to have a mentoring session. It was snowing heavily outside and, other than a wooden desk and a few chairs, there was no other furniture inside not even a portable heater. The prosecutor, a young man in his thirties, wore a traditional headdress made of cloth and a long cloak. When he turned to me, he had a strained look on his face. Apparently, there were troubling things on his mind.

"What do you want to talk about today?" I asked, pulling my head scarf closer. It was chilly.

"We have been having a problem with our salaries," the prosecutor explained, sighing heavily and pulling his long cloak closer too. "We have not been paid for months."

I was quiet as he went on. It was no surprise that the government of Afghanistan had been having financial problems. We had been hearing about it here and there. Still, it was a surprise when one of my mentees said it to my face and told me how it directly affected him and his family.

"I've had to take a second job selling vegetables," the prosecutor mumbled. "It's difficult. I have a family to support."

I took notes. This was important.

"What about your supervisor?" I asked. "Have you spoken to him?"

"Yes, but what can he do?" the prosecutor exclaimed, throwing his hands up in the air.

This conversation was troubling and it was even more disturbing when I heard it repeated subsequently by other Kunduz prosecutors on separate occasions. A few colleagues from Kabul confirmed that they had heard the same complaint from their prosecutors.

I decided to include it in our weekly report.

From the very first when I landed in Kunduz Province, I was assigned to write the weekly report. These reports were fairly standard in the industry and I had seen them in Kosovo and Iraq. They usually contained what one's team accomplished during the week and would be sent to the funding agency. In Kunduz, ours reflected the team's activities in rule of law for the week and provided statistical information about our students. Every one of our offices in Afghanistan submitted one. In Kabul, a company administrator would compile a summary based off of these reports and submit a weekly comprehensive version to offices in the U.S. Department of State and the U.S. Embassy.

The lack of salaries being paid was a highly disturbing issue. It made these prosecutors more vulnerable to corruption, and corruption was the archenemy of rule of law. It was imperative that everyone associated with this field in the country be informed in the hope that outside pressure could persuade the government of Afghanistan to take action.

I submitted my draft of the report. As usual, it went through various channels of review. Alas, when the comprehensive summary was issued, no mention was made of payroll problems the Kunduz prosecutors were experiencing.

"I wrote it in there!" I exclaimed to Ralph.

Ralph shrugged and told me to review the strict guidelines about writing this report.

I did. They were not hard to follow. Most of the rules were about form: margins, font, color, and sizes of pictures. What I wrote met all the criteria. It *should* have stayed. But I had an eerie feeling that something else was going on. In this industry, as in any other, many did not wish to raise awkward issues. No one wanted to discuss problems that seemed to have no solutions. I even heard that payroll problems were technically not a rule of law issue.

But they were.

They were a critical part of the administration of justice. Though it wasn't our mandate to resolve Afghan payroll problems, by not reporting them I was doing rule of law in the country a disservice.

If a prosecutor, police officer, or anyone in the system of administering justice was not receiving a regular salary, what will he or she resort to? Taking another job? Perhaps. But wouldn't he or she be more vulnerable to creative ways of getting paid? If rule of law programs in Afghanistan were turning a blind eye to this vital issue, they were ignoring an important factor that could undermine everything they had worked so hard for.

Moreover, what about those on the receiving end of our reports? If these weekly summaries always reported projects progressing, wouldn't, shouldn't this raise eyebrows? For anyone remotely paying attention to the news, it was no secret that the government of Afghanistan had a number of problems, among them financial. Institutional payroll issues were not unknown, but here I had specific examples of how it was affecting our justice actors, not just a rumor.

Perhaps the failure to dig deeper was indicative of further systemic problems on the U.S.'s end. Understandably, no individual in any of our federal agencies or Congress wanted to be the "champion" of a program or programs that had problems with no easy solutions. By not raising and or pursuing sensitive issues, certain American interests and egos, on both sides, were protected—at least for the time being.

◆ ◆ ◆

Going to Malaysia for vacation to "cool off" was a godsend. Yet even the few innocuous days leading up to it opened my eyes. Right before flying out of Kunduz, I was sitting in the cafeteria talking to a fellow American. We were just shooting the breeze. I mentioned that I was going to Malaysia. His brow furrowed. He volunteered that he had never thought of that place as a vacation spot.

"Is it even clean?" he asked.

It was my turn to furrow my brow.

When I reached Newport in Kabul, another American asked where I was heading.

"Malaysia," I answered.

"Where is that?" he asked, looking clueless. "It sounds more like a disease."

We were in Kabul on the continent of Asia but this man did not know where Malaysia was.

To heighten my dismay, I overheard a colleague reveal his travel inhibitions. Usually, when we flew from Afghanistan to the U.S., the normal route included changing planes in Dubai. Many times this involved an overnight stay with expenses paid by an employer. This colleague, who abhorred being in unfamiliar cities, refused to leave the Dubai International Airport. Instead of going to a hotel, he would park himself at the gate of his next flight and sleep an uncomfortable night there.

On the plane, I mulled over these revelations. Often in my overseas assignments, I would meet people who were sophisticated world travelers. Some were so well traveled that they could tell the difference between food from Taiwan and from Hong Kong. Others just puzzled me. In Afghanistan I had not only met a number of Americans who needed a refresher course in world geography but those who failed to show an interest in world affairs or a desire to travel. This latter group only flew between Afghanistan and the U.S., skipping all the interesting places nearby and in between.

◆ ◆ ◆

Returning from the well-needed rest, I jumped right back to work in Kunduz. Sadly, February 2012 was a delicate time to be in the Muslim world. An American preacher in Gainesville, Florida, had announced that he planned to publicly burn the Koran, the holy text of Islam. His statement "rocked the boat" in many Islamic countries, including inside the Kunduz RTC.

A few days later I was folding laundry in my trailer. I was told by our security officers not to venture too far from my room. The several hundred police trainees at our camp had learned what this American preacher intended to do and they started to grumble. Discontent brewed. Verbal anger was directed at foreigners, particularly Americans.

I had no idea what was going to happen. All I remembered was that I was the only female at this camp, and that alone made me more vulnerable.

Suddenly, there was a knock on my door. It was B.

"Are you there, Jade?" he asked. "I need to talk to you. It's important!"

I opened the door. B was out of breath. Apparently, he had been running around telling the Americans under his wing to be ready.

"Be ready for what?" I asked.

B asked me about my ready-to-go backpack. We were advised to always have a backpack ready with our U.S. passport, money, flashlight, penknife, bottle of water, and a change of clothing. If all else fails and we had to leave in one minute, we would grab this pack and go.

My pack was ready, but B said that we weren't due to leave yet.

"Just remain calm," he said. "If and when we need to get out of here, I will come and get you."

The next several days passed in anxiety as trainers and security officers at our camp tried to calm the police trainees. I wondered if the American preacher had *any* idea of the number of Americans he put at risk. If Muslims in remote Kunduz learned of his threat, then many in not-so-remote places had learned of it too.

Slowly, by the end of the week, things seemed to quiet down. Camp management announced there would be a "training" about the Koran for all the foreigners on the RTC. I signed up and attended.

To the international community's credit, this training was to educate people unfamiliar with the Koran. Several Americans stood in front of the room, talking about the holy text and how to physically handle this holy book.

"You need to be careful about touching the Koran," the camp manager said sternly, looking at all of us. "If you are not Muslim, you should wrap the book in a clean white cloth before picking it up."

It was a brief, bare-bones informational session.

But I was surprised. None of the bilingual Afghan staff had conducted the training. Indeed, they were not even in the room. Moreover, the training was given in reaction to the preacher's announcement. It would have been better if it had been given prior to everyone's deployment. Thinking back, the Koran was mentioned in our pre-deployment orientation but only briefly. Nothing had been said about how to physically handle this book.

Leaving the presentation, I thought about how lucky we were to have avoided an in-compound mutiny. Things could have turned out differently and very much to our detriment. The preacher's announcement had only reinforced how seriously the Afghans took their religion. It confirmed for me that, between different cultures, even whimsical things like jokes should be used sparingly.

31

West Knows East?

It was close to the end of the workday when Bob came into my office.

"We just got this form from State and all our students need to sign it," he said matter-of-factly.

He put a copy on my desk. It was a one-paragraph acknowledgment stating that the signatory was not involved with and did not use mind-altering substances. Apparently, there were those in the State Department concerned that U.S. government money was benefiting Afghans involved with this kind of activity.

I looked up at Bob. I had never seen this form before. It was not one of the documents our students were required to fill out prior to beginning a course.

"When does the form have to be signed by?" I asked, trying not to sound sarcastic. I had my own opinion about the effectiveness of such an acknowledgment.

"Now. I have the Dari version. We should send the forms over to class before the students leave," he said.

Bob wanted to get it right. As the head of our office, he was responsible. Moreover, he always crossed his "t's" and dotted his "i's."

We looked at the clock. In less than forty minutes the law seminar would be over for the day. Bob handed a stack of the Dari version forms to Sameer and explained what needed to be done.

I heard the office door close as Sameer headed over to the classroom. His English was fairly good and he was a man with a great deal of common sense. Yet I could tell by his body language that he saw the ridiculousness in this situation right away.

Twenty minutes later, Sameer returned with a stack of papers in his hand.

"Mission accomplished?" I asked, looking up from my computer.

It was Sameer's turn to try not to sound sarcastic.

"Well, yes, the students signed," he said, sighing. "But some of them asked me why now. Why sign this form today? Class began weeks ago!"

I was aching to say something contemptuous about the State Department but I held back.

"A few students asked me what would happen if they didn't sign. Will they be removed? Graduation is just days away," Sameer continued, looking at me.

Removed? Wasn't part of the American effort in Afghanistan to inculcate its people with democratic values? To be successful, shouldn't it be as inclusive as possible?

I had no idea what State would do in such a situation. It was apparent that this form was more offensive than useful. After all, how were we to check whether someone was or was not involved with such activities? This piece of paper had caused eyebrows to be raised and questions to be asked. But what did it accomplish?

Yet State was our funding agency. What it wanted done was going to get done irrelevant of how difficult, untimely, offensive, or ludicrous.

This wasn't the first time American policies made at one level did not translate well on the ground.

Weeks earlier State had asked for very specific bio-data information from each student and his nuclear family. We had not come across this type of request before. Fair enough, most Westerners might think. Yet this was Afghanistan, a rural country where customarily many people did not record or keep records of such things.

"Oh no," Ralph groaned as he saw the bio-data form.

The Afghans were partly at fault. Afghan government agencies that sent us students rarely told us ahead of time who they were. If we needed thirty prosecutors for a class, the agency would send them, but which thirty was not decided until the last minute.

State's request asked for names, gender, dates of birth, places of birth, and so forth. Many of our students didn't even know their own exact dates of birth let alone those of their children and wives. Some only knew their dates under the Islamic calendar, which had to be converted. Worse, the Afghan culture, in its "protection" of the female gender, was not inclined to discuss its women. It was culturally unacceptable for anyone on our team, even one of our Afghan staffers, to approach a student and ask him about his wife and daughters.

But State was our funding agency and it demanded this information.

Little by little, we got it done, but it was a painful process, one which offended some students who did not understand why this information was needed.

Trying not to let things get to me, I went for a walk. I needed to get away from the office for a day. Running into Jeff Sarnes who was coming out of the gym, we ended up shooting the breeze. Jeff was a tall, blond, good-looking man from Arkansas. He worked as a correction facility specialist. Wiping his sweat, he told me he was going to the Kunduz men's prison the next day to ensure that rules and regulations were followed.

"Can I shadow you?" I asked, hopeful. "I'd like to see a prison."

Though not part of my job, I thought it would be useful for me to expand my horizons and see where those who violated the law ended up.

"Sure," Jeff said. "We'll leave around nine."

The next morning was extremely cold. Snow had fallen the night before so heaps of it were everywhere. As we pulled up to several dilapidated buildings surrounded by a rusty iron gate, I was glad that I had worn my knee-high winter boots. We were going to have to tread through mud, puddles of water, and melting snow to get to the entrance of the prison.

When we passed through the main door, we were told that my security guards could not enter the grounds with their weapons. They could either leave their rifles outside or remain outside with their weapons while Jeff and I entered. They chose the latter. I was nervous as we stepped in without any protection.

A large Afghan man with a dark mustache, wearing thick glasses and a uniform, stepped forward to greet us. He was Mr. Habib, the warden of the prison. Apparently, he and Jeff had met on prior visits. Now they shook hands as he ushered Jeff and me into his office. Jeff explained who I was. For the next twenty minutes, Mr. Habib, Jeff, and I discussed prison issues while tea was served. I was never more thankful for hot liquid. Then

Habib nodded his head in my direction and asked what I wished to see. I told him that I wanted to visit cells and see the programs he had for the inmates. He chuckled.

"You wish to see cells?" he asked, eyes big. "Follow me!"

The next thing I knew we had exited his office and stepped outside. It was hailing so I immediately opened my pink umbrella and followed him. The three of us hurried through a rundown courtyard with mud everywhere. We passed a clothesline where some inmates hung their laundry. Many pairs of eyes stared at me through windows, doors, and other crevices. Jeff giggled.

"It's your umbrella!" he shouted through the hail. "The hot pink color!"

As we entered an old building, Jeff told me that he used to work for the U.S. federal prison system. He revealed that he had been sued a few times for "excessive use of force." I turned and looked at his arms. There were some huge biceps. When I asked what the results of the lawsuits were, he shrugged and said that things were settled out of court. I nodded and told him that if anything odd happened here today I was going to need his protection. He nodded. He understood.

Habib led us into a small square-shaped room where twenty inmates jumped up and stood as we entered. Since I was five foot two, the only female around, and not trained in martial arts, I decided to be the last to enter. I wanted to be closest to the door.

Habib explained that this was one of the cells. The inmates had to share these rooms and collectively keep them clean. There was no furniture but large cushions that lay on the floor. The room was well swept. It was a lot neater than I had expected.

Then I looked at the prisoners. They were all relatively clean too, wearing long tunics and turbans. They respectfully nodded at us.

But their eyes would not stop following me.

Contrary to my frightening experiences as a female criminal defense attorney in American male prisons, these male prisoners were surprisingly deferential. Likely the warden's and Jeff's presence had something to do with it. Though these inmates stared, they smiled and stayed quiet.

Habib walked us through cell after cell. The rooms all appeared the same. They were simple, clean, and each occupied by at least twenty men. Surprisingly, there was less sewage odor than I had expected.

Then I nudged the warden, reminding him I wanted to see the programs too.

Walking back across the muddy courtyard, Habib took us to two large rooms. One was a bakery. Apparently, some of the prisoners had joined together and formed a baking business. The other was shop but that room was closed for the day.

Walking into the bakery, I could not help but take in the fresh aroma of baked goods.

"Mmm," I said, breathing in deeply. The smell gave me a nice, homey feeling.

When I looked around, I saw boxes of cookies everywhere: on tables, chairs, and even on the ground. The inmates told us about their business, and I ended up buying several boxes of sugar cookies, as Bob had requested, to take back to our office.

Watching these men measure flour and roll the dough, I was touched by how hard they worked. I looked at Habib and told him what a fine job he was doing.

"Come," he said. "There's something else I want to show you."

Jeff and I followed him. We came upon a small gift shop on the premises. It sold home-made beaded necklaces, earrings, and small purses. Jeff explained that some of the inmates got together to form this store as their business.

"What would you like?" Habib asked, looking at me. "I will buy it for you!"

I was surprised. I wasn't expecting the warden to spend any money on me. I looked at Jeff.

But Habib insisted. So I chose a necklace and watched as the warden pulled out his wallet. He handed some Afghanis to the inmate running the cash register. I was touched by Habib's gesture of goodwill. It reminded me again of the warmth I felt from the Afghan people.

When the visit was over and we returned to the RTC, I thanked Jeff for allowing me to accompany him. I headed back to my office and put the boxes of cookies on my desk. In the next two days, Bob and I kept one box for office staff and gave the other boxes to our students.

Subsequently, someone in our office informed me that he found a dead insect in one of the cookies and said that someone else had found

Figure 31.1. Me with the warden and his staff, Kunduz Men's Prison, 2012

a piece of human hair in another. All I could do was sigh. This incident reminded me again that what we Americans expected of the Afghan people and what we actually got were two entirely different things.

◆ ◆ ◆

"Jade, I have to tell you something," our chief of mission said quietly into my ear.

We were getting ready for a graduation ceremony of one of our law classes in Kunduz and the American ambassador Ryan Crocker was expected to attend. My chief of mission, Joseph K. Atsmie, III, known as Joey, had flown up from Kabul just for the occasion.

"That man from State has a request to make," Joey whispered, pointing to a tall African American in the distance who was busily talking to others in his spiffy Columbia brand jacket.

I had met that man before, although his job title and responsibilities were never clearly explained to me. His name was Harry. He had visited our RTC months ago, stating that he covered Mazar-i-Sharif and Kunduz Provinces.

The day before, anxious for the graduation ceremony to go smoothly, Harry had arrived and spent the day discussing program logistics with our staff.

"He's going to propose that each of our students send him an email every week reporting his or her progress after graduation," Joey said, shaking his head. It was apparent that Joey didn't think it was a good idea.

I was surprised. How were our students going to do that?

Without focusing on Harry's motivations, I thought about this anticipated request. Even if our students were willing to comply, how would they do it? Computers in the area were scarce as were the knowledge and skills to use them. I did not believe that even half of our students were computer proficient, not to mention the fact that internet access was often unavailable. About ninety-nine percent of the local offices I had visited had no computers on desks. Kunduz was a rural place.

And there was another problem. Assuming these challenges could be overcome, what language would the Afghans communicate with Harry in?

I looked down at my shoes.

Here it was again: West does not know East. Beyond the computer, internet access, and language challenges there was one more obstacle: culture. Afghans did not measure progress by emailing reports to their management regularly. Most of our students would find it odd and not know what to write.

But this idea came from an American and it showed how little he or his office understood the country's professional dynamics. Moreover, ours was a rule of law program, focused on the complex mixture of law, culture, and religion, and how these affected the notions of right and wrong. Ours was *not* a widget-producing factory. There was no exact way to measure its success. Only time and patience will show if and how the Afghan criminal justice system had changed.

I looked at Joey, who sighed. But then another thought occurred to me.

Perhaps I did not give Harry enough credit.

Thinking back to my issues with our weekly report, perhaps there was a good reason why Harry wanted direct communication with our students. He wanted to hear from them, without any party in between, about the utility of our program. Many in *our* government wanted to see measurable results and soon. Given the amount of money, time, and lives the U.S. had poured into Afghanistan for peace-building, reconstruction, and stabilization, no one wanted to wait generations to see change.

But given that the length of the West's presence in Malawi, Kosovo, and Iraq had not resulted in great improvements in the local people's quality of life, was it reasonable to expect huge strides in Afghanistan in a little more than a decade?

Mind the gap.

Ambassador Crocker arrived. We had our ceremony. The students loved meeting the ambassador and sitting down to lunch with him. Afterward, either someone had a talking-to with Harry or he changed his mind because he never made his pitch. In fact, he left the RTC without me noticing. I never saw him again.

With Ambassador Crocker as an exception, as he had a great deal of experience in developing countries, I thought about many of the high level Americans who flew into Afghanistan for a few hours or even days and then left. What can they really see? All the latent problems that we deal with will not necessarily surface during their visit. If all they saw were the polished surfaces of programs, how useful will their policy decisions in Washington be?

A friend who worked for DynCorp International in Kabul told me about his experience during one U.S. congressman's visit. When the congressman and his staff arrived in Kabul, they visited various offices on a compound. Up until that point, the group was only shown things that were in order. Eventually, they ended up in a remote section of the grounds. Suddenly, one of the congressman's staffers needed to use the restroom. My friend pointed to a port-a-john nearby. When the staffer opened the outhouse's door, a heap of fecal matter and smell swooshed upon him.

This unscheduled event may have made more of an impression on him and his colleagues than a week's worth of dog and pony shows.

32

Not at Any Cost

Without warning on a gray winter's day, a huge explosion took place in Kunduz city. I was sitting in my office working on the computer when an email message suddenly interrupted my screen. It was from security informing us that minutes earlier a bomb had exploded in the city. Many were dead. Lots were injured. There was chaos in town.

I looked at the clock. It was nearing the end of the workday and my Afghan staff were getting ready to go home. By the way they joked and laughed I saw they had not learned of the bombing. A few seconds later they got up, said goodnight to me, and left.

I looked out the window. Should I go after them and warn them? I only had seconds to act. I knew some of them had to pass through town to get home. But our security rules were strict. Internationals were not allowed to share security details with Afghan staff. It was based on the age-old belief that we cannot entirely trust them—and with good reason.

But these were my staff!

They assisted and interpreted for me. They helped me in so many ways. I couldn't do my job without them.

Without wasting another second, I bolted out of the office, down the stairs, and toward the gate. I shouted after them to come back. They saw me and waited. They were surprised. No one ever ran after them at the end of the day.

"Wait! Wait!" I yelled, breathless. "There's been a huge explosion in town! Lots of people are dead! Find another way home!"

I saw the looks on their faces change to horror. They nodded and dashed off.

"My family! My family!" one of them screamed.

I walked slowly back to my office, still breathing hard from the running. I had downcast eyes. It was not my proudest moment. Why were these Afghan employees always the last to know? Weren't they and their families affected the most? Didn't they risk a great deal working for us? Why can't our security office relate information directly to them, especially when the incident had already happened?

I didn't know whether I had violated any security rules that day and I didn't care. It was difficult to understand why that critical email had only been sent to foreigners on the compound—foreigners who didn't have to commute. The Afghan staff were people too. If I were in their shoes that day, I would have wanted to know.

Surprisingly, for weeks thereafter no one spoke to me about this explosion at work. Our Afghan staff went about their duties and said nothing, not even a hint about how their friends or relatives had fared. Then one day, I had to pay a visit to the local Department of Women's Affairs, an office I had never been to. I needed to ask their head for a favor regarding our program.

When I arrived, the head was not in but her deputy was.

Mr. Rohullah was second in command at the Department of Women's Affairs in Kunduz Province. Wearing a collared long-sleeve shirt and slacks, he welcomed me into his office and apologized that his boss had to step out. We exchanged greetings and he offered me some tea.

Before I could say anything more, Mr. Rohullah looked straight at me saying, "I know who you are."

I was surprised and began to say that we have never met.

"Ah yes," he said. "But *I know* who you are. You see, my best friend is one of your interpreters. He is like a brother to me. He told me about your kindness that day when the bomb exploded in town."

I was speechless. I was touched. Time had stopped. A number of emotions went through me in that split second. It should have been no surprise that our employees talked outside the office. Still, I was amazed at how it came back to me.

Then Mr. Rohullah caught on that I came to discuss something.

"You have come here to ask for something?" he inquired. "If we can help, we will do it."

I related that we wanted to give a legal seminar and use the board-room on his premises. We were trying to encourage local female attendance, and his location would be better suited than an RTC filled with men.

Rohullah agreed to this request immediately. I was relieved. He opened a drawer and pulled out a new pen.

"This is for you," he said humbly. "You are worth much more than a simple pen, I know. But this is what I have."

Surprised and touched, I accepted the gift. It was amazing how many times the little things we did mattered the most. We could spend millions of dollars building schools, roads, houses, and conduct program after program, but if we failed to treat the Afghans as people, very little of our efforts would make a difference.

I looked at the pen. It was indeed inexpensive but Rohullah's precious words were the way the Afghan people were quietly thanking me. Though only coming from one man, they were enough.

As the weeks passed and our program continued, security became worse in Kunduz. Car bombs, roadside bombs, and suicide bombers all added to it. Yet the security officers who lost their jobs when our protection was cut were not restored. Little by little our safety and well-being as Americans in Afghanistan were eroded.

To make matters worse, the layers of bureaucracy in the peace-building, stabilization, and reconstruction industry continually made it difficult to change or improve anything quickly if at all. In the several compounds I visited in Kunduz and Kabul, frustration was prevalent.

Frustration was evident in the group of people I worked with, the American judges and lawyers. Though I found many of them to be smart, interesting, hard-working, and eccentric, very few questioned why things were done the way they were. Even fewer spoke up when things needed to be said to those in authority for improvement. Out of the fear for reprisal, many just went by the "golden rule": *don't make waves, just lie low and keep your head down.*

While that "rule" may work to temporarily preserve an individual's job, it certainly did not help the long-term interests of a program or further American national interests. It did not make our efforts more effective in a war zone where there were a myriad of challenges.

In conflict zones where billions of dollars were spent and lives were at risk, honest communication was essential. Whether that was communication for the better or for the worse, Congress, the federal government, funding agencies, contractors, chiefs of mission, and subcontractors all needed to be part of the giving and receiving of information, particularly when things were fluid on the ground. More importantly, the unvarnished truth needed to reach the higher levels. Those who had information, even if it might mean to end a project, needed to speak up. Sometimes "rocking the boat" was necessary and common sense. I deeply admired those few colleagues who had the courage to do this.

Eventually, in March 2012 I was instructed to leave Kunduz and return to Kabul. Instead of teaching and coordinating seminars, I was to join another department that dealt with other aspects of law. As I did so, bureaucratic problems did not improve despite my best efforts.

Then came the fateful day when, after weeks of deep thought, I submitted my resignation.

I remember that moment. Time stopped. All was quiet. I was sitting in my room in Newport. I felt sad. Very sad. I didn't want to leave my position, but I could no longer do this, *not at any cost*. It had been surprisingly difficult to get here. Due to the high salaries and the economic recession, competition among potential hires was fierce.

In a war zone where the field was dominated by men, being female made the chance of being hired slim. Being female and a minority made the chances even slimmer. As a first-generation immigrant, my family and I struggled a great deal when we first came to America. There were *not* a lot of first-generation Chinese American women in third world development, particularly in conflict zones. It was not what their families considered a prestigious field to be in. The "proper" jobs were as lawyers, doctors, and engineers in metropolitan U.S.A.

This was an exceedingly difficult decision for me—at so many levels. Like everyone else, I had bills to pay. But I didn't see improvement in things that, I believe, could and should improve.

I was just a number in Afghanistan.

Interrupting my thoughts, my cell phone rang. It was Abdul. Abdul had been one of the Afghan lawyers on our staff in Kunduz. Around the time I rotated back to Kabul, he joined the local staff there too. He had a fiancée who was attending the University of Kabul.

"Jade, how are you?" Abdul asked cheerfully.

"Fine," I mumbled, feeling very down. Then I couldn't keep it in anymore. "Abdul, I just resigned. I'm leaving."

"No! No!" he yelled, horrified. "You can't go! I'm sorry. It's our fault! If Afghanistan was safer you would stay! It's our fault!—It's *our* fault!"

I was surprised by his words. Without apportioning fault, I assured Abdul that security was only one of the reasons and that there were many more that were complicated.

To Joey's credit after receiving my resignation, he tried to retain me. The afternoon I was sitting in his office, he was all ears. A lawyer in his sixties with wisps of white hair growing at the temples, he had spent a great deal of time in the development world. The Balkans, Iraq, and Afghanistan were only a few of the places he had worked in.

In a black collared shirt and khakis, Joey sat in his armchair and looked at me intently as I explained to him my reasons.

Without saying more, he made me a counteroffer.

"Think about it," Joey said quietly, referring to his pitch.

He wanted me to stay.

This touched me because it told me that the office still saw me as an asset. Yet something was troubling. The issues I raised in my resignation letter were not addressed. Likely, Joey felt that he couldn't because many of them were systemic, well beyond the borders and control of one entity. They were ingrained within the larger culture of big money in overseas development, contracting, and subcontracting.

As news of my resignation flew through our offices, colleagues who passed me in the halls made their sentiments known. Some said they were saddened and others wished me luck.

Separately, two men said to me, "Sorry to hear you're leaving, but I've got bills to pay so I have an excuse to stay."

I heard them. I didn't like what it meant and what it inferred about me.

The day I flew out of Kabul in the spring of 2012 there was no exhilaration. No celebration whatsoever. Many Americans at home would find that hard to believe.

Is it a universal "truth" that one *must* be happy to leave a war zone?

Not for me. I love working in adventurous places, meeting new people, learning new things, and submerging myself in a new culture.

At Kabul International Airport I looked out a large window. The mountains were still as beautiful as they were the day I arrived. Their color, mystique, and allure were all there. They beckoned and tempted me to stay.

As my plane took off, the dust around me became a great beige cloud. In a flash of several minutes the view of Afghanistan faded away like a dream, but the realities of what happened and the lessons learned and not learned—remained.

V

Bureaucracy in Washington

Flashback Five

Taking a stroll around the Chinatown district of Washington, D.C., I saw a huge truck ahead parked in front of a restaurant. Its side panel was open and I could hear people inside talking. Suddenly, as I passed, a lifeless naked body was thrown from the truck and thump, landed right in front of me—almost hitting me! Jumping back in horror, I looked down and saw a large dead pig. Its skin was white and its eyes stared straight into me. As its corpse was frozen and heavy, I could have been badly injured or killed. I thought it ironic that I could return home unscathed from three war zones only to be smashed by a dead beast. Life was fragile indeed. Time was precious.

33

A Route Less Taken

"That's $18.99, please," the cashier said loudly to a customer, trying to talk above the noise.

We were in a busy eatery on L and 19th Streets during lunch hour. I was telling my friend, John, about the time a bomb exploded near Newport. He, like many Americans, was distracted by his iPhone.

"There was a loud explosion near our compound," I said, straining for the second time.

"Wh-what?" he said looking up from his phone. "You were saying?"

"A bomb exploded near my compound in Kabul and I went—."

"Just a sec," John said, holding up a finger. His phone was ringing again. He mouthed an apology and answered it.

Walking down the streets of Washington, D.C., it seemed as though Afghanistan never happened to me, that it was all a dream, and one from which I suddenly woke. Friends and family listened to my stories but many could not relate. One minute I was telling them about insurgent activities and the next minute they were looking down at their mobile devices. Their attention was scant, sparse, and given out of politeness.

It was October 2012. Life went on and I returned to work in D.C. Yet something about me had changed. I saw things differently. I felt different. I was more confident in myself, my observations, and conclusions. I had seen repeated immaturity, irresponsibility, willful ignorance, and greed overseas. Moreover, I had had a taste of the complex relationships among the giving and receiving entities, the host country and the U.S. government, and the foreign and local populations.

I decided to put my knowledge to good use.

But I had no illusions.

I had lived in our nation's capital before. I had seen the politics, the artificiality, and the deception that swirled through the city. Many times money, connections, and power prevailed. Rebuilding Afghanistan was a political, controversial, and complicated issue. Reaching out to decision makers was not going to be easy.

To make matters worse, many of the U.S. contractors winning these overseas projects try to mute their employees, discouraging them from speaking out and sharing precious lessons learned. This was done purportedly to protect trade secrets and to preserve a company's competitive edge. However, the lack of accessible, fluid, and unvarnished information from the ground inhibited many of our government officials from making sound policies. This is a critical point and an unfortunate aspect of our overseas contracting industry.

Nevertheless, there is a compelling national interest and a right of the people to know how exactly money was spent and what should be continued, discontinued, or changed—particularly when American lives and billions of dollars are at stake.

Therefore, I felt compelled to do something about it.

I contacted my former employer's headquarters in the D.C. area to arrange a meeting. It was crucial to give feedback and recommendations on its rule of law program. This would benefit all parties concerned, including its current and future employees and the recipients of the program.

A company's representative named Paula agreed to meet with me. The day I arrived at headquarters, I saw how tastefully decorated the lobby was. Paula, a tall, slim woman wearing a white form-fitting dress and heels, greeted me and led me to her office. After initial small talk, I pulled out a list of items that I wished to discuss. Diplomatic and realistic, I did not expect her to agree with me on everything.

"The program has good intentions but it needs work," I began.

I related the positive aspects of the program and the items that needed improvement as well as suggestions on how they could be improved. Paula took notes, but I could see from the tenor of our conversation that she understood very little. With her perfectly coiffed hair, manicured nails, and an elegant office, she was a corporate figure. She revealed that she had taken short visits to countries where the company had programs but she never actually worked in these places. She had never been a rule of law advisor, nor had she ever been stationed overseas for any length of time where the local culture, economy, religion, and language were challenges. Additionally, she did not have to navigate through a program's complicated link to American politics, dollars, and lives.

But Paula did focus on one thing.

"Do you have a complaint against anyone?" she asked, eyes looking straight at me.

I was surprised. I was there to give constructive feedback, not to lodge a complaint against someone. Yet while we were on the subject, I said it was necessary for a company to better screen its applicants. Given the attitudes and behavior I saw repeatedly overseas, in-depth screening was crucial, not only for contractors but for nonprofit organizations, nongovernmental organizations, and private companies that send people abroad.

Paula looked at me quizzically. If a job candidate had the qualifications on paper and jumped through all the right hoops, what else was there to look for? She did not understand that years of experience as an American lawyer in the U.S. did not necessarily equate to suitability for an overseas rule of law program.

Each candidate has his or her own reasons for wanting to work overseas, particularly in a war zone. There was a difference, however, between a person who was mainly in it for the money and another who cared about the outcome of a program, its effectiveness, and the difference it made in the lives of the local population. The latter concept had never been raised as a requirement in any of my overseas job interviews.

Perhaps this concept was hard to reconcile in an industry where stiff competition existed for contracts, and where profit and the bottom line were of utmost importance. Nevertheless, a program in tune with the local population's needs was more likely to be successful and continued than one that was not.

There were many Americans in Afghanistan who simply followed directions. Whether their projects were helpful to the Afghans or even fitted to local needs was not a priority. They did their jobs according to the job description and expected to be paid. Period. They didn't speak up, question program goals, or ever challenge the policies and methods used to obtain these goals. This was not about laziness as these people reported to work. But their main purpose, which was often the driving force, was income and not the welfare of the locals, advancement of U.S. interests, or even the health of the peace-building, stabilization, and reconstruction industry. This was true from the worker-bee level to individuals in top management.

I contrasted this kind of employee with one who thought, asked questions, proactively made recommendations, and stood up to authority when necessary. The latter type was never encouraged. In fact, those few who were brave enough to speak up were often ignored and found to be no longer needed in their positions.

"Don't worry," Paula said reassuringly before we ended. "This information will be passed on to the higher-ups."

I left Paula's office that day feeling that I had accomplished little. I had not only wanted a program more suitable for the Afghans but one that advanced American interests while watching the budget. I wanted there to be communication from the ground up without fear of reprisals. I envisioned a union or advocacy group for subcontractors, particularly American women: one that would represent and protect the members' needs and interests.

Weeks passed. I was still in touch with colleagues in Afghanistan and heard that nothing much had changed. It did not appear that anyone had heard me. The issues I raised were complicated. If anyone at headquarters was remotely interested, I would have been contacted.

Then suddenly I had an idea.

I sat down and wrote an essay about the Afghan women I met in Kunduz, focusing on the little details that can make or break a project.

Two days later my cell phone rang. It was a call from Paris.

"Hello, is this Jade Wu? Jade, this is Greg Jones from the *International Herald Tribune*. We are interested in your piece and would like to publish it."

"You are?" I asked, surprised.

I was amazed that someone actually saw the worth in what I had written.

"Yes, and it will be in the *New York Times* too because the *Times* owns the *International Herald Tribune*."

The article was published shortly thereafter, and I appreciated the publicity it got for the Afghan women.

Yet I had more to say. I composed another essay urging that there be a channel of communication outside the normal chain of command, anonymous if necessary, for all American subcontractors and employees who work in war zones. An employer should be required to have a company email address, chatroom, or some communication route through which concerns could be raised and the message would reach someone with the authority to look into to it. The *Washington Diplomat* published this article.

But were my essays making an impact?

I still had the contact information of a few people who were our liaisons in the State Department, our program's funding agency. We had met at my pre-deployment training. I decided it was a good time to give them a call and provide constructive feedback while my memory was still fresh.

Again, I had no illusions. I was not wealthy, famous, or politically connected. I did not have special access to State.

But I had something to give.

I made my call and was ignored. So I called again and was ignored again. This went on for several weeks. Then I got on the computer and started emailing these contacts. After a few more days of no-answer, I finally received a response that led to an appointment.

Unfortunately, the appointment that was made was cancelled by State at the last minute. A new time was scheduled for our meeting but it was not with the rule of law director whom I had wanted to see. It was with one of her deputies.

It was a gray winter's day in November 2012 when I took the D.C. Metro to Foggy Bottom to meet Kiva at State. Kiva had told me ahead of time that Ronanne, also a State employee, would be joining us.

We headed straight for the conference room.

When we sat down I brought out my list of items to discuss. As with Paula I began with the things that went well and eventually moved on to items that needed improvement. I explained to her how, many times, requests from State ended up not translating well on the ground. Both Kiva and Ronanne listened politely. During the course of our conversation, I found out that Kiva was new in her position and Ronanne had never been to Afghanistan nor worked on a law project overseas.

"Often we'd get directions from you to do or change something and it would usually be at the last minute," I explained. "If you want quality and accuracy, you really need to give us ample time."

Ronanne stared at me while Kiva took notes.

"And once you've asked that a method be changed, you need to give it some time. You need to see the results before you ask us to change the method again," I related and then gave an example.

After I spoke, Kiva told me she appreciated my time and that she could see I came from experience. Yet something about her manner told me she did not understand the depth of the challenges I raised. She was a bright young lady in her early thirties who seemed to have risen quickly in her profession and was well connected within State. But her years of experience in the field were unclear. She told me she had made brief trips to Afghanistan and thought that things were going fairly well.

"It's a good program," she said nodding enthusiastically. "Just needs a bit of tweaking."

I pointed out that, while it was a plus that she traveled there, brief visits do not allow much to be discovered, especially where latent issues were hidden from view.

Then, thinking of the detrimental behavior and attitudes I witnessed in the field, we talked about the hiring standards for subcontractors. At this point, Kiva turned her body away and did not look at me.

"That responsibility has been contracted away," she said quietly. "I'm uncomfortable with getting involved."

She related that the responsibility was the duty of the contractor, not the Department of State's. I told her that her manager was a panelist at my interview. Moreover, I told her that I was informed in Kabul that the funding agency always retained the right to review and remove anyone it wished. I recommended that State play a closer role in the interviewing, reviewing, and monitoring of these individuals, and establish criteria for suitability. The success of a program largely depended on the quality of those in the field.

After a pleasant but otherwise sterile meeting, I left Kiva and Ronanne. I saw I had accomplished very little that day. They were not the best ones at State to meet with but they were what I was given.

As the months passed, I pondered many questions. Was it right for me to reach out and speak up? Should I have shared the hard-earned knowledge I gained with those who could best put it to work, particularly where money and lives were still at stake?

Or should I have just stayed silent, like many others, because it was not my "job" and speaking up wouldn't make a difference anyway? After all, I was only an implementer, a worker-bee, one of the little guys and not a director or some high-flying policymaker.

And yet does being a little guy mean one should *not* speak up? What if more little guys spoke up—not only to their bosses but to their congressmen and women? I believe there could be a positive impact. Since we were the ones closest to the ground, the information we had could help educate decision makers in Washington who could not visit each country and every program funded.

As I continued to walk down the streets of D.C., deep in thought, I knew I had attempted the right thing.

Suddenly, *thump*! A large frozen pig landed right in front of me in Chinatown. A truck had been unloading. I was so alarmed I almost stopped breathing. I couldn't believe that I almost got hit by this corpse. I could have been killed. Life was fragile indeed.

Pulling myself together, I walked on. I picked up the day's *New York Times*. Sure enough, there was yet another article about the U.S.'s involvement in Afghanistan. It talked about American lives, billions of dollars, and reputations at stake. It went through a number of problems I was already familiar with and concluded with observations on politics, egos, corruption, lack of understanding, and the failure to see the bigger picture.

I continued walking, thinking of those who had written astutely, perceptively, and courageously on similar issues. Among them were Max Boot, David Ignatius, Sarah Chayes, and Rajiv Chandrasekaran whose analyses on American foreign policy have highlighted certain trends. Yet no matter how much criticism and praise these authors had received, they continued to write what they believed to be true.

In time I met up with Dylan, a family friend. Dylan lived in northern Virginia and was an active Rotarian. He had had a successful career in the State Department and, although retired, still worked there part-time.

We met for lunch one day and I shared a few tales from the field. His eyes went big.

"You should come speak to the Rotary," he suggested. "These are *very* good stories."

I chuckled. Were there people interested in what I had to say?

So I attended a Rotary meeting with Dylan and spoke subsequently about my experience in Afghanistan. The presentation had a good response and received interesting questions from the audience. Little did I know this was going to be the first of many presentations I was to give to foreign affairs and community service organizations.

Meanwhile, I continued writing foreign affairs analyses and getting them published. Each time I wrote, I linked it to something I saw or did and another memory flashed before my eyes.

And maybe, just maybe, someone out there will learn something from what I have shared and put it to good use. This goes for all professionals who, regardless of their field, position, or job security, have spoken up to authority and given constructive feedback, speaking truth to power.

Epilogue

It was early on the morning of February 11, 2015, when I received an email from Mohammad Walid. It had almost been three years since I left Afghanistan and we had only kept in touch sporadically. Walid, a native of Kunduz, was a judge and a lawyer. He was one of our finest rule of law advisors in Kunduz Province. The last time I saw him was in March 2012 when he was busily planning a seminar. Months later, Walid was hired by another foreign entity to continue the promotion of rule of law in Kunduz.

Curious, I clicked open the email. In it, Walid wrote that life had become more dangerous for him and his family. He had received numerous threats from the Taliban for working with the Americans and asked if I could help him.

He wanted a Special Immigrant Visa (SIV) to the U.S.

Before responding, I went to the U.S. Department of State's website and reviewed the requirements for the SIV. One of the requirements was that the applicant had to be experiencing an ongoing threat based on his employment by or on behalf of the U.S. government. It appeared that Walid met all of the requirements and all I had to do was write a letter to support his application, showing that indeed his life was in danger. Moreover, the website indicated my letter would be stronger if I could *vouch* that Walid was a good guy, a nonthreat to U.S. interests and the American people.

I winced at that last phrase.

How could I, or any American who worked in Afghanistan, vouch that a local staff member was a nonthreat to the U.S.? Didn't the lawmakers know how things worked on the ground? Didn't they know how little qualified any of us were to vouch for anyone under these circumstances?

While the Afghan might be an excellent employee, we did not know what he was doing when he was not in the office.

I sighed and turned my head. My eye caught a picture in a frame on my bookshelf. It was a photo of me and my Afghan interpreter during a mentoring session. He was translating what a judge was saying. The photo reminded me that without our local staff our programs overseas would be nothing, least of all successful.

Then I understood.

Congress had passed the SIV law mainly to protect Americans, not the Afghans or Iraqis or the various ethnic groups that would fit under this legislation. It was a way to buy loyalty from the locals, offering a safe haven in the U.S. for those who supported the American mission so that people like me, working in these dangerous countries, would be safer.

I emailed Walid and told him I would help him.

Days later he sent me a copy of his statement outlining his threats from the insurgents. Like many of my former Afghan staff, he had been polite at work, rarely ever raising an issue or complaint about his employment. Now as I read his words, chills went down my spine. For the first time, it brought out his side of the story.

Walid cited two incidents, one in 2011 and the other in 2012, where he had accompanied me on visits to justice institutions in Kunduz. In both, Taliban members were sitting nearby and monitoring us. Walid knew who they were and vice versa. Shortly thereafter, he received phone calls from unknown callers who had threatened him and had ordered him to stop working with the foreigners, the "infidels." His unidentified callers had told him they would cut off his head if he did not quit his job. In the last few years these threats have only increased, causing Walid to move his family several times within the province. Recently, after seeing a death note posted on his door, Walid moved his family again, this time to a building in front of his office. He stated he and his family were severely restricted in their movements; even going to the local market was a problem. He reminded me and anyone else reading his statement that Kunduz was a rural place. Almost everyone there knew who was working for the U.S. mission. Should anything happen to his job, he would no longer have the protection of the security personnel provided during work hours.

Sitting in front of the computer, I held my head in my hands.

What have *we* done?

Have we helped Afghanistan?

While some Americans had sacrificed their lives and limbs, and others had shown great courage and commitment, many had primarily enriched themselves—with some taking action that was detrimental to the U.S. effort. Bob was still there, and so were other Americans I had known, including a number of the contracting companies I had seen.

Walid was the perfect example of an educated Afghan who believed in due process. Ironically, he was among those whom top people in Washington would want to *stay* in Afghanistan and lead it into a new era of progress. But now the dangers in his country were increasing. He wanted to come to the U.S. and begin life anew, even in the face of anti-Islamic sentiment.

Walid had spoken up and told me what was not working.

Troubled, I wrote a letter in support of his application.

Months passed and no visa came for Walid.

Then, in late September, the unspeakable happened. Kunduz fell to the Taliban. Days later U.S. aircraft mistakenly attacked the Doctors Without Borders hospital, causing great loss of life. Everything seemed to be going fast in a downward spiral.

Then there was a period of deadly silence as I wondered what happened to Walid.

Finally, in October, he resurfaced, telling me he had passed many difficult days. Insurgents had broken into his office and gotten all the staff's personal information. Walid and the others had fled for their lives. Without revealing his whereabouts, he described the slew of dead bodies he saw, the collapsed buildings, the lack of organization in the Afghan government forces, and the fact that he was in even graver danger.

Still there was no visa.

Without wasting another moment, I contacted four U.S. congressmen who had previously shown an interest in Iraq and Afghanistan, asking for their help with the SIV. Two returned with useless responses and the others did not even bother to respond.

I held my head in my hands again.

The disconnect between what the U.S. preached and its actions kept reappearing.

If our government failed to keep its word to Walid and those like him in their time of need, those who had risked their lives for the American effort, how would this affect our current and future involvements abroad?

Have we learned any lessons yet?

Afterthoughts

Working overseas has taught me a great deal about life, people, and myself. No amount of money could buy what I have seen and experienced, good or bad, with much of it still left untold: one, to *tease* the reader, and two, to save material for a future book.

Each time I returned from another country unscathed, I was terribly grateful. Somehow life had given me another chance. Seizing this chance after Afghanistan, I wrote *this*. I wanted my memories fresh, the facts accurate, and the emotions raw. I did not wish to wait until I was an old woman, with bad eyesight and poor health, to tell a story that should have been told long before.

I shared these moments not to discourage, embarrass, defame, or punish anyone but to stimulate thought and encourage improvement in the field of U.S. foreign assistance, especially in the peace-building, stabilization, and reconstruction industry. Like many young people, I had entered the field with ideals and had happy and fulfilling moments. Yet over time as my eyes were opened and skills were honed, I witnessed a great amount of immaturity, ignorance, frustration, absurdity, and inefficiency. It made me question people, things, and ways of doing things. Moreover, I had the horrifying opportunity to witness these events repeating themselves in various forms in more than one country. From Peace Corps volunteers to high-salaried subcontractors, it was amazing how many projected attitudes and behavior that were detrimental to their programs—and eventually to U.S. national interests.

This field will never be perfect; perfection is in the eye of the beholder. But it can progress for the better. It can be more focused, better budgeted, more culturally and gender inclusive, have better channels of communication, fewer layers of bureaucracy, and less opportunities for greed and waste.

From the subcontractors, contractors, and federal employees to the congressmen, politicians, and lobbyists—many in this field have to earn a living. Oftentimes each person was a prisoner in his or her own shoes. Caught up in the momentum of a job description, status, organizational politics, personal finances, and ego, he or she had very little time to stop and think. He or she just *did*, particularly when deadlines and personal gain were involved.

Then there was the pack mentality. If one stood up, spoke up, and took the minority view, one would risk being an outcast, a pariah. Our society has a way of "demonizing" those who are different. Jobs may even be lost, and criticized programs could lose funding.

What then?

Are these good reasons to stay silent and continue things as they are, or should we speak up in hopes of improvement?

Though I do not have all the answers, I take the latter sentiment and realize that many may not agree with me. In some ways the field is changing and there are those who share my feelings, including some reform-minded institutions. Currently, there is a wave of Islamic radicalism breaking over many countries causing the deaths of thousands of innocent people, including Americans, and threatening the personal well-being and liberties of others. The U.S. *will* remain involved, fighting terrorism and ultimately rebuilding and reconstructing societies again. The questions are *how* will we be involved, *whom* will we send, and *what* methods will we use.

We *must* learn from our lessons past.

Acknowledgments

As I did not major in journalism or take many writing courses, I must thank those closest to me for encouraging me to write. This was a work of will and purpose, not one of talent, chance, or luck.

First and foremost, I must acknowledge Bruce Beardsley. He is a man whose accomplishments and understanding of the world cannot be imitated. He stands alone. His ideas and feedback, as well as his laughter, encouragement, generosity, and patience, were priceless. Without them I could not have survived the many agonizing moments during this project.

Second, I must acknowledge my family, in particular my two grandmothers Sui Jen Wu and the late Chung Yook Tong for their enormous strength and support.

Third, I am grateful to many overseas who have helped me while I worked. This list includes Malawians, Kosovars, Iraqis, Afghans, and many of other nationalities whom I cannot name due to security reasons. Those I can identify include Joseph Ziyemi, Marjorie Maluza, Joseph and Virginia Phiri, Stephan Walter, Vyrle Owens, Paul Dever, Emine Emini, Pranvera Raci, Gezim Kunoviku, Miriam Adman, Dale Jacobs, Iliac Lopez, Vasconcelos Bulmaro, Bashkim Zeneli, Ella Lacey, B. Marston, Eric Bone, Hasna Kadem, and Antigona Bardhi Bikliqi.

Fourth, I must also acknowledge my teachers who made learning a joy, particularly the subjects of history and world affairs. Among them are Marlene Felix, Beverly Underwood, Geraldine Baird, Margot Epstein, Frank J. Frost, and the late but great C. Warren Hollister.

Last but not least, despite my frustrations, disenchantment, disappointment, and sometimes dismay, I must acknowledge appreciation for the quirks, curious behavior, and odd comments of the many acquaintances I came across during my time working abroad. Were it not for these individuals, the material in this book would be far less interesting, unquestionably boring, and stand little chance of titillating my readers.

Index